Research Into Translation and Training in Arab Academic Institutions

Research Into Translation and Training in Arab Academic Institutions provides insights into the current issues and challenges facing in-service and trainee Arabic translators and interpreters, both professionally and academically.

This book addresses translators' status, roles, and structures. It also provides Arab perspectives on translation and translation training, written by scholars representing academic institutions across the Arab world. Themes in this collection include training terminologists on managing, promoting and marketing terms; corpora and translation teaching in the Arab world; use of translation technologies; translators training and translators' methodologies and assessment of translators' competence; research on translator training; and the status quo of undergraduate translation programs in a sample of five Arab universities.

A valuable resource for students, professionals and scholars of Arabic translation and interpreting.

Said M. Shiyab is Professor of Linguistics and Translation Studies and Director of the Arabic MA Translation Program at Kent State University, USA. Professor Shiyab served as the Graduate Studies Director in the MCLS Department at Kent State University (2016–2019); he has also been teaching in the MA and PhD programs since 2014.

Research Into Translation and Training in Arab Academic Institutions

Edited by Said M. Shiyab

Routledge
Taylor & Francis Group
LONDON AND NEW YORK

First published 2022
by Routledge
2 Park Square, Milton Park, Abingdon, Oxon OX14 4RN

and by Routledge
605 Third Avenue, New York, NY 10158

Routledge is an imprint of the Taylor & Francis Group, an informa business

© 2022 selection and editorial matter, Said M. Shiyab; individual chapters, the contributors

The right of Said M. Shiyab to be identified as the author of the editorial material, and of the authors for their individual chapters, has been asserted in accordance with sections 77 and 78 of the Copyright, Designs and Patents Act 1988.

All rights reserved. No part of this book may be reprinted or reproduced or utilised in any form or by any electronic, mechanical, or other means, now known or hereafter invented, including photocopying and recording, or in any information storage or retrieval system, without permission in writing from the publishers.

Trademark notice: Product or corporate names may be trademarks or registered trademarks, and are used only for identification and explanation without intent to infringe.

British Library Cataloguing-in-Publication Data
A catalogue record for this book is available from the British Library

Library of Congress Cataloging-in-Publication Data
A catalog record for this book has been requested

ISBN: 978-0-367-47284-9 (hbk)
ISBN: 978-0-367-47282-5 (pbk)
ISBN: 978-1-003-03466-7 (ebk)

Typeset in Times New Roman
by Apex CoVantage, LLC

Contents

List of figures vii
List of tables viii
List of contributors x
Acknowledgments xv
Foreword xvi
MIKE BAYNHAM

Introduction 1
SAID M. SHIYAB

1 **Crucial insights into translator training, assignments, and assessment** 7
EYHAB A. BADER EDDIN

2 **Corpora and translation teaching in the Arab world** 21
MAI ZAKI

3 **Trainee translators' and professional translators' source text comprehension and reproduction: problems and solutions** 41
OMAR F. ATARI

4 **Training translators: a case for Arabic orthographic reforms** 58
MAHER BAHLOUL

5 **Analytical translation quality assessment: insights for translators' training** 89
HEIDI VERPLAETSE AND AN LAMBRECHTS

6 **Toward training terminologists on promoting and marketing terms from a language planning perspective** 113
FAWWAZ M. AL-ABED AL-HAQ, ABDEL-RAHMAN H. ABU-MELHIM AND SUHAIB F. AL-ABED AL-HAQ

7 **New forms of translation: the need for new professional profiles** 142
LAHOUSSEINE ID-YOUSS, ABIED ALSULAIMAN AND FRIEDA STEURS

8 **The trials and tribulations of the teaching of CAT: the case of Oman** 153
RAFIK JAMOUSSI AND ALADDIN AL ZAHRAN

9 **Epilogue: where do we go from here?** 165
ERIK ANGELONE

Index 171

Figures

1.1	Three translators never distinguish between the positive and negative connotations linked to the usage of the two words in focus	13
2.1	Word cloud of most frequent words from course descriptions	33
2.2	Summary of undergraduate and graduate programs in Arab universities related to corpora and/or translation technology	40
4.1	Transliteration of the voiced velar stop consonant /g/	65
4.2	Map of the Arab-speaking countries	86
4.3	Arabic languages and their linguistic environment	87
4.4	Worldwide use of the Arabic script	88

Tables

2.1	Summary of surveyed courses in Arab universities	32
2.2	Variation in course titles relating to corpora	33
3.1	Comparison of the two groups' translation of six source text segments	48
3.2	Professional translators' unacceptable and acceptable solutions and identified and unidentified problem segments	48
4.1	Sample of common transliterated English words	60
4.2	English vs. Arabic consonant graphemes and phonemes	61
4.3	English vs. Arabic vowel sounds	62
4.4	Transliteration of the /g/ sound in 'hamburger'	63
4.5	Transliterations of the voiced velar stop sound /g/	64
4.6	English to Arabic transliterations of the voiceless bilabial stop /p/	66
4.7	Transliterations of the voiced labiodental fricative /v/	67
4.8	Frequency and percentage of translation strategies/techniques	73
4.9	Transliteration of acronyms containing the voiceless bilabial stop /p/	74
4.10	Transliteration of acronym pairs	75
4.11	Transliteration of challenging acronyms	77
4.12	Graphemes for /p/, /g/, and /v/	78
4.13	Acronyms with /p/, /g/, and /v/ graphemes	79
4.14	Arabic script base and diacritics for /p/	80
4.15	Arabic base and diacritics for /g/ and /v/	80
5.1	Error analysis HT versus MT+PE (based on Daems et al. 2013)	99
5.2	Error analysis MT versus MT+PE (based on Daems et al. 2014)	100
5.3	Error analysis in SMT and RBMT (based on Costa et al. 2015)	101
5.4	Error analysis in SMT and RBMT (based on Tezcan et al. 2018)	102
5.5	Most common error categories in TM-based, MT-based, and new translation segments (based on Guerberof 2009)	104
5.6	Sample of common error types per translation method (based on Guerberof 2009; Daems et al. 2013, 2014; Costa et al. 2015; Tezcan et al. 2018)	106

5.7	Overview of error typologies and common error categories	108
6.1	Knowledge	126
6.2	Evaluation	127
6.3	Usage	128
6.4	Proficiency	129
6.5	Adoption	131
6.6	Correlations (all students)	133
6.7	Correlations (Translation students)	134
6.8	Correlations (English language students)	135
6.9	Attitudes toward the Arabicization of sociolinguistic terms	136

Contributors

Abdel-Rahman H. Abu-Melhim was born on February 14, 1958, in Jerash, Jordan. He is a Jordanian American, currently teaching as Full Professor of English Language and Literature at Al-Balqa Applied University in Jordan. He graduated from Texas A&M University, College Station, in 1992. His PhD degree was in English with emphasis on sociolinguistics. So far, he has published a total of 41 peer-reviewed articles in international academic journals along with a book titled *Communication Across Arabic Dialects: Code-Switching and Linguistic Accommodation in Informal Conversational Interactions*, published in Germany (2018). In addition, in collaboration with Prof. Fawwaz Al-Abed Al-Haq, *A Dictionary of Sociolinguistics* was translated from English into Arabic and published in the Kingdom of Saudi Arabia in (2019). His research interests include sociolinguistics, applied linguistics, translation, psycholinguistics, English literature and cross-cultural communication.

Fawwaz M. Al-Abed Al-Haq is a Professor of English and Linguistics at Yarmouk University, Jordan since 1986. He currently serves as the president of the Hashemite University and prior to that, he had been the Vice President for External Relations and Student Affairs at Yarmouk University, Vice President for Academic Affairs at the Tafila Technical University and Dean of the Faculty of Arts and Humanities in Al al-Bayt University. Professor Al-Abed Al-Haq published extensively and presented locally and globally in the following fields: language planning, Arabicization, sociolinguistics, psycholinguistics, syntax, applied linguistics, contrastive analysis, error analysis, discourse analysis, language acquisition, and TEFL. He participated in more than 250 examining committees for MA/PhD theses and supervised more than 50 postgraduate students.

Suhaib F. Al-Abed Al-Haq was born on April 29, 1994, in Irbid, Jordan. He is a Jordanian citizen, currently teaching as an English language instructor at the Hashemite University in Zarqa, Jordan. He graduated from Yarmouk

University in 2019. His MA degree was in translation. His research interests include translation, sociolinguistics, applied linguistics and discourse analysis.

Abied Alsulaiman is Professor of Arabic at KU Leuven, Campus Sint-Andries in Antwerp, Belgium. He is also a co-founder of Arabic Translators International (ATI), an international association uniting translators of Arabic worldwide, and is co-editor of its series *ATI Publications*. He lectures in history of Arabic culture, legal translation, business translation, and interpreting. His research interests include translation studies and translation technology, legal translation and legal terminology, literary and religious translation, Arabic language and linguistics, Islamic studies and history, Semitic languages and linguistics, Hebrew studies, and Judeo-Arabic literature. He has published on translation studies, Arabic linguistics, Semitic languages, and Judeo-Arabic literature.

Aladdin Al Zahran received his BA in English language and literature from Aleppo University, Syria, and has an MA in Arabic/English translation and interpreting and PhD in interpreting studies from Salford University, UK. Dr Al Zahran is currently Assistant Professor of Interpreting and Translation Studies at Sohar University, Oman. Dr Al Zahran has been serving as the English Language and Translation Program Coordinator since 2018. Dr Al Zahran's research interests lie in intercultural mediation and the interpreter/translator's role, interpreting strategies, interpreter and translator training, corpus linguistics and interpreting/translation studies, and translation policy. Dr Al Zahran is also a freelance interpreter, translator, reviser, external examiner, and translation consultant.

Erik Angelone is Associate Professor of Translation Studies at Kent State University, USA. He received his PhD in translation studies from the University of Heidelberg, Germany. His research interests include translation pedagogy, process-oriented translator training, cognitive processes in translation, intercultural communication and language industry studies. He co-edited the volumes *Bloomsbury Companion to Language Industry Studies* (2019, with Maureen Ehrensberger-Dow and Gary Massey) and *Translation and Cognition* (2010, with Gregory Shreve). He has close to 20 years of experience in training future language industry professionals at Kent State University, ZHAW Zurich University of Applied Sciences, Switzerland and the University of Heidelberg, Germany.

Omar. F. Atari is Professor of Applied Linguistics and Translation Studies at the University of Petra, Amman, Jordan. He is currently the chair of the English department. His research interests center on the interaction between text analysis of the source text at the micro-/macro-levels and the translator's interlingual competence. He has published in several international refereed journals: *Meta, Babel, The Translator and Interpreter Trainer, Turjuman, Journal of*

Literary Semantics and *IRAL*. At present, he is working on a project for incorporating workplace translation norms and conventions into the translator training program of the English department at the University of Petra.

Eyhab A. Bader Eddin, BA, MA, PhD, CL, MCIL, MITI, is Assistant Professor of Translation at King Khalid University, Abha, Saudi Arabia. He has extensive teaching experience in such countries as Syria, Oman, Kuwait, and Saudi Arabia. Dr Bader Eddin has been teaching exclusively in the MA programme for the past four years. With a PhD titled *Semantic Problems in A. J. Arberry's Translation of the Suspended Odes (Mu'allaqat)*, Dr Bader Eddin is passionately interested in Classical Arabic and how it can be functionally translated into English. He has published extensively in the fields of linguistics and translation in such refereed journals as *Translation Journal,* the *British Journal of Middle Eastern Studies*, etc. Dr Bader Eddin's research interests include, but are not limited to, theory of translation, translation competence, literary translation, stylistics, translation training, systemic linguistics, discourse analysis, and the salient features of the Gracious Quran in translation.

Maher Bahloul holds a PhD from Cornell University, USA, in linguistics and an MA in linguistics from Sorbonne University in Paris, France. He has taught courses in language (English, Arabic, and French), translation, and linguistics for the past 30 years. His research interests cover issues in theoretical linguistics, applied linguistics, the sociology of language, teaching and learning pedagogy, and the use of arts in education. He has taught in the United States, North Africa, and the Middle East. Dr. Bahloul has been very active with academic publishing and professional activities. He has presented a variety of papers and conducted several workshops in regional and international venues. With around 100 talks and workshops and 30 peer-reviewed books, book chapters, and articles, Dr. Bahloul continues to promote the fields of teaching and learning pedagogies. After his 2012 book with Carolyn Graham titled *Lights! Camera! Action and the Brain: The Use of Film in Education*, he has just published a monograph titled *Providing Students with Creative Spaces: The Power of Edutainment* (see www.maherbahloul.com/mb/) for more information.

Mike Baynham is Emeritus Professor of TESOL at the University of Leeds, UK and a fellow of the Academy of Social Sciences. His monograph *Translation and Translanguaging*, jointly written with Tong King Lee, was published by Routledge in 2019. He translates poetry from Spanish and increasingly from Arabic. His translations of poems by the Moroccan poet Abdallah Zrika, accompanied by a commentary, have been published in the poetry translation journal *Transference*.

Lahousseine Id-Youss is affiliated with KU Leuven, Belgium. He lectures on translation from Arabic into Dutch of media and business documents and

Contributors xiii

administrative texts. The title of his doctoral thesis is: *Legal Translation: A Comparison of Concept Systems. Arabophone Morocco versus Francophone Belgium*. He has published in the areas of translation studies, legal terminology, parallel corpora, and translation technology.

Rafik Jamoussi is Associate Professor of Translation Studies at Sohar University, Oman. He has been teaching at Sohar University since 2009, where he served as the English Language and Translation program coordinator from 2013 to 2018. He has taught courses addressing terminology management and technology in translation as well as courses on literary and legal translation. His research interests include translator training, translation technology, and corpus linguistics.

An Lambrechts obtained her MA degree in translation at KU Leuven, Campus Antwerp, Belgium, in 2014. She worked as a professional in-house translator for ten years, specializing in medical, legal, and technical translation, before embarking on a research project in translation and linguistics at KU Leuven in September 2016. The focus of her research is the impact of CAT tools and corpora on the quality and efficiency of specialized (medical/legal) translations from English into Dutch. Her research interests include specialized translation, phraseology, corpus linguistics and translation technologies. She has also worked as a technical writer and currently works as a translator for a municipality of Brussels.

Said M. Shiyab is Professor of Linguistics and Translation Studies at Kent State University, Ohio, USA. He has been teaching at Kent State since 2014. Currently, Professor Shiyab is running the MA Program in Translation and has served as the Director of Graduate Studies in the Department between 2016–2019. Professor Shiyab has published extensively in the fields of linguistics, discourses analysis, and translation. In addition to over 160 refereed articles, Professor Shiyab published a few books; among those are *Translation: Concepts and Critical Issues* (2017), *Writing Business Letters across Languages* (2015), *Translation and the Structure of Argumentation* (2013), *Globalization and Aspects of Translation* (2010), and *A Textbook of Translation: Theoretical and Practical Implications* (2006). Professor Shiyab's research interests include, but are not limited to, theory of translation, translation competence, translation and pedagogy, intercultural communication, and translation training, systemic linguistics, and discourse analysis.

Frieda Steurs is Full Professor at the KU Leuven, Faculty of Arts, Belgium. She works in the field of terminology, language technology, specialized translation, and multilingual document management. She is a member of the research group Quantitative Lexicology and Variation Linguistics (QLVL). Her research includes projects with industrial partners and public institutions. She is the founder and former president of NL-TERM, the Dutch terminology association for both the Netherlands and Flanders. Since 2016, she has been the head of research of the INT, the Dutch Language Institute in Leiden. In this capacity, she is responsible for the collection, development and hosting of all digital language resources for the Dutch language. In 2018, she was elected Secretary-General of CIPL, the international committee of linguists.

Heidi Verplaetse is Associate Professor of Linguistics and Translation at the Antwerp Campus of KU Leuven, Belgium, where she currently teaches English in the domains of translation and writing (medical/scientific, business, journalistic) and external communication. She has also worked on research projects in the domain of knowledge management based on automatic retrieval of semantic relations and anaphora. Her PhD in English linguistics (Ghent University, 2008) was situated in the domain of modality. She has also published in the domain of business communication. Her current research interests and recent publications are situated in the domains of specialized (medical) translation and health care communication, translation quality and translation assessment and the use of CAT tools and corpora as translation resources, trans-editing of journalistic texts, (the evolution of) translation work and processes in students, as well as the expression of epistemic modality and related semantic categories for the expression of author commitment in historical science writing and modality in present-day texts.

Mai Zaki is Associate Professor of Arabic and Linguistics at the Department of Arabic and Translation Studies at the American University of Sharjah, UAE. She has a PhD in linguistics from Middlesex University, UK. She has taught courses in linguistics and translation in Egypt, the United Kingdom and the United Arab Emirates. Her research interests include corpus linguistics, corpus stylistics, translation studies and teaching Arabic as a foreign language. She has published papers in corpus-based linguistic studies, translation and using corpora in Arabic language teaching. She is currently compiling the first parallel corpus of modern literary Arabic texts and their English translations with full-length texts.

Acknowledgments

I would like to express my warmest and deepest gratitude to all those who contributed to this volume and have spurred me to read their work and further my knowledge in some areas I was unaware of. I would also like to thank my colleague, Dr. Erik Angelone, Kent State University, for making the efforts during the coronavirus's trying and challenging times to write the epilogue and giving me the opportunity to share my ideas with him.

A special thank you goes to Professor Mike Baynham, University of Leeds (UK), whom I have only recently known and worked with on an accreditation case. Even though our collaborations were brief, I feel as though I have known Mike for years and did not hesitate to ask him to read the volume and write the foreword. I truly value his immense knowledge and plentiful experience and encouragement.

I am extremely grateful to the Routledge team for their time, patience and, above all, confidence in this project. In particular, I would like to thank Ellie Auton and Andrea Hartill for their kindness and help in the creation of this project.

Finally, this project would not have been possible without the help and love of my family, particularly my wife (Tammy) and my daughter (Amy), who endured the impossible and managed to create a comfortable environment through which I was able to work and focus. Their support and generosity with their time made the difference between completing this project and losing hope in its completion. I am deeply indebted to them.

Foreword

Mike Baynham

It gives me great pleasure to introduce this diverse collection of research-informed contributions to the study of translation training in the Arab world, ably introduced by its editor. Papers are drawn from a range of national contexts, including Jordan, the UAE, Saudi Arabia, and Oman. While many of the practical and theoretical concerns of translation are not language and culture specific, some necessarily are determined both by the affordances of a specific language, its potential relation with other languages of translation, its sociolinguistic constitution and of course the prevailing social/cultural/political context. One of the well-known affordances of Arabic, for example, is its capacity to incorporate loan words productively into its morphology, so film can become فلم/أفلام. Of course, this is not an unproblematic tendency, as language ideological debates over the merits of loan word incorporation and تعريب or Arabization testify. Such issues surface in the book, and I will return to them later.

The chapters in this book in the main explore issues related to translation training into and from Arabic in the Arab world. They bring together perspectives from across the Arab world and beyond, revealing a diversity of foci in different countries and different social conditions, this diversity impacting on translation into and out of Arabic. Examples of this are the multilingual translation needs generated by the annual Hajj pilgrimage to Saudi Arabia, the public service translation needs generated by the large body of migrant workers in the Gulf States and the sociolinguistic diversity of Arabic, with its many regional varieties, though contributions also show us that the written language (Modern Standard Arabic) has its diversity. When a speaker of one regional variety of Arabic is translating for a speaker of another, even from neighboring states, significant failures of understanding can occur. A contribution to this book shows how translation is a necessary component of such humanitarian interventions, with distinctive challenges. In the standard variety of Modern Standard Arabic and its written texts, lexical differences can be detected, for example, as another chapter shows, in relation to the naming of legal concepts or government institutions in different countries, which can influence, even hinder, effective translation. Contributions to the book also address other sociolinguistic issues such as language planning and implicitly through this language ideology, for example in considering, as mentioned earlier, the impact of strategies for the Arabicization of technical lexis. Calls are made for the standardization of newly introduced technical lexis and the ongoing revision of the orthography of Arabic. Again, this can be taken as distinctive to the pivotal if perhaps changing role of the standard language in the Arab world, though it also has echoes in efforts elsewhere, for example in strategies aimed at managing the influx of foreign language terminology (notably English) undertaken by organizations such as the Académie Française in France.

And yet, as the last point suggests, despite the specificity of the book's topic, on translation training in the Arab world, problems and issues arise in its chapters that are not region specific but commonplace in different contexts: for example, a pervasive reliance on nonqualified translators, often in high stakes contexts such as health. Unsurprisingly, therefore, there is a strong emphasis across the chapters on professionalization of the translation field, translator education and training as well as issues of assessment, not to forget issues of quality.

The chapters variously show the methodologies currently advocated in translation education include problem-based and task-based approaches and roleplay, focusing on contextualized practice and learning, which can serve as a preparation for the translator transitioning effectively into the field. This raises another key issue: transition from translator education and training into the workplace and the workplace preparedness of newly graduated translators. Here the importance of engaging with "authentic" texts is also emphasized. Here, as elsewhere across the world, the inclusion of a placement or practicum in the translation course is considered a fundamental of good practice in preparing novice translators for the workplace.

Alongside influences from contemporary methodologies for teaching and learning there have of course been very rapid and transformative developments in technologies that support translation, for example online dictionaries and linguistic corpora and machine translation. Corpora are another way of investigating "authentic" distribution of items in a text and have become invaluable to the contemporary translator, who has arguably become more and more of a *cyborg*: a human/machine composite. Corpora enable the perception through the processing of large amounts of linguistic data of regularities of lexicogrammar, genre and register, invaluable in translation. Corpora are shown to have a significant place in the translation classroom. In this context I might mention a specialist corpus, the Quranic Arabic Corpus, an invaluable resource for translators and others, developed and housed at my university, the University of Leeds.

In short, this book engages in a research-informed way both with themes specific to translation training in the Arab world and with those of very general concern for practitioners and researchers the world over. I see the thematic concerns informing the book as engaging, in particular with the ongoing professionalization of translation in the Arab world; its emergence as an academic discipline; issues of expertise and the development of expertise; and a concomitant emphasis on assessment of competence, both in the classroom and the workplace. To all of these it makes an important contribution.

The book concludes with a call for both routinized and adaptive learning in the education of translation students. Routinization will develop the core skills, knowledge and attitudes of the students, though the delivery of the curriculum should of course be anything but routinized. Adaptiveness is what will enable the student to enter and thrive in the workplace, with its rapidly changing roles and opportunities and equally rapidly developing technological scenarios. In drawing our attention to these issues, illustrated with copious grounded examples drawn from many settings, this book is to be welcomed.

Introduction

Said M. Shiyab

Over the past three decades, many studies have been conducted on various issues related to translation or translation studies, and these issues range from the notion of translatability, equivalence and fidelity to intercultural communication. Out of the many publications that have been conducted, an increasing proportion of published articles on translation focus on specific and technical components in which the emphasis is largely on terminological and psycholinguistics issues. Despite the increase of publications on translation, a small number of such publications involve translators training, simply because there is a lack of recognition as to the role training plays in the translators' education.

Let it be known that one significant topic in writing about translation is writing about translators training. Only recently in translation training, it has been increasingly acknowledged that formal training in academic institutions is the most practical and more effective approach, not only in the way translation is taught but also in the way academic institutions teach and test abilities to fulfill the needs of the market and translation industry and provide them with reliable and qualified professionals.

Studies on the nature, adequacy and possession of the required and needed skills of translators have grown, and studies on translators training have gained momentum. However, the different parameters, needs and situations that ought to be enforced when it comes to translators training are still a challenge. This means that scholars and translators, particularly in Arab academic institutions, have a long way to go before empirical research findings can even claim to have the knowledge and skills to differentiate between effective and ineffective means of training translators. Therefore, training translators is still in its infant stages and is largely based on professional experience, reflection, personal judgment and discussions between training institutions as to the means and ways of training translators. This kind of situation does not exclude theoretical or philosophical foundations for translators training, particularly in programs run by academic institutions.

When it comes to Arab institutions, the translation movement is generally weak, and the issue of training translators is even more complicated. Jacquemond

(2009: 2) argues that the Arabic translation situation in the Middle East is astonishingly weak; it is an indication of lack of seriousness and "a blatant illustration of the cultural lag of Arab societies and their faulty insertion in the international economy of knowledge".

Although this representation may seem highly questionable to some Arab or Middle Eastern scholars, Jacquemond argues that such representation has "been reproduced in countless official discourses, both Arab and non-Arab, and now constitutes the first and main justification for most of the translation programs currently undertaken".

Although there have been good advances in translation studies, the literature review on translators training in Arab academic institutions is scarce. Most of the studies conducted on translation and training focus on general descriptive issues, such as error analysis, contrastive linguistics, etc. Fallacies about the nature and method of teaching translation are one of the many impediments facing translators training at Arab academic institutions. In addition, there is no common denominator that unites teachers, academic institutions and translation organizations. This is exacerbated by the lack of understanding of what translation is all about and what constitutes good translation training programs. Up to this moment, there is no proper methodology that can provide translators with the means and tools that would train translators on the linguistic, social, cultural, cognitive and professional skills to a level where they can meet the demands of the job market. Even if there have been attempts to incorporate translators training in the curriculum, those attempts have not contributed to creating a systematic approach in which efficiency and higher-level of translators' competency are guaranteed. This is coupled with a lack of interest on the part of the translator, educator and institution to create an environment in which translators are trained on the tools and skills required by a fast-changing market. That being said, this collective work has developed as a result of my personal interest in Arab translators training, and therefore, this introduction provides the reader with some new knowledge about different but always valuable research topics relevant to translators training. While this volume is primarily written for Arab translators who teach one or both professions (i.e., also interpreting), some chapters present a global perspective or a perspective on different aspects of translators training. In addition, Western scholars can find this volume particularly illuminating in the sense that they become familiar with the current trends regarding the profession of translation and translators training in Arab and Middle Eastern institutions. Scholars who are not involved in teaching translation or translation training may also find this volume extremely useful, as it may enhance their ability to explore areas of interest other than what they are already pursuing. It may also deepen their sense of awareness of what translators are going through in this digitized world.

Without any exaggeration, this volume can be regarded as the first comprehensive compilation of scholarly works on translators training. It is written by scholars known for their contributions to the field of translation studies in general as well as Arabic translators training in Arab universities, in particular. Their innovative research on translators training and the distinct and smooth interrelated aspects of their work make this volume unique and crucial for those who are involved in translators training.

This volume consists of 12 chapters. Chapter 1 breaks new ground in the field of innovative approaches to translators training and explores new translators methodologies and assessment of translators competence. The chapter is the fruition of first-hand experience, taking the form of questions, training and assignments that pin down the results of this chapter in relation to the new methodologies and translators training. The subjects of the results provided in the chapter are MA translation students at King Khalid University. The chapter occasionally touches upon some of the challenges facing educators in translators training and provides tangible examples taken from actual courses in legal and Islamic translation.

Since corpora resources have a significant role to play, not only in translation studies research but also in translation practice and teaching, Chapter 2 discusses corpora and translation teaching in the Arab world and outlines existing Arabic corpus resources as well as efforts in incorporating corpora in translation and training classes. The chapter also introduces an ongoing project at the American University of Sharjah to build a parallel corpus of Arabic-English literary texts and its potential uses in courses on translating literature and in translators training.

Translators training in undergraduate programs is also an important issue in Arab universities, and Chapter 3 reports the results of a comparative study conducted on a sample of undergraduate Arabic-speaking trainee translators' renditions and on a sample of professional translators renditions of a source text exhibiting a set of grammatical constructions. Furthermore, this chapter examines the two group processes of identifying or not identifying the source text segments as problems and the solutions offered.

In Chapter 4, the author examines the current writing systems in Arabic using scripts such as Farsi and Urdu and calls for a serious consideration of a reform of the orthographic system of Arabic, adding three new graphemes, namely /v/, /g/ and /p/, so that the Arabic orthography overcomes certain handicaps such as dealing with loan words, in order to put an end to current problems for translators and others. The author argues that academics, not only those involved in translation and interpreting but also linguists and language academies throughout the Arabic-speaking countries, are called more than ever to get involved and initiate badly needed orthographic reforms to eliminate current transliteration inconsistencies. The author concludes by highlighting the importance of translators training programs in overcoming pertinent orthographic challenges, especially in an era where the world is becoming more relevant and largely interconnected as the result of the proliferation of media technologies throughout the world. Indeed, social media has turned national and international, cultural and intercultural, translation and transliteration communication and practices to constant, fast-paced changes.

Like Chapter 1, Chapter 5 discusses assessment of translators competence. While the former chapter is based on a Saudi Arabian context, the latter provides a global and Western perspective, thus bridging assessment of translators competence from both a Middle Eastern and a Western perspective. In determining the completeness of error taxonomies for translation training, Chapter 5 presents the most frequent error types made with different translation aids and analyzes whether the most frequent error types fit into the preestablished categories from five different error taxonomies, viz. the Canadian Language Quality Measurement System (Sical), the SAE J 2450 quality metric, MeLLANGE, the Multidimensional Quality Metrics (MQM) framework and the Smart Computer-Aided Translation Environment (SCATE) error taxonomy. The authors also compare the frequent errors made with different translation aids with the ATA Framework for Standardised Error Marking and conclude that most of the error taxonomies pay great attention to language quality in the target text, in addition to the source text, to target text transfer, and that this also has great importance for translation training. In addition, it is concluded that awareness of and insight into error taxonomies will benefit both students and professional translators. While not specifically focused on the Middle East, this chapter provides transferrable insights, making comparisons or uniformization of different error typologies that will indeed benefit translators' trainers both in Arab and Middle Eastern institutions and also worldwide and hence also benefit student translators and interpreters as well as professional translators. Within this context, translators trainers and trainees specifically will benefit from the application of analytical error typologies, particularly when concrete guidelines are provided to distinguish error types. Such concrete annotation guidelines will then not only promote inter-annotator reliability, and hence research purposes, but – even more importantly – didactic translation contexts.

Promoting and marketing terminology in Arabic is a serious issue in translators training, and from a language planning perspective, the authors of Chapter 6 propose a strategic model for training terminologists on managing, promoting and marketing terms. A commendable model is proposed on how to plan coining and Arabicizing terms through different processes and strategies acquainting and raising term awareness, usability of terms including proficiency and evaluation of such newly coined or Arabicized terms.

Chapter 7 sheds light on several new and developing areas within the fast-growing field of translation technologies; it examines some of the technicalities that translators must be familiar with within each of these areas. The fields in question include wiretap interpreting, software localization, website localization, screen translation, etc. The authors recommend that the solution to resolve this problem lies in constant updating and putting forth proper and practical trainings in which translators can develop their competences in order to meet the new qualification requirements established by these new translation modes.

While a detailed discussion of translation technologies may not seem to be directly relevant to translators training in Arab institutions, in fact it constitutes a valuable contribution and unique invitation for Arabic translators to take a hard look at the kind of technology they use in teaching translation. It is within this context that this chapter becomes extremely significant, as hiring bilingual professional translators with no or little technology background is in the current context counterproductive, making them unable to meet the market demand for high-qualified and technology-oriented professional translators, not only in Arab institutions but also globally. Similarly, paying good translators who were trained to deal with traditional forms of translation to carry out such a task does not solve the problem, either. The solution lies in putting forth adequate training in which translators take the necessary steps to broaden their competences in order to meet the new qualification requirements established by these new translation modes. This way, one can ensure that the localized product will undoubtedly live up to the highest standards possible.

In Chapter 8, the authors investigate the integration of computer-assisted translation (CAT) tools within higher education institutions (HEIs) in Oman and makes use of both qualitative and quantitative approaches to reach an accurate depiction of the situation in Oman. This chapter focuses on: (a) the types of tools involved, (b) software packages used and (c) balance between education and training as reflected in the course components. Toward the end, the chapter provides a discussion of the findings that emerge from the results and concludes with the necessary recommendations for what could arguably represent a more appropriate integration of technology-related translation tools into the curriculum.

In the final chapter of this volume, Chapter 9, the author presents a critical evaluation of contemporary approaches to translators in Arab universities and highlights the impediments facing Arabic translators and interpreters. The chapter proposes strategies and calls for further investigation of the current situation of Arabic translators in Arab universities.

Over the years, and due to the scarcity of information about translators training in the Arab world, I have become convinced that contributions in this direction are badly needed and deserve to be highlighted in order to benefit all scholars in the field. Chapters in this volume are valuable contributions written by knowledgeable scholars largely representing the Arab world and/or Arab institutions. In addition, some of the chapters provide global and Western perspectives on translation, written by scholars representing Western universities of direct relevance to the context of Arab academic institutions. In this manner, a fruitful exchange of Arab and Western didactic practice may be promoted.

It is hoped that the basic issues of translation and the impediments facing Arabic translators presented in this volume will provide new insights to the reader.

It is also hoped that the experiences and ideas along with the suggestions made by the contributors would provide a platform for the continuing optimization of translators training in the Arab world and for fruitful exchange with Western didactic practice and perspectives.

Reference

Jacquemond, Richard. 2009. "Translation Policies in the Arab World Representations, Discourses and Realities". *The Translator*, 15(1): 15–35.

1 Crucial insights into translator training, assignments, and assessment

Eyhab A. Bader Eddin

1.1 Introduction

Translation has been seen as an activity that pulls down the language and cultural barriers among languages. It is how previous civilizations came in contact with each other to exchange knowledge, philosophy, religion, and even at peace and war. Translation proficiency is an alloy of what to translate (declarative knowledge), how to translate (operational knowledge), why to translate (explanatory knowledge), and 'when to translate' (conditional knowledge) (Hurtado Albir 2015). The current chapter sheds light on translator training, assignments, and assessment, as components falling under declarative and operational knowledge.

The field of translation has never seen such rapid change in the plateau and blueprint of translator training, assignments, and assessment as is the case nowadays. The area of translator training has been the focus of attention because it is the stage in which the translators' skills are refined and honed to be qualified enough to join the job market and meet its ever-growing, demanding needs.

One problem that faces translation departments at Arab universities is the assignment of instructors who are not fully qualified to teach in MA programs. Many of them are specialized in literature or linguistics. It is often the interest that an instructor shows to teach translation that guarantees him/her to be assigned to teach translation.

Contrary to the common expectations, training translators is not and should not be confined to the academic path; rather, it is an ongoing in-service professional vocational training (Al-Qinai 2010). Translator training, according to Pym (2003), aims at developing multicomponent competencies, namely skills at the linguistic, cultural, technological, and professional levels. Although translator training is a field that is unanimously agreed on as imperative, it remains an open field that calls for experiments and new successful approaches (Wilss 1996). Various ways of training have been introduced, and still many more are arriving on the scene.

1.2 Approaches to student translator training

Translator training has become an area that is gaining momentum amid the high demand for qualified translators as a result of the rapid expansion of translation. In a world mostly characterized by a constant change in information, it is important to highlight the importance of translators' skill to research. Research goes inextricably hand in hand with the knowledge of terms in the translation process. At Durham University, students are trained to develop their research skills using reference tools (Burukina 2013). The 21st century has seen a dramatic shift to information mining, highlighting the importance of how to find reliable information and filter, select, and use it correctly (Way 2016).

To echo Dmitrienko (2017), translator training is viewed as a dynamic process that is honed toward the transfer of relevant specialization-specific declarative and operational knowledge. Professional education and training cannot be limited to declarative knowledge. Today's student translators should be trained enough to be equipped; this involves putting to practice the previously acquired theoretical knowledge, as set out by Dmitrienko (2017). Declarative knowledge represented by the theoretical background provided to students at the outset of their instruction needs to be followed by a thorough in-classroom training to activate the skills they already possess.

Until recently, most Arab universities used to teach translation as an academic subject subsidiary to the theoretical courses on linguistics and literature (Al-Qinai 2010). The traditional long-standing approach to translator training is represented by assigning selected texts from an array of subjects to all students. The problem with this approach is that it does not produce translators who are fully prepared for the job market. The case is that it usually takes graduates years to possess the skills required for translation for specific purposes. Meanwhile, they are prone to running the risk of translational pitfalls due to their inadequate experience in the field in question (Al-Qinai 2010). Because of the inadequacy of student translators' level of proficiency to translate into a language that is not their mother tongue (English), the student translators often fall prey to such problems as literal translations and unnatural renditions. Thus, it takes them years to create enough competence to possess a mastery of that language. Abdel-Fattah (2011) states that the amount of instructional time given to prepare students to translate into English is far from enough to achieve the necessary command required. This approach in teaching is called the transmissionist teacher-centered approach. This approach focuses on the individual differences of students' performance. Students are not able to benefit from their peers' mistakes unless the instructor makes it known or discusses it in public before the whole class.

Team or group work is another strategy commonly used in translator training. Students are expected to gain a useful learning experience with a view to bolster their understanding to embark on a career in translation. The task-based translation teaching approach is an imitation of the real-world experience in which students work through groups to achieve a common goal (Al-Qinai 2010). In the task-based approach, students share information to identify translational problems and consequently seek resources to solve the detected problems collectively. This approach engages all team members in the process of translation and allows them to look at the text from different perspectives, depending on each student's background and angle of analyzing the text. Usually, students parcel out the work among themselves. Such subtasks include text analysis, looking up vocabulary, search for terminology, editing, revision, structure analysis, semantic change, etc.

At some universities, the graduation project of MA students includes translation criticism of a work or an exploration or analysis of a theoretical issue in translation. Alternatively, students are asked to parcel out a large text (possibly a book) among themselves. Some of them are tasked with translating a section of the text while others act as editors or revisers. This approach is designed to put to practice collaboration to obtain some firsthand experience. It also enables students to shoulder their responsibility and establish rapport with other team members, a simulation of real-world experience in the job market.

1.3 Assessment of translators' competence

The world has been abuzz with 'quality' of translation in general, and legal translation in particular, since poor legal translations have drastic consequences. The standards applied to translation in general may not necessarily work for legal translation, for reasons to be shown in the next section.

Researchers have been pursuing various paths to look for the key to improving translator training, all of which take 'developing competence' as the point of departure. Sparer (1988) states that it is possible to train legal translators without their necessarily being legal experts or lawyers. Most student translators are not legal experts or lawyers, thus having little or no grounding in the legal profession or system (Way 2016).

Developing student translators' competence involves an amalgam of further sub-competencies and skills including such communicative skills as reading and writing, a professional use of wide-ranging knowledge, and intercultural awareness, along with problem-solving strategies and the successful transfer of ideas from a source language into a target language (Espunya 2014).

Canale and Swain (1980) propose a four-component model of competence made up of (a) grammatical, (b) sociolinguistic, (c) discourse and (d) strategies. It is mostly the grammatical and discourse components of this model that are emphasized in teaching. They both share the command of two language systems and the ability to understand texts accurately.

Translation assessment has always been a matter of great concern to translators. Apart from the bone of contention whether the final product (target text) is the translator's own job or others', an assessment of a translation involves tracing the text from its authorship to its final product (Mason 1982). He goes further to put forward the principles of 'acceptability' and 'readability' as yardsticks on which the process of assessment rests. Both principles should be gauged according to the source text author's intention. This involves checking if the impact or effect left by the source text has been maintained in the target text, echoing Nida's dynamic equivalence (Nida 1964; Nida and Taber 1969). In other words, the translator's ultimate goal is to come up with a translation that is equivalent in response to the source text (Shiyab 2006). This echoes one approach in the psychological school of behaviorism. It heavily relies on the fact that an assessment should be based on the recipients' reactions to a text (response-based behavioral views) (House 2009). A student may find it very useful to compare the source text and its target text with a view to analyze problems and find how they are solved. Any assessment of a translation considers two factors: fidelity and naturalness (Shiyab 2006).

Because each text type has its own salient features, each target text of a different text type should by logic bear its own features, too. The general rule says that a good translation must achieve its intention. For instance, an informative text must convey its facts quite acceptably, whereas in an expressive text, the form and content are equally important, etc. (Newmark 1988).

I was told once that a native speaker of English who did not know Arabic did mark Arabic translations. The story occurred in Baghdad in the sixties of the past century when an announcement seeking English–Arabic translators was made, and many applied for that post. The applicants were given an English text to translate into Arabic. Once done, they were asked to come back a month later. To their amazement, they were given the texts they themselves had produced unmarked, and they were asked to translate it back into English. The marker, who was a native speaker of English and who did not know Arabic, marked their back-translations by comparing their new attempts to the original text they first received when they came to translate. The more similar the translation was to the original, the better score their translation got.

1.4 Hands-on experience in training and assessment

Legal translation is viewed as a challenge, except for cases in which the translator is exclusively required to fill out data into already-done forms of certificates of death, birth, and passports. The difficulty of legal translation is aggravated by such factors as (a) obsession with words and terminology and (b) lack of experience (Way 2016).

Legally binding documents are very sensitive to translate, and they often involve high risks, making Robert (2012) consider the legally astute translator a more than important factor. Burukina (2013) likens the legal translators to military men who should be always alert, often stressed out, and sometimes on the verge of a crisis. Way (2016) gives her voice to Burukina (2013) in stating that a legal translator is considered a crucial nexus for effective communication. This makes legal translation more restricted than any other form (Newmark 1981). Farghal and Shunnaq (1999) explain it by saying that legal discourse is far different from other discourses because it requires disambiguation and use of exact legal jargon. Way (2016) points out that legal translation carries the added burden of keeping in mind legal aspects that are not found in other genres of texts. This is because of the difference between legal systems that are different, again owing to strong sociocultural and historical influence exerted on them. For instance, while common law is applied in the United States and England, it is not applicable in Scotland, though the latter is part of the United Kingdom.

Structural and stylistic differences between the English and Arabic legal discourses pose a challenge to translators (Emery 1989). Seeking too literal translations from a source text produces an unnatural rendition and swerves away from the jargon used in legal profession. Under this category comes what Farghal and Shunnaq (1999) call 'syntax problems' in legal translation. Because of the disparity in the language systems of English and Arabic, translating legal texts poses a formidable challenge. One syntax-related example is وإذ تعي أن. It is a legal cliché that is handled with difficulty and uncertainty. Most inexperienced translators would translate it literally as 'conscious that'. The problem arises from the fact that most UN legal texts in English consist of nonfinite English clauses (Farghal and Shunnaq 1999). To give a functional effective translation, the target text should be natural and existent in the jargon of the genre in focus. One possible UN-adopted translation could be 'bearing in mind that'.

Of crucial importance are problems related to 'layout', which is an umbrella term to include paragraphing, capitalization, indentation, etc. For instance, a bold or italicized word in an English legal text must keep its emphasized status in Arabic. One perfect example is '*The PARTY*', '*the CONTRACT*', etc., which retain their capitalized status throughout the legal document.

Based on firsthand experience of teaching translation in an MA program, I have collected a few thoughts on the translation of legal and Islamic texts. In legal translation, the student is required to be able to identify all the terms in the text, along with knowledge of their notions. For instance, a sharp distinction must be made between 'arrest', 'detain', 'round up', 'capture', 'hunt down', etc. Using the exact term in the text which belongs to a certain country is extremely important. For instance, what is known in English as 'the Court of Cassation' is known by different terms in different countries. While it is known as محكمة النقض in Abu Dhabi and Egypt, it is known as محكمة التمييز in Syria and Jordan. It is also known as محكمة التعقيب in Tunisia, whereas it is known as المحكمة العليا in Sudan and Libya. One more example is the reference to the Ministry of Labor in the Arab Gulf countries as وزارة العمل, while it is referred to as وزارة الشغل in Tunisia.

On the other hand, in Islamic translation I usually start with my students translating 'particles' and move on to cover 'lexical choices' and end with 'texts', i.e., verses from the Noble Quran. Bader Eddin (2019) gives a detailed explanation of the difference between the particle هل (*hal*) and how it takes on different meanings in different contexts. Widely read translators of the Quran could not differentiate between them. Bader Eddin explores uncharted territory in translation and syntactic analysis, bringing to focus the preposition ب (*baa*), signaling 12 uses. I discuss with my students some other particles like كم (*kam*) and اللام (*lam*). The spiritual nature accompanying its very carefully selected lexical choices of the Quran poses a daunting challenge for translators. Some examples from the Quran that are considered a formidable task to tackle in translation are اليم والبحر، الرياح والريح، الأجداث والقبور and جنات.

Elaborating further on some of these words that are seemingly synonyms, and whether the Quran's choice of words is meticulously selected or not, let us bring into focus the words أجداث and قبور in the Holy Quran. Translators do not seem to have reflected on whether any difference can be spotted, making them use the same word in English for both, i.e., 'graves'. The word أجداث appears three times, whereas القبور appears five times throughout the Holy Quran. Both lexical items have the same referential meaning in Arabic. That is perhaps why translators view them both alike and consequently use the same word for both in English.

Interestingly enough, the Holy Quran uses them meticulously and with infinite accuracy. Etymologically, the singular of أجداث, i.e., جَدَث, belongs to the same root that the word جدثة belongs to. جدثة in Arabic means the sound of friction of animal hooves against the soil they walk on, and it also means the sound of munching on flesh in an explicit reference to the sound probably uttered when the flesh of the bodies of the dead is decomposed in their graves (Al-Fairouzabadi 2008). Here there is a unique use of the word أجداث, which is not found in the use of القبور. The word أجداث appears in the Quran only when a picture of motion of the dead is given, as the dead rush for the Assembly Day for the Judgment Day after resurrection. Note the three verses that use أجداث: يَخْرُجُونَ مِنَ الْأَجْدَاثِ كَأَنَّهُمْ جَرَادٌ مُنْتَشِرٌ - فَإِذَا هُم مِّنَ الْأَجْدَاثِ إِلَىٰ رَبِّهِمْ يَنسِلُونَ and يَوْمَ يَخْرُجُونَ مِنَ الْأَجْدَاثِ سِرَاعًا كَأَنَّهُمْ إِلَىٰ نُصُبٍ يُوفِضُونَ. It is crystal clear that the word أجداث goes hand in hand only with the scenes where the dead are brought to life and rush for the Judgment Day. The word أجداث is used in this particular context or situation, as if it intends to tell us that the sound they produce as rushing is like the sound of friction produced as animal hooves walk, after the flesh of those bodies are munched on in their graves. Keeping these details helps conjure up a full accurate picture of how the scene unfolds, creating an audiovisual picture. In the translations provided by the three translators in question, it is found out that their translations deal with both أجداث and قبور alike.

On the other hand, the lexical item القبور never appears where أجداث does in the Holy Quran. The word القبور is held through the Quran in contexts of situation where the dead in their dormant status are the focus of attention. The dead are described as motionless and still bodies. Some examples supporting the argument can be found in (60:13) (قَدْ يَئِسُوا مِنَ الْآخِرَةِ كَمَا يَئِسَ الْكُفَّارُ مِنْ أَصْحَابِ الْقُبُورِ), and

(أَفَلَا يَعْلَمُ إِذَا بُعْثِرَ مَا فِي الْقُبُورِ) (100:9) (They have despaired of [reward in] the Hereafter just as the disbelievers have despaired of [meeting] the inhabitants of the graves) (60:13) and (But does he not know that when the contents of the graves are scattered) (100:9).

One final example showing the uniqueness of vocabulary usage in the Holy Quran is the usage of the words ريح and رياح which both have received very little attention by translators. The two words are usually translated as 'winds', sometimes modified with certain epithets, but the head of the relevant noun phrases is always 'winds'. The word الرياح in the nominative case appears 10 times in the Quran, whereas الريح in nominative, accusative and dative cases appear 18 times, one of which carries the meaning of 'smell' in the Chapter of Yusuf (12:94).

As shown in Figure 1.1, the three translators never distinguish between the positive and negative connotations linked to the usage of the two words in focus. They view the two words from the same perspective, spotting no difference in the semantics of the two senses carried over by each of the words.

The matchless stylistic usage of the Holy Quran limits using الرياح to glad-tidings-bringing contexts of situation, whereas الريح is limited to contexts of situations characterized by chastisement and events with dire consequences (Al-Jahiz 2010). Some

Source Text	Abdullah Yusuf Ali	Muhammad Khan & Al-Helali	Pickthall
يَخْرُجُونَ مِنَ الْأَجْدَاثِ كَأَنَّهُمْ جَرَادٌ مُنْتَشِرٌ (54:7)	They will come forth,- their eyes humbled - from (their) graves, (torpid) like locusts scattered abroad	They will come forth, with humbled eyes, from (their) graves as if they were locusts spread abroad	they come forth from the graves as they were locusts spread abroad,
وما أنت بمسمع من في القبور (35:22)	But thou canst not make those to hear who are (buried) in graves.	But you can make hear those who are in graves	Thou canst not reach those who are in the graves.
كَمَثَلِ رِيحٍ فِيهَا صِرٌّ أَصَابَتْ حَرْثَ قَوْمٍ (3:117)	likened to a wind which brings a nipping frost	The likeness of a wind which is extremely cold	as the likeness of a biting, icy wind which smiteth the harvest of a people
وَهُوَ الَّذِي أَرْسَلَ الرِّيَاحَ بُشْرًا بَيْنَ يَدَيْ رَحْمَتِهِ (25:48)	And He it is Who sends the winds as heralds of glad tidings, going before His mercy	It is He Who sends the winds as heralds of glad tidings	And He it is Who sendeth the winds, glad tidings heralding His mercy

Figure 1.1 Three translators never distinguish between the positive and negative connotations linked to the usage of the two words in focus

of the examples proving the association of الرياح with desired results are وَأَرْسَلْنَا الرِّيَاحَ 15:22) (لَوَاقِحَ فَأَنزَلْنَا مِنَ السَّمَاءِ مَاءً فَأَسْقَيْنَاكُمُوهُ) (And We have sent the fertilizing winds and sent down water from the sky and given you drink from it) and وَاللَّهُ الَّذِي أَرْسَلَ الرِّيَاحَ 35:9) (فَتُثِيرُ سَحَابًا فَسُقْنَاهُ إِلَىٰ بَلَدٍ مَّيِّتٍ فَأَحْيَيْنَا بِهِ الْأَرْضَ بَعْدَ مَوْتِهَا ۚ كَذَٰلِكَ النُّشُورُ) (And it is Allah who sends the winds, and they stir the clouds, and We drive them to a dead land and give life thereby to the earth after its lifelessness. Thus is the resurrection). By contrast, the usage of الريح is always associated with disastrous consequences, as shown in the following verses: 46:24) (بَلْ هُوَ مَا اسْتَعْجَلْتُم بِهِ ۖ رِيحٌ فِيهَا عَذَابٌ أَلِيمٌ) (It is that for which you were impatient: a wind, within it a painful punishment) and (41:51) وَفِي عَادٍ إِذْ أَرْسَلْنَا عَلَيْهِمُ الرِّيحَ الْعَقِيمَ) (And in 'Aad [was a sign], when We sent against them the barren wind). One striking exception to the rule stated above is found in:

هُوَ الَّذِي يُسَيِّرُكُمْ فِي الْبَرِّ وَالْبَحْرِ ۖ حَتَّىٰ إِذَا كُنتُمْ فِي الْفُلْكِ وَجَرَيْنَ بِهِم بِرِيحٍ طَيِّبَةٍ وَفَرِحُوا بِهَا جَاءَتْهَا 10:22) (رِيحٌ عَاصِفٌ وَجَاءَهُمُ الْمَوْجُ مِن كُلِّ مَكَانٍ) (It is He who enables you to travel on land and sea until, when you are in ships and they sail with them by a good wind and they rejoice therein, there comes a storm wind and the waves come upon them from everywhere).

(10:22) جَاءَتْهَا رِيحٌ عَاصِفٌ وَجَاءَهُمُ الْمَوْجُ مِن كُلِّ مَكَانٍ

(there comes a storm wind and the waves come upon them from everywhere)

The reason why ريح is described as 'fair' and 'moderate' is that 'one wind' in the singular is needed to push the sails of a ship to carry on smoothly in the sea. In case a plural form of wind was used, then the ship would have not sailed smoothly. It is important that this short scene is immediately followed by a tragic event as shown in the verse as reading

The translators never distinguish between the positive and negative connotations linked to the usage of the two words in focus. They view the two words from the same perspective, spotting no difference in the semantics of the two senses carried over by each of the words. By the same token, the Holy Quran uses اليم and البحر, and many people believe they are interchangeable and thus in free complementary distribution. The three translations of both words are the same (see Figure 1.1). This shows that the translators in question understand the two words to be alike. From a different angle, the two words appear in a unique way in the Holy Quran. The word البحر is used generally in the Quran, including but not limited to Moses' story, and the sea is used as a blessing and a source of fish and jewels, etc. The word البحر appears 33 times throughout the Holy Quran in general contexts. By contrast, the word اليم appears eight times, and only in horror and frightening contexts of situation in relation to Moses' story. One example is 28:7) (وَأَوْحَيْنَا إِلَىٰ أُمِّ مُوسَىٰ أَنْ أَرْضِعِيهِ ۖ فَإِذَا خِفْتِ عَلَيْهِ فَأَلْقِيهِ فِي الْيَمِّ) (And We inspired to the mother of Moses, "Suckle him; but when you fear for him, cast him into the river"). One more interesting point to draw attention to is that the word اليم has its etymological roots in Syriac and Hebrew, the latter of which Moses spoke as an Israelite. So the word اليم is particularly used in the contexts of situation revolving around Moses. The translators have shown no sensitivity regarding what each word reflects in the Holy Quran. So the usage of اليم is intentionally associated with Moses, who spoke that language. The Quran includes no complete synonyms that can be used interchangeably. The style must be described as 'sui generis', whose matchless expressions make up an enormous challenge that has long faced the translators.

On the other hand, the sensitivity of legal terms in the legal profession is where the translator must keep in mind the audience for whom the text is being translated to select the terms used in the target country. I have found it very useful to give the legal terms to be used in their future texts beforehand in the form of exercises. Working on a text whose vocabulary has been already given to students in useful sentences in exercises helps students pick up the exact word and use it correctly. One good suggestion is to use Wyatt's (2006) *Check Your English Vocabulary for Law*, a book that is thematically categorized and provides very useful exercises, introducing terms in the legal profession. Such exercises provide contextualized terms, showing the characteristic features or more technically 'diagnostic properties' of such legal terms. I have found this strategy very useful because students often make unjustified decisions regarding lexical choices and dictionary use, an experience that Dam-Jensen (2012) finds true for the MA students in Denmark. This strategy helps students refine their skills of lexical choices in legal translation. Decision making is very crucial, since the assessment methods measure the success or failure of trainees' decisions (Way 2016).

It is useful to have a look at the judicial system of the area being translated in the two languages. Having a look at original texts in both languages would help get student translators familiarized with the diction, layout, syntactic structures, etc. If a too literal translation is provided blindly, then an awkward text will naturally be produced.

It has been found that the 'back-translation' approach is effective, particularly on the pre-final product, to ensure the target text's faithfulness to its source text. This involves comparing the texts by translating the target text back into the source text to check if the same or at least a very similar text can be obtained. Back-translation remains a very interesting option, where student translators are expected to bring back the original source text out of the target text (Thawabteh and Najjar 2014).

Adopting a social constructivist approach has proved more effective than the traditional instructor-centered approach. The former engages students in real experiences in which they view what their mistakes really are. Discussing the translational problems equips students with the skills needed for their future encounters with texts. The traditional approach is seen as monotonous and unidirectional, detaching students from interaction, making them only passive recipient objects of material. They are mainly absorbed in copying what is written on the board. They are absorbed in writing down the 'authoritative', 'correct' rendition according to their professor, who acts as the guardian of translating truth (Kiraly 2000). This contradicts Newmark's (1988) corollary that there is no final translation. A translation is prone to development and improvement, and the way we produce a translation today may not necessarily be produced the same verbatim in the future. The shift from product-oriented to process-oriented approaches has been found instrumental in translator training and assessment (Way 2016). It heavily relies on decision making. To make students get the maximum from their translation classes, they must be placed at the center of the translation process to be able to analyze and judge their work (Delisle 1988). Keeping them passive as mere recipient objects in the class would add very little to their repertoire of translation skills. It is the interpretive theory proposed by Marchand (2011) that is of most interest to us in class, since it pays attention to the meaning of the conveyed message rather than to the linguistic forms (Seleskovitch and Lederer 2001).

Urging students to self-evaluate themselves or to get their attempts evaluated by their peers is an effective approach, as this would bolster their self-confidence. However, their evaluation must be upheld by the instructor. Identifying their mistakes on their own, students are most probable to make more progress in translation.

Having spent many years in translation teaching, I have found it useful to discuss the students' attempts on the board so that everyone can derive benefit from their peers' mistakes. It is useful to give the student some time, depending on the length of the chunk to be translated. A text is divided into chunks, and each chunk is given some minutes during which the students try to translate it. I then indulge them to give some general remarks on the source text to be followed by a detailed analysis of the attempts received in terms of lexical choices, grammatical issues, stylistic remarks, etc. One important yet interesting principle I establish in classes is the 'What-if Principle'. This principle applies to all unsuccessful attempts made by students in the class while working on any text. In this principle, I take on the students' attempts and explain to them why the translation given is not correct. So I take their unsuccessful attempts as a point of departure for further analysis to pursue the path of arriving at a successful translation. This principle takes its strength from the fact that it discusses what the meaning becomes if we take students' attempts. It usually sheds light on seeking answers to the following questions: What is the wrong message we would get IF we went for 'the lexical choices' made in the students' attempts? How would that change the source text's intended meaning? What different meaning would we get IF we kept that structure, etc.? All these answers must be provided with justifications and solutions.

I always urge my students to reflect on each sentence they translate and pose the following questions to themselves: Does my translation make sense? Is it meaningful? What would a recipient understand when reading it? Try to develop the habit of always providing a mental back-translation of what you produce to check it bi-directionally.

Revision of a translation is usually preferred to be carried out by a different person from the one who produces the translation. The reason is that translators are sometimes unable to detect their own problems. This is very useful and feasible for group work, especially in graduation projects. Alternatively, translators can revise their own translation after some time. They put time and effort to see their work better than when immediately revising it once done. In revision, the goal is to screen out the translations, improve the translation quality, and get an error-free text. It is convenient here to make a sharp distinction between self-revision and a revision carried out by others. The former is when the translator is the same person who revises the translation, a process known as 'checking' (Al-Qinai 2010). The best way to make use of the errors found when marking students' translations is to analyze them systematically so as to bring to light the difficulties encountered. One solution technology has provided is the use of computer corpora, which plays a central role in translation and is gaining momentum in translator training with the arrival of the data-driven learning approach on the scene. Such corpora list monolingual original texts in the learners' second language (Granger et al. 2009).

It has become a pressing need nowadays to put more effort on establishing projects that gather student translations in electronic format form, compiled from text banks to form complete annotated corpora. One example is the ENTRAD, in Spain, a project with a collection of translations aligned with their respective source texts, first established in 2005 at the University of Zaragoza (Serrano and Sanz 2008). Such corpora are effective for students to identify errors and how they can be avoided and for instructors because they help them propose hypotheses, interpret the existing errors, and can consequently apply newly obtained knowledge for designing future materials.

Revision is not confined to correct punctuation mistakes, spelling, or grammatical errors. Rather, a reviser delves into the source text, its author, the extent of faithfulness to the source text, readership, etc. Nord (2001) argues that a reviser takes on a moral obligation to follow certain strategies in revision, to be listed in a preface, footnotes, or endnotes.

Advances in technology have taken the field of translator training a step forward by introducing parallel corpora, that is, collections of the same texts in two or more languages. House (2009) defines a parallel corpus as a set of texts and a set of their translations into another language. Parallel corpora have proved more useful, providing more information than that obtained from monolingual corpora. It is under data-driven learning (DDL), a term first coined by Tim Johns in 1993 and subsequently in 1997, that parallel corpora fall. DDL is a corpus linguistics-based approach that gives central importance to developing the learner's ability to 'puzzle out' how the target language operates from examples of authentic usages (Odlin 1994).

Student translators can be encouraged to familiarize themselves with parallel corpora because such experience enables students to carefully explore authentic language and how much the languages differ or bear resemblance to each other. Students are provided with an opportunity to explore naturally occurring language including but not confined to grammatical features, word usage, semantic and pragmatic features, etc. (Flowerdew 2015). Using DDL makes students less dependent on their instructor, making it an autonomy-promoting approach (Boulton 2013). It represents a radical shift from an instructor-centered approach to a student-centered approach where the emphasis is placed on the instructor as a facilitator, when needed, to guide students forward. Using a parallel corpus in translation helps student translators pin down the type of routine translation shifts by comparing instances of lexical and syntactic structures in both source and target texts using 'concordance software' (House 2009).

Despite the enormous significance the use of parallel corpora has taken on in language teaching, contrastive linguistics, and translation, Arabic remains a language that still lacks a satisfactory general-use parallel corpus resource (Alotaibi 2017). Using parallel corpora for translator training purposes has been gaining currency over the past decade or so. A parallel corpus is an effective tool that can be a recourse in translation training programs, so students can make use of it in translation projects (Singer 2016). It is a widespread practice to put parallel corpus use into practice, urging students to compile their own corpora depending on the typology of their projects (legal, scientific, religious, medical, etc.). This is usually accompanied by instructors' opening their students' eyes to further corpus-related skills such as corpus types, corpus analysis and search tools (Alotaibi 2017). Using parallel corpora helps students compare their translations with other professional translators' works (Pearson 2003). More features that are helpful for a student translator are concordances that support bilingual search queries, other filtering options, etc. One real feather in the cap of Saudi universities is the 10 million-word parallel corpus that is being established by King Saud University in Riyadh since 2017. It is useful as a resource for translation training (Alotaibi 2017). Among the most common reliable Arabic–English parallel corpora are the 5,392,491-word EAPCOUNT, 300 million-word MultiUN, and the 51 million-word EuroMatrix.

1.5 Conclusion

A considerable acrimonious debate has been raging about the training of translators and the challenges they face to be qualified enough for the labor market after graduation. Translation teaching, assignments, and assessments are indispensable in that an assessment is carried out to check the correctness of the assignment, given as a fruit of teaching translation. Various approaches have been adopted to measure their efficiency in translator training. The learner-oriented approach has proven most useful since it treats learners as active participants rather than recipient objects who are absorbed only in copying what their instructor has written on the board. Advances in technology have helped student translators to delve into the self-experienced real world of translation through parallel corpora, which provide students with natural authentic texts in both source and target texts. Some firsthand experience-based strategies were introduced to match the text type in question. Much has been written on translation teaching and assessment, and much more still is to be expected in the future.

References

Abdel-Fattah, Mahmoud. 2011. Role of contrastive text analysis in teaching translation for language learning purposes: Prepositions as a case. *Forum: International Journal of Interpretation and Translation*, 9(2), 1–22.
Al-Fairouzabadi, Majd Eddin M. 2008. القاموس المحيط *Al-Kamous Al-Muheet* (The Comprehensive Dictionary). Cairo: Dar Al-hadeeth.
Al-Jahiz, Abu Othman. 2010. البيان والتبيين *Al-bayan wa Tabyeen* (Elucidation and Illustration). Cairo: Ibn Sina Bookstore.
Alotaibi, Hind M. 2017. Arabic-English parallel corpus: A new resource for translation training and language teaching. *Arab World English Journal*, 8(3).
Al-Qinai, Jamal. 2010. Training tools for translators and interpreters. *Journal of Pan-Pacific Association of Applied Linguistics*, 14(2), 121–139.
Bader Eddin, Eyhab Abdulrazak. 2019. Inconsistent linguistic functional behaviours of particle لـه in the Holy Quran: A critique of the Holy Quran translation. *AWEJ for Translation & Literary Studies*, 3(1).
Boulton, Alex. 2013. Separating fact from fiction: The real story of corpus use in language teaching. In L. Bradley and S. Thouesny (Eds.), *20 Years of EUROCALL: Learning from the Past, Looking to the Future: Proceedings of the 2013 EUROCALL Conference* (pp. 51–56). Dublin: Research-publishing.net
Burukina, Olga. 2013. The legal translator's competence. *Contemporary Readings in Law & Social Justice*, 5(2), 809–826.
Canale, Michael and Swain, Merrill. 1980. Theoretical bases of communicative approaches to second language teaching and testing. *Applied Linguistics*, 1(1), 1–47.
Dam-Jensen, Helle. 2012. Decision-making in translation: A pilot study of students' translation processes. *Fachesprache*, 3–4, 146–164.
Delisle, Jean. 1988. *Translation: An Interpretive Approach*. Translated by Patricia Logan and Monica Creery. Ottawa: University of Ottawa Press.
Dmitrienko, Gleb. 2017. Translator training in Canada and Russia. *Translation & Interpreting Studies: The Journal of the American Translation & Interpreting Studies Association*, 12(2), 310–331, 22p. John Benjamins Publishing Co.
Emery, Peter. 1989. Legal Arabic text: Implications for translation. *Babel*, 35(1), 35–40.
Espunya, Anna. 2014. The UPF learner translation corpus as a resource for translator training. *Language Resources and Evaluation*, 48(1), 33–43. Springer.
Farghal, Mohammed and Shunnaq, Abdullah. 1999. *Translation with Reference to Arabic and English: A Practical Guide*. Irbid, Jordan: Dar Al-Hilal for Translation and Publishing.
Flowerdew, L. 2015. Data-driven learning and language learning theories. In A. Lenko-Szymanska and A. Boulton (Eds.), *Multiple Affordances of Language Corpora for Data-driven Learning* (pp. 15–36). Amsterdam: John Benjamins
Granger, S., Dagneaux, E., Meunier, F., and Paquot, M. 2009. *International Corpus of Learner English*, Vol. 2. Louvain-la-Neuve, Belgium: Presses universitaires de Louvain.
House, Juliane. 2009. *Translation*. Oxford: Oxford University Press.

Hurtado Albir, Amparo. 2015. The acquisition of translation competence. Competences, tasks, and assessment in translation training. *Meta*, 60(2), 256–280. https://doi.org/10.7202/1032857ar

Kiraly, Donald. 2000. *A Social Constructivist Approach to Translator Education: Empowerment from Theory to Practice*. Manchester, UK and Northampton, MA: St. Jerome Publishing.

Marchand, Chantale. 2011. *De la pédagogie dans les manuels de traduction. Analyse comparative des manuels anglais-français publiés en Amérique du Nord et en Europe depuis 1992*. (Mémoire de maîtrise en traduction). Montréal: Université de Montréal.

Mason, Ian. 1982. The role of translation theory in the translation class. *Quinquereme*, 5, 18–33.

Newmark, Peter. 1981. *Approaches to Translation*. London: Pergamon.

Newmark, Peter. 1988. *A Text Book of Translation*. New York: Prentice Hall.

Nida, Eugene A. 1964. *Toward a Science of Translating: With Special Reference to Principles and Procedures Involved in Bible Translating*. Leiden: E.J. Brill.

Nida, Eugene A. and Taber, Charles. 1969. *The Theory and Practice of Translation*, 2nd ed. Leiden: E.J. Brill.

Nord, Christiane. 2001. Loyalty revisited: Bible translation as a case in point. *The Translator*, 7(2), 185–202.

Odlin, Terence. 1994. *Perspectives on Pedagogical Grammar*. Cambridge: Cambridge University Press

Pearson, Jennifer. 2003. Using parallel texts in the translator training environment. In F. Zanettin, S. Bernardini, and D. Stewart (Eds.), *Corpora in Translator Education* (pp. 15–24). Manchester, UK: St. Jerome.

Pym, Anthony. 2003. Redefining translation competence in an electronic age: In defense of a minimalist approach. *Meta*, 48(4), 481–497

Robert, Nadine. 2012. The success factors for reliable legal translations. *The Legaco Express for Paralegals*, 2(10), October. www.legaco.org/article/the-success-factors-for-reliable-legal-translations.

Seleskovitch, Danica and Lederer, Marianne. 2001. *Interpreter pour Traduire* (1984), Vol. 4. Paris: Didier Érudition.

Serrano, Florén and Sanz, Lorés. 2008. The application of a parallel corpus (English–Spanish) to the teaching of translation (ENTRAD Project). In M. Muñoz-Calvo, C. Buesa-Gómez, and M. A. Ruiz-Moneva (Eds.), *New Trends in Translation and Cultural Identity* (pp. 433–443). Newcastle upon Tyne: Cambridge Scholars Publishing.

Shiyab, Said M. 2006. *A Textbook of Translation: Theoretical and Practical Implications*. Antwerp, Belgium: Garant Uitgevers Publishing House.

Singer, Néstor. 2016. A proposal for language teaching in translator training programs using data-driven learning in a task-based approach. *International Journal of English Language & Translation Studies*, 4(2), 155–167.

Sparer, Michel. 1988. L'enseignement de la traduction juridique: une formation technique et universitaire [Teaching legal translation: Technical university training]. *Meta*, 33(2), 320–328.

Thawabteh, Mohammad and Najjar, Omar. 2014. Training legal translators and interpreters in Palestine. *Arab World English Journal*. Special Issue on Translation, 3, 41–52.

Way, Catherine. 2016. The challenges and opportunities of legal translation and translator training in the 21st century. *International Journal of Communication*, 10, 1009–1029.

Wilss, Wolfram. 1996. *Knowledge and Skills in Translator Behavior*. Amsterdam and Philadelphia: John Benjamins.

Wyatt, Rawdon. 2006. *Check your English Vocabulary for Law*. London: A & C Black.

2 Corpora and translation teaching in the Arab world

Mai Zaki

2.1 Introduction

Corpus linguistics has greatly influenced translation studies over the past few decades. With the growing number of corpora and corpus resources, more work has been done to assess the need for translation students and professionals to benefit from corpora. Hu (2016: 28), for example, explains that the use of corpora in translator training "allows students to better understand the regularities and patterns of language transfer by observing large numbers of existing translation samples". Similarly, Bernardini et al. (2007) insist that translation pedagogy should benefit from parallel corpora to help students of translation develop translation awareness and improve their competence as translators. Therefore, corpus linguistics courses can be now seen as part of many translation programs in the West. However, the story is a little bit different in the Arab world. Technology is no stranger to translation programs in Arab universities, but it seems to be more generally linked to aspects of machine translation and/or computer-assisted translation (CAT) tools rather than corpora per se. Knowledge and use of corpora and corpus analysis tools have not yet claimed their rightful place in translation programs in the Arab world.

Within the increasing role of technology in the age of globalization, this chapter aims to highlight the importance of corpora for translation teaching and the need for academics in the Arab world to catch up with the latest corpus-based pedagogies in the translation classroom. The chapter proceeds as follows. Section 2.2 discusses the importance and benefit of corpora for translators training. Section 2.3 outlines existing Arabic corpora and corpus resources that could be easily adapted to translation courses. Section 2.4 reviews some major efforts in universities throughout the Arab world which incorporate corpora in translation classes. Finally, section 2.5 concludes with some remarks on the future of corpora in translation programs in the Arab world.

2.2 Corpora in the translation classroom

The translation market now is largely synonymous with translation technologies, where translators are both required and expected to be familiar with terms and tools such as machine translation, translation memories, computer-assisted translation, SDL Trados, Déjà vu, and the like. This occurs in tandem with the exponential growth in both the volume and variety of texts in need of translation in the modern world. Dealing with a large number of texts in a machine-readable form is also at the core of the discipline known as corpus linguistics, which developed dramatically since the 1960s. Corpora, or digital repertoires of texts which can be searched and analyzed using a concordance software, have been increasingly used in a variety of areas from stylistic analysis to second language teaching. It was not long before translation scholars realised that corpora can also be beneficial to translators and translation students. Bernardini (2006: 20) highlights the idea that using corpora can "result in better-documented, more accurate, as well as more fluent translations". While computers and translation for many academics simply mean machine translation, use of corpora in a translation classroom or for a translation task is fundamentally different. Gradually, there have been calls to integrate translation tasks based on corpora into translation curricula (Zanettin 1998, 2001; Aston 1999; Bowker 2003, 2004 inter alia).

The literature on incorporating corpora in a translator's education is growing, especially studies reporting on actual case studies. Corpora can help translation trainees to acquire essential skills they need to enter the professional translation market, as well as provide a rich resource for translation teachers. Such skills include use of specific software, information management, and analysing, interpreting, and extrapolating data. Bernardini (2006) considers translation to be an ideal field for corpus applications because it makes it easier to identify stylistic features and genre-specific characteristics of texts, in addition to "providing the translator with an inventory of attested units of meaning". Whether they are monolingual, parallel, or comparable corpora, they could help the translator to produce more naturally sounding translations. She stresses the need to raise awareness of the benefits of corpora among translation educators, and she even goes one step further to suggest that the use of corpora in translation classrooms should aim to integrate with computer-aided translation technology.

Beeby et al. (2009), on the other hand, clarify that there are two approaches to integrating corpora in translation classrooms. One proposes "corpus use for learning to translate", i.e., teachers provide the students with corpora along with corpus-based translation-related tasks. The other advocates "learning corpus use to translate", i.e., translation students learn how to build corpora and autonomously use them as part of their translator competence. Frérot (2016: 40) adds that whichever approach is used, corpora "are meant to provide students with translation solutions that cannot be found – or at least hardly be found – in other electronic resources".

Looking at the literature, it can be argued that the first approach is the more common one, probably because it can produce faster results. Inés (2009: 129) directly states that "electronic corpora and corpus analysis tools are resources that can improve the way students acquire translation competence". Therefore, Inés (2009: 141) presents a model for a study evaluating the appropriateness of using corpora and concordance software to solve specific translation problems. While such evaluations would vary depending on the learning outcomes of the course, this study outlines a few basic skills which could be used to assess students' corpus-use abilities. Upon responding to a translation task using a corpus, students could be assessed on the appropriateness of the corpus selected, the search string entered, the search restrictions applied, the sorting of results in the concordance, the use of available software functions, and finally the acceptability of the translation equivalent proposed. Such a model could be adapted to suit a variety of translation tasks. The underlying approach in this study is a student-centered, task-based model of incorporating knowledge of corpus use and analysis in translation courses. In fact, Kruger (2012: 509) adds that this student-centeredness focus is one of the main advantages of using corpora because they "reduce the role of teacher's intuition in the translation classroom".

The ability to use corpora to create teaching and testing materials for a translation class is as important as the ability to "extract translationally-relevant information" from a corpus, as Vaezian (2019: 7) puts it. Vaezian (2019) adds that, among other things, corpora have been shown to enhance a translation student's source text understanding, knowledge of specialised terms, knowledge of different text types, and identification of discourse-based features. Bermúdez Bausela (2016), for example, reports on a study where the use of an ad hoc specialised comparable corpus of English–Spanish texts on microbiology helps in the translation process. Using Wordsmith corpus analysis tools, a translator would be able to study more closely the "terminological, phraseological and textual patterns" in both languages and ultimately arrive at the most appropriate natural equivalents in the target text. Moreover, parallel corpora – corpora which contain source texts and their translations aligned at some level – could also be used to confirm intuitions regarding collocations, syntactic structures, idiomatic expressions, or terminological problems.

However, Frankenberg-Garcia (2015) reminds us that there are challenges when it comes to practically using corpora in translation; chief among them is lack of training for translation teachers on how to incorporate corpora in their classrooms. Issues such as how to choose or build an appropriate corpus, confusion resulting from using different corpus analysis software, and even the lack of resources for some languages are all practical hurdles which have to be dealt with. From the students' perspective, the challenge lies in the fact that using corpora effectively in the translation process requires double competencies: linguistic and technological. Yet most would agree that the direct contribution of corpora to translation practice is a very achievable and adaptable goal whose benefits go beyond the immediate field of translation.

2.3 Arabic corpus resources

Given that the technical difficulties the Arabic language itself poses to computer processing cannot be underestimated (Farghaly and Shaalan 2009; Habash 2010), there are a good number of corpora and corpus resources for Arabic now compared to 20 years ago. (Al-Sulaiti and Atwell 2006; McEnery et al. 2019). The World Wide Web itself is a great source of data for any corpus-compiling activity in many languages. With the growing use of the Arabic language on the web (Arabic is currently the fourth most used language on the web), it becomes an invaluable supplier of data for many varieties of Arabic and in many text types and genres.[1] Atwell (2019) mentions a few examples including the Corpus of Contemporary Arabic and the Arabic Internet Corpus, both developed at Leeds University, by scouting for websites with appropriate data. The latter, in particular, made use of web-crawler tools "to automate harvesting of webpage text" (2019: 102) in order to produce a 176 million-word corpus that was also automatically lemmatised. There is also the tagged Arabic web corpus (ArTenTen) provided by the commercial corpus management software Sketch Engine, which stands at 7.4 billion words crawled from the internet in 2012.

Translation teachers looking to incorporate the use of Arabic corpora in their classroom activities could pursue the major data providers such as the European Language Resources Association (ELRA) and the Linguistic Data Consortium (LDC).[2,3] The most famous corpora on offer there are news corpora, and they come in different forms and sizes, in addition to a license fee. Examples include Arabic Gigaword (400 million words), Arabic Newswire corpus (80 million words), Al-Nahar text corpus (24 million words), and Al-Hayat Arabic Corpus (18 million words), among others. Free and reliable Arabic corpora are harder to find. A great example is arabiCorpus, which currently holds 173,600,000 words, organized into six main categories: newspapers, modern literature, nonfiction, Egyptian Arabic, Pre-modern, and learner corpus.[4] With its built-in concordance tool, features such as word forms and collocations, and an easy-to-use interface, it is a great resource both for teachers and students. Zaghouani (2017) includes a useful survey of free Arabic corpora, and there are even annual workshops and conferences on open-source Arabic corpora and corpus resources (e.g., OSACT workshops). Corpora of spoken Arabic dialects, on the other hand, are understandably fewer. The added challenge of transcribing spoken language makes it more difficult to find resources for the various Arabic dialects. Most of the available resources would be small corpora compiled by linguists or computational linguists for specific purposes. Examples include the Tunisian Arabic Corpus, which currently has over 880,000 words of 4 million (McNeil 2019); the Gumar corpus of Gulf Arabic, which encompasses over 100 million words collected from online novellas composed in the dialects of Bahrain, Kuwait, Oman, UAE, Qatar, and Saudi Arabia (Khalifa et al. 2016); the Shami Dialect Corpus, comprising tweets from Syria, Palestine, Jordan, and Lebanon (Abu Kwaik et al. 2018); and the Corpus al-Logha al-Musriya (CALM), which has 2 million words of internet texts and transcripts from films and scripted television programs (White and Lonsdale 2019).

Parallel corpora, rather than monolingual ones, would be particularly apt for translation classes. Zantout and Guessoum (2015), however, admit that "Arabic parallel corpora are not as abundant as in other languages" (232). Yet there are some large parallel and multilingual corpora which include Arabic that are available for download. Examples include the United Nations Parallel Corpus, containing UN official documents in the public domain; the TED Parallel Corpus, made of TED talks and their translation into Arabic as well as eight other languages; and the Open Parallel Corpus (OPUS).[5] There are also other resources which are not freely available and require paid access from the large language data providers. For example, the LDC offers the GALE Arabic Newswire Parallel Text Project, and ELRA offers TRAD-Arabic-English Mailing Lists Parallel Corpus. Apart from those large parallel corpora, various research teams have endeavoured to build parallel corpora including Arabic for research purposes. Examples of such corpora include Al-Raisi et al. (2018), a monolingual corpus of texts translated into Arabic; Inoue et al. (2018), an Arabic–Japanese parallel corpus; Samy et al. (2006), a parallel multilingual Arabic–Spanish–English corpus; and Bouamor et al. (2014), a multidialectal parallel corpus of Arabic which includes five Arabic dialects in addition to standard Arabic and English. Finally, a great resource for an English–Arabic web-based parallel corpus that is freely available is described in Alotaibi (2017).[6] This ongoing project aims to include 10 million words of various genres and provide a much-needed resource for researchers and students of translation.

In addition to corpora themselves, anyone who is interested in corpus analysis would want to make use of the various tools made available by corpus and computational linguists. While tools such as concordancers, morphological analysers, part-of-speech taggers and syntactic parsers abound for the English language, the same cannot be said about Arabic. The most commonly known concordancers which can deal with Arabic texts include MonoConc, ParaConc, WordSmith, Xaria, and aConCorde. Alfaifi and Atwell (2016) present a useful comparison of seven Arabic corpus analysis tools following certain evaluation criteria such as the ability to read Arabic files in various formats, the ability to display diacritics and the ability to upload own corpus. It is also noteworthy to mention the various computational modeling of Arabic tools which are produced at the CAMeL Lab at New York University Abu Dhabi.[7]

With all these available resources, the field of Arabic corpus linguistics is no doubt progressing at a good pace. However, what is still missing is the link between corpus linguistics and translation in the Arab world. The next section highlights some of the programs which attempt to fill this gap.

2.4 Corpora and teaching translation in the Arab world

The picture for Arabic corpora and corpus resources, as described in the previous section, is a positive one, considering the amount of work that has been done to develop it in the last decade. However, we cannot say the same for the use of corpora in teaching translation. After reviewing many translation programs in universities across the Arab world, which are detailed here, it is obvious that more effort is needed for corpora to be part of normal translation training. Despite the growing number of translation programs in the Arab world, especially on the graduate level, corpus use is still trying to find its feet in the world where computers/technology meet translation. In many Arab universities, working with Arabic corpora still seems to be mainly relevant in the training of machine translation and information retrieval software. Therefore, it is not surprising to see several references to corpora within translation programs as part of a course on machine translation or any other course that falls under the umbrella of translation technology. However, other courses which are collectively concerned with how computers assist in translation miss an important opportunity to include the use of corpora and suffice with the expected use of translation memories, software, and dictionaries.

Therefore, the next section presents an evaluative review of the role of corpora in translation programs at both undergraduate and graduate level in the Arab world. For this purpose, 19 different courses in major universities of nine Arab countries were reviewed on the basis of information in the course title and course description. One caveat to bear in mind is that although the main concern for the purpose of this study is translation programs, the review of courses had to maintain a broad scope of search to also include language and linguistics programs/departments in Arab universities, which may or may not be paired with translation. In American-style universities, this was particularly important since courses offered in one department may be offered as electives for students majoring in another department. The review below includes universities in Egypt, Jordan, Lebanon, Tunisia, Morocco, Oman, Qatar, Saudi Arabia, and the United Arab Emirates. These are divided in two geographical groups for presentation. Where possible, through the university website (as documented) or personal communication, information has been extracted from course descriptions. The term "corpus" and "corpora" are italicized for emphasis if they occur in the course description. Appendix A includes a tabled summary of programs, graduate and undergraduate, and the courses within each one which relate (or not) to corpora. The list of universities and/or courses mentioned here is by no means exhaustive; however, it provides a good starting point to shed some light on the current situation of programs incorporating corpora and translation in the Arab world.

2.4.1 North Africa and the Middle East

There are not many direct examples here related to corpora in translation programs. In fact, there is only one example of a corpus linguistics course being offered, at Ain Shams University in Egypt, and another example from Tunisia on incorporating corpora in translation teaching. Other universities, however, offer a variety of courses related to computer-aided translation or machine translation.

In Jordan, Yarmouk University offers through its Department of Translation a BA in translation, as well as a master's degree in translation. In the BA program, a course titled "Computer-assisted Translation" is offered with the following description:

> This course trains the student to translate various texts from both languages using the computer; it also introduces necessary programs and the advantages of electronic dictionaries. Students should be able to figure out problems of material produced by computers and how to deal with them.
> (http://admreg.yu.edu.jo/en/index.php?option=com_docman&task=cat_view&gid=114&Itemid=159)

The University of Jordan, School of Foreign Languages, on the other hand, offers a course on "Machine Translation" as part of its MA program in translation. Here is a general description of what the course entails:

> This course introduces students to the history, the nature, the problems and the applications of machine translation. Special emphasis is laid on the contrastive, structural analysis of source and target language and how to resolve such problems (phonological, syntactic, lexical, etc.). In addition, students will be familiarized with the notion of context and the rhetorical dimension of texts.
> (http://languages.ju.edu.jo/StudyPlans/MA%20in%20Translation%20English%20Language.pdf)

In Lebanon, the Lebanese American University offers a BA in translation. Within this program there is a 300-level course titled "Computer Applications and Tools". However, it is clear from the brief course description on the website (http://sas.lau.edu.lb/humanities/programs/ba-in-translation.php) that it is mainly concerned with computer aids and translation software. In Morocco, the King Fahd School of Translation (Abdel Malek Essaadi University) offers a Diploma in Translation, which includes a course titled "Translation Technology" (www.esrft.uae.ma/portal/index.html). Unfortunately, no further information could be obtained about the nature of this course.

In Tunisia, Salhi (2010) reports on an experiment at the University of Tunis where translation students were given access to small comparable and parallel corpora to use in order to overcome linguistic, pragmatic, or cultural problems that they encounter in their translation assignments. Moreover, students were also encouraged to collect their own small corpora and build glossaries of collocations and terminology. Salhi (2010: 54) states that the current changes in the translation market and profession as a result of interaction with technology require that "an upgrading of the translator training classroom should be performed in the Arab

World". Although it is not clear if this is a continuous approach at the department, it provides a practical example of a successful integration of corpora in a translation classroom.

Finally, in Egypt, there are a couple of promising examples. At Ain Shams University, Faculty of Al Alsun (Languages), the English Department offers a course titled "Introduction to Corpus Linguistics" as part of the master's program in translation and interpreting. The course is described as follows (description obtained via personal communication):

> This course offers a practical introduction to *corpus* linguistics, an extremely versatile methodology of language analysis using computers. Course participants will be equipped with skills necessary for collecting and analyzing large digital collections of text (*corpora*) and introduced to a number of topics demonstrating the use of corpora in areas as diverse as translation, journalism, political science, discourse analysis, sociolinguistics, and language learning and teaching.

The other example comes from Alexandria University, Faculty of Arts, Department of Phonetics and Linguistics. The BA program there offers a course titled "Corpus Linguistics", which includes various aspects of corpus building, analysis, and representativeness, as well as representing speech corpora. The postgraduate course is offered under the linguistics program and includes topics such as applications of corpus linguistics, corpus annotation, corpus design, part-of-speech tagging and parsing (personal communication). It is also worth mentioning that the Arab Academy for Science and Technology in Alexandria offers a course titled "Computer-assisted Translation" through its Language and Translation Department. Unfortunately, no further description about this course could be obtained.

2.4.2 The Gulf

Gulf universities fare better when it comes to corpus-related courses, as the review of universities in four Gulf countries shows. This could be a reflection of the state of Arabic corpora and corpus resources development, which occurs mostly in Gulf universities and research laboratories with more financial resources to fund such developments. That being said, this does not necessarily mean that awareness of the benefits and uses of corpora should be limited to these universities. At the least, such universities provide shining examples of courses to emulate across the Arab world.

To begin in Oman, Sultan Qaboos University, the College of Arts and Social Sciences offers a master of science in translation where there is a course titled "Translating Skills and Translation Technology". The course is described as:

This course offers extensive practice in ancillary translating skills such as summarizing, paraphrasing, editing and revising, speed-reading, and on-sight translation. It also forms an introduction to computer-aided translation CAT tools such as translation memories TM (Memoq, Memsource and Wordfast) as well as online resources for translators such monolingual and bilingual *corpora* and integrated translation workbenches.

(www.squ.edu.om/ps/Programs/College-of-Arts-and-Social-Sciences/Translation)

The program also includes a course on "Machine Translation". It is understood (via personal communication) that, at the time of writing this chapter, the program was being reviewed to put more emphasis on the technological aspect of the courses.

In Qatar, the College of Humanities and Social Sciences at Hamad bin Khalifa University offers a master of arts in translation studies. This includes a course titled "Translation Technologies", where it is described as follows:

This is a practical course that introduces students to a selection of language technology tools with a focus on their professional practice. These will range from widely used open access tools to the industry standard SDL TRADOS (Getting Started level). Students will create and manage translation memories and terminological databases. They will integrate the use of *corpora* into their translation practice. They will also reflect on the role of machine translation and its application

(www.hbku.edu.qa/en/chss/ma-translation-studies).

Universities in Saudi Arabia present impressive examples of corpus-related courses directly linked to translation programs.[8] Starting with Imam Muhammad Bin Saud University, the master's in translation program there offers a course on "Machine Translation" described as follows (description has been shortened for reasons of space):

The course serves a number of interrelated objectives. First, it introduces level 2 MA students to the area of machine translation (MT) as a new curricular topic. The course focuses on a number of related sub-topics, including artificial intelligence, machine translation software, and machine translation architectures. Three generations of MT design are briefly reviewed: direct (dictionary-based), rule-based, and *corpus-based*. The review addresses their mode of functioning, the technical requirements, the capacity, and their respective limitations.

(https://units.imamu.edu.sa/colleges/LanguageAnd Translation/ma/Documents/machine.pdf)

They also offer a PhD in translation, where there is a course on offer with the title "Computer Applications in Translation". However, the course description could not be obtained. Also, at the undergraduate level, Prince Sultan University offers a BA in translation. Within this program, the department offers a 300-level course titled "Computer Applications in Translation", which is described as follows:

> This course is an introduction to the topics and methods in the field of applied linguistics. The course emphasizes the application of applied linguistics theories to problems of second language teaching and learning and to language in social context. Topics discussed and developed include grammar and vocabulary, discourse analysis, psycholinguistics, sociolinguistics, pragmatics, *corpus* linguistics, functional linguistics, non-native reading research, writing, listening and speaking as well as assessment.
> (http://psu.arabia-it.net/CH/acd-eng-descript.html)

Effat University offers translation programs on both the undergraduate and graduate levels. At the undergraduate level, they offer an elective course in "Corpus Linguistics" for linguistics majors and a course on "Computer Applications in Translation" for translation majors. While the latter does not seem to be associated with corpora, the former is described as follows:

> Students learn that *Corpus* Linguistics is the analysis of naturally occurring language, through corpora – large collections of machine-readable texts. They see how the field has advanced considerably due to advances in computer power. Students become familiar with the specialized software required for a corpus linguist to find and analyze data.
> (https://www.effatuniversity.edu.sa/English/Academics/ Catalogues/Pages/default.aspx)

The Master of Science in Translation Studies Program, on the other hand, offers a course titled "Computer-assisted translation". However, it is evident from the course description that it is mostly related to CAT tools, especially translation memory applications, and does not mention the term corpus per se, although it mentions the notions of "alignment" and "parallel texts":

> The course introduces students to automated and computer assisted translation and mobile translation. The topics covered include bilingual word processing; automated dictionaries and terms banks; alignment of texts and their translations for the purpose of compiling translation memories; internet searching for documentation and parallel texts. Appropriate software is used throughout the course.
> (www.effatuniversity.edu.sa/English/Academics/ Catalogues/Pages/default.aspx)

Finally, three examples from the United Arab Emirates are worth mentioning. Sharjah University offers a master of arts in translation, where the course "Machine-aided Translation" is described as follows:

> This course provides an overview of the use of computers in translation and the practical and theoretical problems encountered. Central issues include machine translation and its limitation, machine-aided translation, terminology banks, translator workstations, online dictionaries, and language *corpora*.
> (www.sharjah.ac.ae/en/academics/Colleges/ahss/dept/eld/
> Pages/Master-of-Arts-in-Translation.aspx)

UAE University does not offer any course on corpus linguistics in their BA in translation studies. However, they do have a related course in the BA linguistics program. The course is titled "Computational Linguistics" and is described as follows:

> This course is an introduction to computational linguistics. It assumes some familiarity with linguistics concepts but no programming is required. It covers topics on automata and finite-state machines and transducers, context-free models of syntax, parsing, and semantic interpretation; *corpus-based* research including probabilistic methods; and some selection of application areas from among such topics as information retrieval or machine translation.
> (www.uaeu.ac.ae/en/catalog/courses/course_4967.shtml?id=LNG420)

UAE University also offers a course titled "Language and Computer Technology"; however, it does not seem to be related to corpus linguistics as such. It is rather generally described as pertaining to "the use of computers for everyday language tasks" including machine translation.

Lastly, the American University of Sharjah offers a master's program in translation and interpreting. One of the recent additions to the pool of elective courses in the program is a course titled "Corpus Linguistics and Translation". The course

> introduces *corpus* linguistics as theory and practice. Equips students with knowledge about types of corpora, criteria for compiling corpora, annotation and concordance. Applies such knowledge to Arabic/English translation, including parallel corpora.
> (personal communication)

The course aims to provide foundational training to students in three main areas: (a) searching, analysing and interpreting results of a corpus; (b) compiling a corpus and uploading it to a corpus analysis software in both Arabic and

English; and (c) using parallel Arabic-English corpora to help in understanding and/or solving specific translation tasks.

2.4.3 Summary

The review in sections 2.4.1 and 2.4.2, while not comprehensive, paints a clearer picture of the state of courses integrating corpora in translation programs and beyond in some of the major universities in the Arab world. Table 2.1 summarizes the findings of the review (see Appendix A for the full list):

Therefore, a little over half of the courses listed here are related directly or indirectly to corpus linguistics and/or corpora. However, only one course at the undergraduate level (Prince Sultan University in Saudi Arabia) is actually part of a translation program, while the others are offered within the linguistics programs. Graduate courses fare better, as all six courses are offered within translation degrees. However, looking closely at the course titles and descriptions of those courses linked to corpora, it is to be noted that this link is not always obvious or, indeed, integral to the course. Table 2.2 lists the titles of the courses which have been found related to corpora on both graduate and undergraduate levels. Interestingly, only four courses mention the term "corpus" in the title, whereas the rest use a variety of terms including "translation technology", "computer", "computational", and "machine".

The course descriptions themselves, on the other hand, display a large array of essential terms expected in such courses. As Figure 2.1 illustrates, the word cloud of all the course descriptions obtained shows an evident occurrence of terms such as "machine", "analysis", and "application" in addition to the most frequent words "translation" and "corpora". However, there is also a noticeable infrequency of the word "Arabic", which might suggest less emphasis on using Arabic corpora and corpus tools in those courses. In fact, it is unclear how many Arabic corpora and corpus analysis tools are used at all in these courses, where English seems to be dominant.

Table 2.1 Summary of surveyed courses in Arab universities

	Undergraduate	**Graduate**	**Total**
Corpus-related	4	6	10 (52.5%)
Not corpus-related	4	2	6 (31.5%)
Unknown	1	2	3 (16%)
Total	**9**	**10**	**19**

Table 2.2 Variation in course titles relating to corpora

Course Title Keyword	Number	Title
Corpus	4	Corpus Linguistics
		Introduction to Corpus Linguistics
		Corpus Linguistics and Translation
Technology	2	Translation Technologies
		Translation Skills & Translation Technology
Computer	2	Computer Applications in Translation
		Computational Linguistics
Other	2	Machine Translation
		Machine-aided Translation

Figure 2.1 Word cloud of most frequent words from course descriptions

2.5 Where do we go from here?

The field of translation studies has developed so much since Holmes (1972) was debating the terms and nature of this area of study in the early '70s. In fact, the translation profession itself has undergone major changes in the last few decades. Changes include the quantity, type and modality of texts which need to be translated, in addition to the speed at which translations are required. Such drastic transformations need to be reflected in the way translation is taught and translators are trained. Pym (1993: 116) stressed more than two decades ago that "we should be teaching translation as a general set of skills that our students can apply and adapt to the changing demands of future markets, and indeed to changing professions". This statement stands as true now as it did back then, especially in the Arab world. Corpus-use skills are now part of our modern world, and translation programs need to acknowledge this. Therefore, and within the growing demands for interdisciplinary skills in our globalised world, translation programs can no longer afford to stand isolated from other close disciplines. We are now seeing more links being forged between translation studies and other fields including corpus linguistics, computational linguistics, computer science, and artificial intelligence.

Universities in the Arab world are admittedly taking positive steps towards integrating graduate and undergraduate translation programs, with more courses geared towards technology and computer applications to translation. However, corpus linguistics deserves more attention as a discipline in its own right, rather than just being one aspect of computer technology in translation. The confusion we have seen in the titles of the surveyed courses reflects a degree of uncertainty about where corpus linguistics fits in translation programs.

This chapter hopes to have highlighted not only the importance of corpus skills in translation training but also areas for improvement. Recommendations for improvement could be presented on the administrative/theoretical level as well as on the pedagogical/practical level. From the administrative point of view, there is a need for increasing the sense of commitment on the part of program leaders to gradually incorporate corpus linguistics courses in their institutions. We have seen that there is a shortage in courses related to corpus skills at the undergraduate level. Secondly, it is recommended for some sort of communication among Arab academic institutions to occur with the objective of ironing out differences in the definition and nature of courses integrating computer applications with translation. A much more difficult aim, indeed; however, it should exploit the fact that Arab universities are still in the early stage of establishing those courses as part of their programs. Some questions which arise from this survey include, for example: should corpus linguistics be taught as a separate course in translation programs? Or should corpus skills be taught as part of computer/technology applications in translation? Other issues which could be discussed include if it would be more useful not to mix up corpus linguistics and machine translation or to stick to a tighter definition of computer-assisted translation courses. Although those issues will vary depending on each institution's goals and directions, raising awareness about them would be hugely beneficial for the future and credibility of those programs.

On the pedagogical level, researchers and academics in the Arab world have a responsibility to explore more heavily this area of teaching corpus linguistics to translation students. Whereas books and journal papers on this topic abound (e.g. Mikhailov and Cooper 2016; Doval Reixa and Sánchez Nieto 2019; in addition to references in Section 2), there is a stark lack of research or case studies which are applicable to the Arab context and the Arabic–English language pairing in translation activities. As was previously mentioned, Arabic corpora and corpus tools are out there, but they are severely underused in translation classrooms. Creating new courses and having actual case studies of applications of corpora in translation teaching are mutually dependent on each other. Moreover, as another practical step to strengthen the case for corpus linguistics courses in translation programs, it is recommended to create a specialised online repository for freely available corpora (monolingual, comparable, or parallel) involving Arabic which are suitable for use in translation classrooms. Apart from the obstacle of licensed corpora, many of the freely available corpora were not designed for a pedagogical purpose in translation classrooms (or in language teaching, for that matter). Many were designed as training corpora for machine translation systems or other tools. But with the growing interest in corpus-based translation studies in the Arab world, it is very common for researchers to build their own corpora with specific translation-related research questions in mind; then, when their research project is over, many do not know what to do with their corpus to make it reusable by others. Therefore, there is a need for such an online repository, which would be a valuable resource for translation teachers in Arab universities and an incentive for them to incorporate the use of corpora in their classes.

One final note on parallel corpora, a particularly needed resource for translation teaching. There are various initiatives around the world for creating parallel corpora to be available for teachers and researchers. Two areas that are in dire need of attention involve what is called "specialised" corpora, that is, translation learner corpora and literary translation corpora. Translation programs everywhere produce a wealth of data from students' translations. This data could be the basis for building translation learner corpora to act as searchable databases and become available for researchers via a web interface. Currently, the author only knows about one such project in the Arab world, specifically in Saudi Arabia, as described in Alfuraih (2020). The Undergraduate Learner Translator Corpus (ULTC) is an error-tagged, sentence-aligned parallel corpus of Arabic, English, and French. The ongoing project is a great starting point and paves the way for, hopefully, more collaborative work in this area, especially given the number of graduate translation programs in Arab universities. A good example to emulate in this regard is the Multilingual Student Translation (MUST) project, which includes parallel corpora of students' translations from 20 countries around the world.[9]

As far as literary translation is concerned, there are two important assumptions to bear in mind. First, literary translation courses are almost a staple in many translation programs, including those in the Arab world. Second, literary translation between Arabic and English and vice versa has been historically a very busy two-way street, so there is no shortage of data. Yet, very little work has been done in this area using corpora and parallel corpus analysis. That being said, literary texts are notoriously difficult to work with due to copyright issues, especially for modern literature. As far as the author knows, there are currently no dedicated parallel literary corpora for modern standard Arabic and English translations available to researchers. Therefore, the author is currently working on compiling such a corpus for modern Arabic novels from all over the Arab world and their published English translations which includes, for the first time, whole texts. This ongoing project would provide a wealth of data for teachers and students of literary translation, in addition to being a rich resource for corpus-based translational stylistic and stylometric studies (see Rybicki and Heydel 2013; Eder et al. 2016). More initiatives in this area are badly needed, including those which involve creating multilingual parallel corpora of an Arabic source text and its translations in multiple languages (e.g., Fraisse et al. 2018).

The intersection between corpus linguistics and translator training is an open-ended debate in the field. It is hoped that Arab academics and universities get more involved in the discussions, driven by a growing awareness of the importance of corpora in the education of translation professionals of tomorrow.

Notes

1 At the time of writing, this information was obtained according to the "Internet World Stats" website (www.internetworldstats.com/stats7.htm), dated April 30, 2019 (last accessed 5 September 2019).
2 www.elra.info
3 www.ldc.upenn.edu
4 http://arabicorpus.byu.edu
5 http://opus.nlpl.eu
6 http://aeparallelcorpus.net/index.php/content
7 https://nyuad.nyu.edu/en/research/centers-labs-and-projects/computational-approaches-to-modeling-language-lab.html
8 See also Almutawa and Izwaini (2015) for a survey of machine translation courses in Saudi Arabia.
9 https://uclouvain.be/en/research-institutes/ilc/cecl/must.html

References

Abu Kwaik, Kathrein, Motaz Saad, Stergios Chatzikyriakidis, and Simon Dobnik. 2018. "Shami: A Corpus of Levantine Arabic Dialects." In *Proceedings of the Eleventh International Conference on Language Resources and Evaluation: European Languages Resources Association (ELRA)*, 3645–3652. www.aclweb.org/anthology/L18-1576.

Alfaifi, Abdullah, and Eric Atwell. 2016. "Comparative Evaluation of Tools for Arabic Corpora Search and Analysis." *International Journal of Speech Technology* 19(2): 347–357. https://doi.org/10.1007/s10772-015-9285-5.

Alfuraih, Reem F. 2020. "The Undergraduate Learner Translator Corpus: A New Resource for Translation Studies and Computational Linguistics." *Language Resources and Evaluation* 54: 801–830. https://doi.org/10.1007/s10579-019-09472-6.

Almutawa, Faten and Sattar Izwaini. 2015. "Machine Translation in the Arab World: Saudi Arabia as a Case Study." *Journal of Translation and Technical Communication Research*, 8: 382–414.

Alotaibi, Hind. 2017. "Arabic–English Parallel Corpus: A New Resource for Translation Training and Language Teaching." *Arab World English Journal* 8(3): 319–337.

Al-Raisi, Fatima, Weijian Lin, and Abdelwahab Bourai. 2018. "A Monolingual Parallel Corpus of Arabic." *Procedia Computer Science* 142: 334–338. https://doi.org/10.1016/j.procs.2018.10.487.

Al-Sulaiti, Latifa and Eric Atwell. 2006. "The Design of a Corpus of Contemporary Arabic." *International Journal of Corpus Linguistics* 11(1): 1–36.

Aston, Guy. 1999. "Corpus Use and Learning to Translate." *Textus* 12: 289–314.

Atwell, Eric. 2019. "Using the Web to Model Modern and Qur'anic Arabic." In *Arabic Corpus Linguistics*, ed. by Tony McEnery, Andrew Hardie and Nagwa Younis, 100–119. Edinburgh: Edinburgh University Press.

Beeby, Allison, Rodríguez Inés Patricia, and Sánchez-Gijón Pilar. 2009. *Corpus Use and Translating: Corpus Use for Learning to Translate and Learning Corpus Use to Translate*. New York and Amsterdam; John Benjamins.

Bermúdez Bausela, Montserrat. 2016. "The Importance of Corpora in Translation Studies: A Practical Case." In *New Perspectives on Teaching and Working with Languages in the Digital Era*, ed. by Antonio Pareja-Lora, Cristina Calle-Martínez, and Pilar Rodríguez-Arancón, 363–374. Dublin: Research-publishing.net.

Bernardini, Silvia. 2006. "Corpora for Translator Education and Translation Practice: Achievements and Challenges." In *Proceedings of the Third International Workshop on Language Resources for Translation Work, Research and Training* (LR4Trans-III). http://mellange.eila.jussieu.fr/bernardini_lrec06.pdf.

Bernardini, Silvia, Dominic Stewart, and Federico Zanettin. 2007. "Corpora in Translator Education: An Introduction." In *Corpora in Translator Education*, ed. by Federico Zanettin, Silvia Bernardini, and Dominic Stewart, 1–14. Beijing: Foreign Language Teaching and Research Press.

Bouamor, Houda, Nizar Habash, and Kemal Oflazer. 2014. "A Multidialectal Parallel Corpus of Arabic." In *Proceedings of the Ninth International Conference on Language Resources and Evaluation* (*LREC 2014*), 1240–1245. European Languages Resources Association (ELRA). http://www.lrec-conf.org/proceedings/lrec2014/pdf/523_Paper.pdf

Bowker, Lynne. 2003. "Towards a Collaborative Approach to Corpus Building in the Translation Classroom." In *Beyond the Ivory Tower: Rethinking Translation Pedagogy*, ed. by Brian James Baer and Geoffrey Koby, 193–210. Amsterdam and Philadelphia: John Benjamins.

Bowker, Lynne. 2004. "Corpus Resources for Translators: Academic Luxury or Professional Necessity?" *TradTerm* 10: 213–247.

Doval Reixa, Irene and Sánchez Nieto María Teresa, eds. 2019. *Parallel Corpora for Contrastive and Translation Studies: New Resources and Applications*. Studies in Corpus Linguistics (SCL), Volume 90. Amsterdam: John Benjamins Publishing Company

Eder, Maciej, Jan Rybicki, and Mike Kestemont. 2016. "Stylometry with R: A Package for Computational Text Analysis." *R Journal* 8(1): 107–121.

Farghaly, Ali and Shaalan, Khaled. 2009. "Arabic Natural Language Processing: Challenges and Solutions." *ACM Transactions on Asian Language Information Processing* 8: 1–20.

Fraisse, Amel, Quoc-Tan Tran, Ronald Jenn, Patrick Paroubek, and Shell Fishkin. 2018. "TransLiTex: A Parallel Corpus of Translated Literary Texts." Paper presented at *Eleventh International Conference on Language Resources and Evaluation (LREC 2018)*, Miyazaki, Japan. https://hal.archives-ouvertes.fr/hal-01827884/document.

Frankenberg-Garcia, Anna. 2015. "Training Translators to Use Corpora Hands-on: Challenges and Reactions by a Group of 13 Students at a UK University." *Corpora* 10(3): 351–380.

Frérot, Cécile. 2016. "Corpora and Corpus Technology for Translation Purposes in Professional and Academic Environments. Major Achievements and New Perspectives." *Cadernos De Tradução* 36(1): 36–61. https://doi.org/10.5007/2175-7968.2016v36nesp1p36.

Habash, Nizar. 2010. *Introduction to Arabic Natural Language Processing*. Synthesis Lectures on Human Language Technologies, #10. San Rafael, CA: Morgan & Claypool.

Holmes, James. 1972. *The Name and Nature of Translation Studies*, unpublished manuscript. Amsterdam: Translation Studies section, Department of General Studies. Reprinted in Toury, Gideon. 1987. *Translation Across Cultures*. New Delhi: Bahri Publications.

Hu, Kaibao. 2016. *Introducing Corpus-Based Translation Studies*. New Frontiers in Translation Studies. Heidelberg: Springer. https://doi.org/10.1007/978-3-662-48218-6.

Inés, Patricia Rodriguez. 2009. "Evaluating the Process and Not Just the Product When Using Corpora in Translator Education." In *Corpus Use and Translating: Corpus Use for Learning to Translate and Learning Corpus Use to Translate*, ed. by Allison Beeby, Rodríguez Inés Patricia, and Sánchez-Gijón Pilar, 129–140. New York and Amsterdam: John Benjamins.

Inoue, G., N. Habash, Y. Matsumoto, and H. Aoyama. 2018. A Parallel Corpus of Arabic-Japanese News Articles. In *Proceedings of the 5th International Conference on Language Resources and Evaluations*, 918–924. LREC 2018. https://pdfs.semanticscholar.org/ff5a/dfeddb3a3a8f077a645f243f887d18591407.pdf?_ga=2.154569592.1360789054.1585907460-995980893.1585907460.

Khalifa, Salam, Nizar Habash, Dana Abdulrahim, and Sara Hassan. 2016. "A Large-Scale Corpus of Gulf Arabic." In *Proceedings of the Tenth International Conference on Language Resources and Evaluation*, Portorož, Slovenia, 4282–4289. Luxemburg: European Languages Resources Association (ELRA). www.aclweb.org/anthology/L16-1679.

Krüger, Ralph. 2012. "Working with Corpora in the Translation Classroom." *Studies in Second Language Learning and Teaching* 2(4): 505–525. https://doi.org/10.14746/ssllt.2012.2.4.4.

McEnery, Tony, Andrew Hardie, and Nagwa Younis, eds. 2019. *Arabic Corpus Linguistics*. Edinburgh: Edinburgh University Press.

McNeil, Karen. 2019. "Tunisian Arabic Corpus: Creating a Written Corpus of an 'Unwritten' Language." In *Arabic Corpus Linguistics*, ed. by Tony McEnery, Andrew Hardie, and Nagwa Younis, 30–55. Edinburgh: Edinburgh University Press.

Mikhailov, Mikhail and Robert Cooper. 2016. *Corpus Linguistics for Translation and Contrastive Studies: A Guide for Research*. Routledge Corpus Linguistics Guides. Milton Park, Abingdon, Oxon: Routledge. https://doi.org/10.4324/9781315624570.

Pym, Anthony. 1993. "On the Market as a Factor in the Training of Translators." *Koiné* 3: 109–121.

Rybicki, J. and M. Heydel. 2013. "The Stylistics and Stylometry of Collaborative Translation: Woolf's Night and Day in Polish." *Literary and Linguistic Computing* 28(4): 708–717. https://doi.org/10.1093/llc/fqt027.

Salhi, Hammouda. 2010. "Small Parallel Corpora in an English-Arabic Translation Classroom: No Need to Reinvent the Wheel in the Era of Globalization." In *Globalization and*

Aspects of Translation, ed. by Said M. Shiyab, 53–67. Newcastle upon Tyne: Cambridge Scholars Publishing.

Samy, Doaa, Antonio Sandoval, Jose Guirao, and Enrique Alfonseca. 2006. "Building a Parallel Multilingual Corpus (Arabic-Spanish-English)." In *Proceedings of the 5th International Conference on Language Resources and Evaluations* (LREC 2006), 2176–218. European Language Resources Association (ELRA). www.lrec-conf.org/proceedings/lrec2006/pdf/238_pdf.pdf.

Vaezian, Helia. 2019. "On Language Corpora in the Translation Classroom." *International Journal of Language, Literacy and Translation* 2(2): 1–12.

White, Michael and Deryle Lonsdale. 2019. "Verbs in Egyptian Arabic: A Case for Register Variation." In *Proceedings of the 3rd Workshop on Arabic Corpus Linguistics* (WACL-3), ed. by Mahmoud El-Haj, Paul Rayson, Eric Atwell, and Lama Alsudias, 60–71. Association for Computational Linguistics. www.aclweb.org/anthology/W19-5608.

Zaghouani, Wajdi. 2017. "Critical Survey of the Freely Available Arabic Corpora." In *Proceedings of International Conference on Language Resources and Evaluation* (LREC 2014), Reykjavik, Iceland, May 2014. https://arxiv.org/pdf/1702.07835.pdf.

Zanettin, Federico. 1998. "Bilingual Comparable Corpora and the Training of Translators." *Meta*, 43(4): 616–630. https://doi.org/10.7202/004638ar.

Zanettin, Federico. 2001. "Swimming in Words: Corpora, Language Learning and Translation." In *Learning with Corpora*, ed. by Guy Aston, 177–197. Houston, TX: Athelstan.

Zantout, Rached and Ahmed Guessoum. 2015. "Obstacles Facing Arabic Machine Translation: Building a Neural Network-based Transfer Module." In *Papers in Translation Studies*, ed. by Sattar Izwaini, 229–253. Newcastle upon Tyne: Cambridge Scholars Publishing.

Appendix A

Country	University	Program	Course	Corpus-related?
Undergraduate Degrees				
Jordan	Yarmouk University	BA Translation	Computer-assisted Translation	No
Lebanon	Lebanese American University	BA Translation	Computer Applications and Tools	No
Egypt	Ain Shams University	BA English Language and Literature	Computer-assisted Translation	No
Egypt	Alexandria University	BA Phonetics and Linguistics	Corpus Linguistics	Yes
Egypt	Arab Academy for Science & Technology	BA Language and Translation	Computer-assisted Translation	Unknown
Saudi Arabia	Prince Sultan University	BA Translation	Computer Applications in Translation	Yes
Saudi Arabia	Effat University	BA Linguistics	Corpus Linguistics	Yes
UAE	UAE University	BA Linguistics	Computational Linguistics	Yes
			Language and Computer Technologies	No
Graduate Degrees				
Jordan	University of Jordan	MA Translation	Machine Translation	No
Morocco	Abdel Malek Esaadi University	Diploma in Translation	Translation Technology	Unknown
Egypt	Ain Shams University	MA Translation and Interpreting	Introduction to Corpus Linguistics	Yes
Oman	Sultan Qaboos University	MSc Translation	Translation Skills & Translation Technology	Yes
Qatar	Hamad bin Khalifa University	MA Translation Studies	Translation Technologies	Yes
Saudi Arabia	Imam Mohamad bin Saud University	MA Translation	Machine Translation Computer Applications in Translation	Yes
		PhD Translation		Unknown
Saudi Arabia	Effat University	MSc Translation Studies	Computer-assisted Translation	No
UAE	University of Sharjah	MA Translation	Machine-aided Translation	Yes
UAE	American University of Sharjah	MA Translation and Interpreting	Corpus Linguistics and Translation	Yes

Figure 2.2 Summary of undergraduate and graduate programs in Arab universities related to corpora and/or translation technology

3 Trainee translators' and professional translators' source text comprehension and reproduction

Problems and solutions

Omar F. Atari

3.1 Introduction

Research into the performance of English/Arabic trainee translators and professional translators is relatively rare. The research by leading scholars on translation with reference to the language pair English/Arabic is focused mainly on translator training in academic settings. It has not sufficiently embraced professional translators' practices in the workplace (cf. Farghal and AlManna 2018; Hatim and Mason 1990; Dickins et al. 2002).

There is an apparent imbalance between research studies on trainee translators' and professional translators' performance. This may not be surprising given the fact that empirical research with reference to English/Arabic translation has largely been conducted in the classroom – not in the workplace. Although undergraduate and graduate translator training programs are available in many Arab universities, the effectiveness of translation teaching methodology has not been directly corroborated by empirical evidence from research on performance assessment of trainee translators and professional translators.

The significance of translation performance assessment cannot be overemphasized because of its invaluable contribution to translation pedagogy, including classroom teaching, curriculum design, and identification of the learning outcomes (Davies 2004; Mahn 2008).

Research on professional translators at the workplace may enable translation trainers to incorporate the workplace context into their classroom practices.

Against this backdrop of an apparently limited empirical research, this study consists of two main phases: (1) an investigation into the translation work of both groups and their errors (i.e., their products) and (2) an assessment of trainees' and professional translators' identification of the source text segments as problems and their solutions (i.e., the process) (Gile 2005; Nord 2005; Kiraly 2005). This will be based on the two groups' responses to a questionnaire's items (see Appendix B).

It should be pointed out here that the term "professional translators" refers to translators working in private translating institutions in some parts of the Arab world. These "professional translators" are usually picked up from the pool of BA or a smaller pool of MA degree holders in translation or English language and literature. However, their employment requirements and their actual performance are not well known to us. Thus, the use of the term "professional translators" refers to translators working in translation agencies and whose work is judged by the owners or managers of those translating agencies. In fact, I cannot think of a specific study of these professionals' competence in translation. Hence, this research aims to fill this gap by studying professional translators' performance in the workplace.

3.2 Data collection

For the purpose of data collection and analysis, I have focused on specific source text segments that can pose problems for translation at the micro- and macro-text levels. These are referred to as "source text significant segments", and they have been listed as follows:

- An idiomatic collocational structure – "Strikes a budget deal" – in the text subheading "A fractious and lengthy meeting strikes a budget deal"
- A subheading: "Cries and gestures"
- A fronted nonfinite clause: "Depending on where you stand"
- An idiomatic phrase: ". . . a return to business as usual"
- An appositive element: "The British, as holders of the EU Presidency in June"
- A fronted idiomatic phrase: "Hard on the heels of the European Constitutions' rejection by French and Dutch voters"

The text, titled "The European Union Summit", that has been chosen for the subjects to translate is taken from *The Economist* (2005) (see Appendix A). This text is an argumentative one, with a blend of embedded elements of exposition, as in paragraphs 2 and 3, but the author's overall intentions are to evaluate and comment on the EU summit meetings in constant disagreements. The reader must utilize their background knowledge and the contextual cues in the text and integrate information both within and between paragraphs while simultaneously linking all the information with the title and subheading of the source text (i.e., top-down[1] and bottom-up[2] text reading processes for comprehension [cf. Carrell 1989; Grabe 1991, among others]).

3.3 The subjects

This study investigated the translation performance of two categories of translators:

- Group A: Eighteen trainee translators in their fourth year of training in a BA translation studies program at an Arab university.

- Group B: Eighteen professional translators who are employed as full-time in-house translators at an established translation agency.

Eighteen trainee translators were asked to translate the first two paragraphs, including the title and subheading, under test conditions. In other words, the test was administered and proctored by this researcher in a university classroom. The students were allowed to use translation aids, dictionaries, their mobiles, etc. The time allotted for the test was 90 minutes. They were provided with a "brief" for this translation task (see Appendix B). These students had successfully completed a series of EFL language courses, including reading, writing, and translation courses that included introduction to translation, translation of English texts, translation of Arabic texts, literary translation, technical and business translation, basic issues in translation, contrastive analysis for translation, and a sequence of Arabic language courses.

Eighteen professional translators were also selected based on their qualifications (i.e., BA in translation or English language and literature) and a minimum of three-year translating experience as full-time in-house translators in a recognized translation agency. They also translated the first two paragraphs, including the title and the subheading of the source text, into Arabic. Information about the subjects in this group was obtained from the director of the translation agency where they work. Professional translators' performance can, presumably, be used as the benchmark against which to measure trainee translators' performances.

3.4 Performing the translating task

The 18 trainee translators performed the task of translating the text from English into Arabic in one classroom at the same time under test conditions. The 18 professional translators also performed the task, but in a large hall at the translation agency. Both groups were allotted the same amount of time for translating the passage and completing the questionnaire. The time allotted for translating the text and responding to the questionnaire was 90 minutes (see Appendices I and II). Both groups had access to electronic and paper dictionaries. The investigation of the translation performance of the two groups was carried out in two phases:

- Phase I: The errors that may be attributed to the lack of comprehension of the source text, reproduction in the target text (i.e., Arabic), and/or the translators' mediation procedures and decisions (i.e., product).
- Phase II: Performance in terms of the identification of a source text segment as a problem and the solution offered by both groups of translators, (i.e., the process) (see Appendix B).

The analysis of the two groups' behavior comprised two components: (1) comparing trainee translators' errors with the professionals' errors and (2) comparing the two groups' identification of the problem segments and their solutions, as evidenced by their responses to the items in the questionnaire (see Appendix B).

3.5 Classification of solutions

The following classification of problem solutions is based on the PACTE Group's taxonomy (2011):

- Acceptable solution (A): The solution activates all relevant connotations of the ST in the context of the translation related to the meaning of the ST, the function of the translation, and language use.
- Semi-acceptable solution (SA): The solution activates some of the relevant connotations of the ST and maintains the coherence of the TL in the context of the translation related to the meaning of the ST, the function of the translation, and language use.
- Unacceptable solution (UA): The solution activates none of the relevant connotations of the ST or introduces connotations that are incoherent in the context of the translation related to the meaning of the ST, the function of the translation, and/or language use.

It should be made clear here that the term "solution" refers to the trainees' or professionals' processes of identifying a source text segment as a problem and how they went about solving it or giving a translation equivalent (i.e., the translation process). The term "error", however, as used earlier refers to the actual translation of a source text segment that is incorrect. So in a way the terms "error" and "unacceptable solution" are used interchangeably. The difference is that "error" refers to the product while "problem solution" refers to the process (Pym 1992).

3.6 Data analysis

In this section, the author presents samples of the six source text segments used in this study. Examples of faulty renditions by both trainee translators and professional translators are given here, although the professional translators' faulty renditions are fewer in number.

Source Text Segment No. 1

Original English: "A fractious and lengthy meeting strikes a budget deal that answers almost no questions about the future."

3.6.1 Samples of faulty renditions by trainee translators

- Blkhusoos sarim Wa taweel?ijtimaʕ?almeezaniyyaṣafqat ʕan?al-idʕrab.

  Regarding strict and long meeting, the budget deal about the strike.
  A long and decisive meeting regarding the strike about the budget deal.

Source text comprehension and reproduction 45

- Wa?anhaa ʕasʕeeb Wa tʕaweel?ijtimaaʕ?al-meezaaniyya ʕala qadʕa

    And . . . finished . . . difficult . . . and long . . . meeting . . . the budget . . . on abolished
    A long and difficult meeting finished and abolished the budget

- Blkhusoos sarim Wa taweel?ijtimaʕ?almeezaniyyaṣafqat ʕan?al-idʕrab.

    Regarding strict and long meeting, the budget deal about the strike.
    A long and decisive meeting regarding the strike about the budget deal.

- Wa?anhaa ʕasʕeeb Wa tʕaweel?ijtimaaʕ?al-meezaaniyya ʕala qadʕa

    And . . . finished . . . difficult . . . and long . . . meeting . . . the budget . . . on abolished
    A long and difficult meeting finished and abolished the budget

3.6.2 Samples of faulty renditions by the professional translators

- ?al-meezaniyya Yuhaajim ʕaneef Wa tʕaweel?ijtimaaʕ

    . . . the budget . . . attacks . . . violent . . . and . . . long . . . meeting
    A long and rowdy meeting attacks/criticizes the budget

- naaqasha?al-lathee?al-Has-sas?al-?ijtimaaʕ

    . . . discussed . . . which . . . the sensitive . . . the meeting
    The critical meeting which discussed the strikes of the budget

3.6.3 Comment

All four translations of the English clause "A fractious and lengthy meeting strikes a budget deal that answers" into Arabic are completely incorrect. Although the professional translators' faulty renditions were fewer in number, the renditions they provided were as faulty as those of the trainee translators. This is surprising given the fact that the professional translators participating in this study had relatively long experience in translation, ranging from three to 12 years in a privately owned translating agency. To interpret the four faulty renditions, one has to note that the four renditions by both groups of translators are centered on the word "strikes", which is one unit of the entire clause mentioned earlier. The two groups of translators, it seems, paid special attention to this part of the text and entirely neglected the preceding and following contextual text analysis – "a fractious and lengthy meeting" and "which answers almost no questions about the future". Not only did the translators ignore the informational input of the contextual phrases such as "fractious . . . meeting" and irrelevance to the future EU summits, but they also ignored the overall general context of "cries and gestures" as typical symptoms of the EU summit meetings. At another level, these four mistranslations indicate the translators' lack of awareness of the norms and conventions of *The Economist*, that usually provides targeted readers the gist of the entire article and its function in one sentence. The translators apparently failed to recognize the function of placing the sentence "A fractious and lengthy . . . the future" immediately after the title and the subheading. This "generic" feature, the one-sentence summary that preceded the opening section of the remaining text, is typical of this genre of news reporting and some journals' news-writing conventions.

The incorrect renditions by the two groups of translators, which were centered on one lexical item, "strikes", has been referred to as the phenomenon of "false friends", which is the negative consequence of the translators' "automatic reflexes", to use Kussmaul's (1995) term. One may add that these translators with their overemphasis on the term "strikes" indicate that they didn't take their time to establish the interconnections between "strikes" and the features of the preceding and the following text, as mentioned earlier.

Here is another sample of both groups' faulty rendition:

Source Text Segment No. 2

Original English: "The budget announced in Brussels on December 17th was a return to business as usual in the European Union."

3.6.4 Samples of faulty renditions by trainee translators

- ʔaʕmaal li sʕaliH ʕaidaʔ.al-ourobi al-it-ti Had

    . . . business . . . to benefit . . . returning . . . the European . . . the Union
    . . . A return to the business interests of the European Union

- ʔilaʔ.al-meezaniyya tarjiʕ Kanat Hadatha kamaʔ.al-ʔiqtisʕadʕ

    . . . to . . . the budget . . . go back . . . was . . . what happened . . . as . . . the economy

    The budget used to go back to the economy as what had happened

3.6.5 Samples of faulty renditions by the professional translators

- ʔal-ʔaʕmaal ʕala taʕuud kanatʔ.al-ourobi bil-it-ti Hadʔ.al-khasʕ aʔ.al-tijaariyya

    . . . the business . . . on/to . . . return . . . used to . . . the European . . . the Union
    . . . concerning . . . the commercial

    The budget used to go back to the commercial business of the European Union

- ʔal-it-ti Hadʔ.aʕmaal li-ʕaidaat bayanʔ.al-ourobbi

    . . . the Union . . . business . . . for the revenues . . . report . . . the European . . .
    The budget was a report on the revenues of the EU business

3.6.6 Comment

In all the four translational versions, there is a distortion of the meaning of the idiom "... a return to business as usual." Both translators' versions put much emphasis on just one linguistic unit of the original English phrase "a return to business as usual" and on its literal meaning as an isolated lexical element with no reference to its context of situation. In other words, there is no connection between the translation "a return to business" given by the translators and the meaning of the idiom in the given context. The idiomatic nature of the phrase "... a return to business as usual" must have been blocked by the dominating schema in the minds of the two groups of translators. In other words, the word-for-word meaning of the term "a return" deprived them of making use of the surrounding elements, namely, a return to business in the European Union, whose meetings have come to be associated with endless disputes and disagreements. The other contextual elements in the text that have not been considered by the translators are the following two sentences: "Depending on where you stand, the deal was" and " burying its head in the sand." Had the translators worked out the connection between "a return to business as usual" and the context of "the Union burying its head in the sand," they would have realized the intended meaning of "a return to business as usual." We are again being confronted with this propensity by the translators to dwell on the lexical item and just automatically rush to a faulty rendition on the basis of the word-for-word rendition of the meaning of the phrase "... a return to business" In a nutshell, this translation testifies to Kussmaul's (1995) use of "automatic reflex" as a typical translation behavior.

These faulty renditions point to one practice and possibly one bad practice followed by trainee translators and, to some extent, by the professional translators. One is actually tempted to assume or hypothesize that these faulty renditions may reflect inadequate training by a few trainers in our colleges or universities.

3.7 Results

Table 3.1 shows the two groups' translations of the six source text segments. The professional translators outperformed the trainees, as shown by Table 3.1 (i.e., the total number of correct renditions by the professional translators was 45, while that of the trainee translators was 27). However, both the trainee translators' and the professional translators' performance show relatively comparable patterns of unacceptable solutions of the source text segments (i.e., a total of 71 instances of unacceptable solutions versus 52 instances by the professional translators).

Table 3.2 shows the correspondence between the professional translators' unacceptable solutions to the source text segments and the instances of their failure at identifying problematic translation segments. The numbers are 71 instances of unacceptable solutions and 64 instances of unidentified problems. Furthermore, there is also correspondence between acceptable solutions and identified

48 Omar F. Atari

Table 3.1 Comparison of the two groups' translation of six source text segments

Source Text Segment	Trainee Translators			Professional Translators		
	Unacceptable	Semi-acceptable	Acceptable	Unacceptable	Semi-acceptable	Acceptable
"...strikes a budget deal..."	12	2	1	8	2	8
"Cries and gestures"	15	2	1	13	4	1
"...a return to business as usual"	13	1	4	7	1	10
"Depending on where you stand …"	13	2	3	9	3	6
"...the British, as holders of the EU presidency"	8	0	10	9	0	9
"Hard on the heels of the European constitution's rejection by the French and Dutch voters"	10	0	8	6	1	11
Total	71	7	27	52	11	45

Table 3.2 Professional translators' unacceptable and acceptable solutions and identified and unidentified problem segments

Source Text Segment	Unacceptable	Semi-acceptable	Acceptable	Unidentified	Identified but Not Solved	Identified and Solved
"...strikes a budget deal..."	12	2	1	13	3	2
"Cries and gestures"	15	2	1	6	10	2
"… a return to business as usual"	13	1	4	15	0	3
"Depending on where you stand…"	13	2	3	9	7	2
"… the British, as holders of the EU presidency"	8	0	10	12	1	5
"Hard on the heels of the European constitution's rejection by the French and Dutch voters"	10	0	8	9	1	8
Total	71	7	27	64	22	22

problems. These numbers are 27 acceptable solutions and 22 identified problems. However, the correspondence between unacceptable solutions and unidentified problems far exceeds the correspondence between acceptable solutions and identified problems.

In the cases of trainee translators as well as professional translators, there is a direct correspondence between faulty renditions and the failure to identify translation problems. However, the professionals outperformed the trainees in translating the six source text segments (i.e., product-based, but not how the process of finding the correct translation was followed).

3.8 Framing trainee translators' faulty renditions

Trainee translators tended to rely heavily on isolated problematic linguistic elements of the "source text significant segments"; they tended to count on their previously stored knowledge/meaning of that linguistic element. They did not observe the contextual surroundings of the significant source text segments (Kussmaul 1995). Most of the trainee translators misinterpreted the meaning of "strikes a budget deal". They misinterpreted "strike" as meaning "to deliver a blow or to hit". Furthermore, they did not even attempt to reflect either on the relation of that expression with the preceding clause or the title. One might contest that these elements are collocational in nature and so the translator reader can guess their meanings. However, this can only apply to a native speaker of English.

The majority also employed the same strategy when confronted by the following two source text significant segments: "a return to business as usual" and "depending on where you stand". In translating both these source text significant segments, most of the trainees depended on their previous knowledge of the word "business" and of the word "stand": They did not consider the two source text significant segments in the context of the immediately preceding text, nor did they think of the title, the subheading, or the overall text type function, as if these basic idiomatic expressions were not within their own register.

In addition, the trainee translators' faulty renditions revealed a lack of knowledge of basic linguistic elements, namely, the use of appositive elements, as in the case of translating the following significant segment: "the British, as holders of the EU presidency".

3.9 Professional translators performance

The translation of the source text significant segments by a few of the professional translators exhibited a more sense-oriented approach to translation. Unlike the form-oriented approach used by the majority of the 18 trainee translators, the professional translators seem to have employed both top-down and bottom-up text processes. In handling the source text significant segments, which are essentially judged as purely linguistic or extralinguistic, few of the professional translators could successfully render into Arabic the expressions "strikes a budget deal", "a return to business as usual", and "depending on where you stand".

These professional translators were able to translate "strikes a budget deal" as "to come to an agreement or to conclude the budget deal". As for the appositive element "as holders of the EU presidency", some were able to recognize this as an appositive element. In the case of "depending on where you stand" and "a return to business as usual", their translations revealed that these two idiomatic expressions were correctly rendered by a few professional translators. However, only a few professional translators were able to recognize that the final significant segment "Hard on the heels" was a linguistic, extralinguistic, and pragmatic textual element. These professional translators, though, were unable to capture the author's intention, which is the circumstance that usually dominates the debates and disagreements of those EU summits on issues of budget. Both trainee translators and professional translators alike exhibited a lack of awareness of the text type and the author's pragmatic intention. This was revealed in their word-for-word renditions of the significant source text segment "Cries and gestures".

3.10 Conclusion

The results of the study indicate that the professional translators performed better than the trainee translators in many respects. This is not surprising. It is noteworthy, however, that though the academic qualifications of both groups are the same (BA degrees in a relevant specialization), clearly, the translation experience of the professional translators at the workplace has contributed significantly to their performance (Nord 214). During their employment as translators, the professional translators perceptibly improved their general comprehension of the language and proficiency in its use to a sufficient degree to significantly outperform the trainee translators.

Thus, the findings of this study point to one pressing issue to be tackled while teaching to translate: the need to upgrade the level of trainee translators' textual competence in L2 reading comprehension (Beeby 2004). Specifically, the findings attest to the significant role of source text analysis training for both trainees and professionals. Source text analysis training should form an integral component of source text reading comprehension for recovering the intended messages conveyed by the writer through the micro/macro text features and their contribution to the writer's pragmatic intentions. This is a prerequisite knowledge of trainees' and professionals' work.

This researcher argues in favor of making language teaching an integral part of translation teaching whereby bilingual competence will be the threshold to translation competence acquisition. These findings raise the following question: What type of language teaching should form the crux of a curriculum design for trainee translators?

In this regard, Wilss (2008) points out that the translator needs a precise conceptual image of training and practice based on two types of knowledge: declarative and procedural. The following are the objectives of language teaching for translator training, which cut across declarative knowledge and procedural knowledge:

a   To employ the strategies of bottom-up and top-down text processes
b   To infer implicit information by utilizing explicit information
c   To recognize unnecessary details and omit them
d   To utilize contextual cues and background knowledge
e   To recognize the source text author's intentionality (i.e., using the text to convince, argue, explain, instruct, etc.)
f   To recognize the subordinate and main clauses and the semantic and pragmatic relations that underlie them, such as situation–problem–solution or hypothesis–real or statement–elaboration–contrast–solution
g   To recognize the function of cohesive connectors
h   To establish the logical connections between the title, subheading, and first and last paragraphs
i   To uncover the author's intentionality

Guided by this set of objectives, the translator trainer can make use of these statements in identifying his/her learning outcomes and matching the learning outcomes up with the teaching material on a weekly basis.

3.11 Modules for training undergraduate trainee translators

I argue that the declarative knowledge (i.e., the know-what) of undergraduate trainee translators should constitute the initial stage of the translating process. The aforementioned declarative knowledge represents L2 reading comprehension and text processing, as well as the use of the contextual cues appearing in the source text for drawing inferences about the semantic/pragmatic ideas and author's intentions. Hence, training will consist of three phases – a pre-translation phase to take care of declarative knowledge, a transfer phase to account for the techniques and procedures of transferring source text messages into the target language as components of procedural knowledge, and a post-translation phase that comprises editing and revising, recognition, and classification of errors and their solutions. This phase constitutes the application of both declarative knowledge and procedural knowledge.

3.11.1 Pre-translation training phase

Module one:

- To employ the bidirectional top-down and bottom-up text processing
- To utilize the immediately preceding textual elements to figure out the pragmatic meaning of a problematic source text segment
- To undertake source text analysis by recognizing the purely linguistic elements, such as fronted nonfinite subordinated clauses and appositive elements and certain idiomatic expressions

Module two: Linguistic knowledge training:

- To raise students' awareness of certain purely linguistic devices and their pragmatic functions
- To link certain linguistic syntactical structures with the title, subheading, and overall text pragmatic interactions

This is essentially an exercise in formulating a training strategy for enhancing students' declarative knowledge to use it in the process of transferring the source text into functionally meaningful and equivalent target text. The syntactical nonfinite subordinated clauses and the appositive elements are elements of the students' declarative knowledge. This type of knowledge, if not possessed by the trainee translators, will severely impair their strategies for transferring the text into the target language.

I would like to emphasize that this type of declarative knowledge of the lexical, syntactical, and idiomatic linguistic textual aspects of the source text should constitute a major phase of the training of undergraduate trainee translators, as it is indeed the initial stage of the entire translating process.

Module three:

- To utilize the contextual cues of the source text at the micro-level
- To link the micro-textual contextual cues with the overall macro-text pragmatic elements

Students tend to dwell on minimal isolated problematic lexical items as separate entities devoid of their contextual environment within the paragraph and, consequently, the entire macro-text context. Students tend to miss out on intra- and inter-sentential cohesive devices, namely, anaphoric reference, substitution, ellipsis, recurrent endo-phoric and exo-phoric reference (Halliday and Hasan 1976). They tend to forget their role as readers who interact with the text for the purpose of reconstructing the source text author's intentions in the target language.

3.11.2 *The transfer phase*

This phase complements the pre-phase training strategy of highlighting the role of declarative knowledge at the initial stage of the translating process (Wilss 2008). It is my contention that translator training strategy and pedagogy should be based on a sensible combination of declarative and processing (procedural) knowledge.

Module four:

- To apply the techniques of reduction, expansion, and transposition to accommodate the syntactical and idiomatic source text elements into their equivalent syntactical and idiomatic target text elements
- To explicate the source text author's pragmatic intentions expressed through his/her deliberate choice of appositive elements and fronted nonfinite subordinate clauses in their respective, immediate micro-text and macro-text environments – for instance, to transfer the fronted nonfinite clauses "depending on where you stand" and " . . . a return to business as usual" can be accurately transferred into the target language only if the micro/macro text elements are taken into consideration
- To transfer the semantic/pragmatic relations across clause relations into the target language's source text comprehension entails an accurate perception of the rhetorical relations that underlie the clausal, sentential, and complex syntactical constructions; this is a prerequisite for source text comprehension and an accurate transfer of those relations in the target language (Mahn 100–108)

This phase is in line with the PACTE Group's model (11) on translation competence, 2003.

3.11.3 *Post-translation phase*

The main goal of this phase is to raise trainees' awareness of their self-concepts as decision-makers (cf. Kiraly 2000).

- To edit early drafts of each other's translations
- To identify the instance of errors
- To classify errors into language and translation errors

Modules three and four are for both trainees and professionals, as both groups tended not to work on the interlingual and intertextual levels and the complementarity between the two.

Notes

1 Top-down processing means interpreting the text on the basis of his/her previous knowledge either stored in his/her memory or gained from previous context.
2 Bottom-up processing means processing the actual text (i.e., complex grammatical constructions) in front of him/her.

References

Beeby, Alison (2004). "Language Learning for Translators: Designing a Syllabus". In *Translation in Undergraduate Degree Programs*, edited by K. Malmkjaer, 39–66. Amsterdam/Philadelphia: John Benjamins Publishing Company.
Carrell, Patricia (1989). "Metacognitive Awareness and Second Language Reading". *Modern Language Journal* 73(2): 121–134.
Davies, Maria Gonzales (2004). "Undergraduate and Postgraduate Translation Degrees: Aims and Expectations". In *Translation in Undergraduate Degree Programs*, edited by K. Malmkjaer, 67–83. Amsterdam/Philadelphia: John Benjamins Publishing Company.
Dickins, James, Hervey, Sandor and Higgins, Ian (2002). *Thinking Arabic Translation: A Course in Translation Methods*. London and New York: Routledge
Farghal, Mohammed and AlManna, Ali (2018). *Contextualizing Translation Theories: Aspects of Arabic-English Interlingual Communication*. Cambridge: Cambridge Scholars Publishing.
Gile, Daniel (2005). "Empirical Research into the Role of Knowledge in Interpreting: Methodological Aspects". *Knowledge Systems and Translation* 149–171.
Grabe, William (1991). "Current Developments in Second Language Reading Research". *TESOL Quarterly* 25(3): 375–406.
Halliday, Michael and Hasan, Ruquia (1976). *Cohesion of English*. London: Longman.
Hatim, Basel and Mason, Ian (1990). *Discourse and the Translator*. London and New York: Routledge.
Kiraly, Don (2005). "Project-based Learning: A Case for Situated Translation". *Meta: journal des traducteurs/Meta: Translators' Journal* 50(4): 1098–1111.
Kiraly, Donald (2000). *A Social Constructivist Approach to Translator Education*. Manchester: St. Jerome Publishers
Kussmaul, Paul (1995). *Training the Translator*, 16–19. Amsterdam/Philadelphia: John Benjamins Publishing Company.
Mahn, Gabriela (2008). "Standards and Evaluation in Translator Training." In *Translator and Interpreter Training and Foreign Language Pedagogy*, edited by P.W. Krawutschke, 100–108. Amsterdam/Philadelphia: John Benjamins Publishing Company.
Nord, Christiana (2005). "All New on the European Front? What the Bologna Process Means for Translator Training in Germany." *Meta* L(1): 210–223.
PACTE (2011). "Results of the Validation of PACTE Translation Competence Model: Acceptability and Decision Making." *Across Languages and Culture* 10(2): 207–230.
Pym, Anthony (1992). "Translation Error Analysis and the Interface with Language Teaching". In *Teaching Translation and Interpreting*, edited by C. Dollerup and A. Loddegaard, 279–288. Amsterdam/Philadelphia: John Benjamins Publishing Company.
Wilss, Wolfram (2008). "Topical Issues in Translator Training at Universities". In *Translator and Interpreter Training and Foreign Language Pedagogy*, edited by P. W. Krawutschke, 91. Amsterdam/Philadelphia: John Benjamins Publishing Company.

Appendix A
Source text

The Economist

Dec 24th 2005

The European Union summit

Cries and gestures

A fractious and lengthy meeting strikes a budget deal that answers almost no questions about the future

THE budget announced in Brussels on December 17th was a return to business as usual in the European Union. Depending on where you stand, the deal was either a triumph or yet another example of the Union burying its head in the sand. A sceptic might reasonably conclude that, in the EU, these are one and the same thing.

The deal sets total EU spending at €862 billion ($1,036 billion) in 2007–13 (the EU draws up budgets in seven-year periods). This was rather over €10 billion bigger than the British, as holders of the EU presidency, were proposing; but it was almost €10 billion less than was suggested by the Luxembourg EU presidency in June. Hard on the heels of the European Constitutions' rejection by French and Dutch voters, that summit then collapsed acrimoniously over the budget.

Britain will also give up around one-fifth of its budget rebate that is attributable to the cost of EU enlargement to the east. The forgone amount is now €10.5 billion over seven years – more than the €8 billion first offered by the prime minister, Tony Blair, but less than the €14 billion that the French government had demanded. Meanwhile, the French stuck firmly to the October 2002 EU summit deal to keep spending on the common agricultural policy (CAP) unchanged until 2013 – but they accepted the proposal for a review of the entire budget in 2008.

France and Germany, and a commitment (sometimes wobbly) to enlargement, the summit displayed all of these.

Appendix B
Translation problems instrument

Translation of a text from English into Arabic (60 min.)

Please translate the text, taking into account the translation brief. You can use all the necessary tools/instruments to help you with your translation, but you must write the names of the tools you have consulted below the brief.

Translation brief: *The text you are called upon to translate has been published in* The Economist. *This magazine publishes articles on political, economic, cultural, scientific, and technical issues to be read by politicians, academics, and scientists all over the world. In other words, the readers of this magazine are your typical highly educated middle-class readers. You are required to translate the text into Arabic to be published in* Chamber of Commerce Magazine. *The targeted readers of your translation will be Arab intellectuals and professionals.*

1 **Do you think the following segments of the text are a translation problem (not just for you, but in general)?**

   A: "Cries and gestures"

      a Yes
      b No

   B: ". . . a return to business as usual in the European Union" (lines 2–3, 1st paragraph)

      a Yes
      b No

   C: "depending on where you stand." (lines 3–4, 1st paragraph)

      a Yes
      b No

Source text comprehension and reproduction 57

> D: "hard on the heels of the European Constitutions' rejection by French and Dutch voters" (lines 8–9, 2nd paragraph)
>
> a   Yes
> b   No
>
> E: "as holders of the EU presidency" (line 5, 2nd paragraph)
>
> a   Yes
> b   No
>
> F: "A fractious and lengthy meeting strikes a budget deal" (subheading)
>
> a   Yes
> b   No

2   **Did you find the following segments of the text a problem to translate?**

> A: "Cries and gestures"
>
> a   Yes
> b   No
>
> B: "... a return to business as usual in the European Union" (lines 2–3, 1st paragraph)
>
> a   Yes
> b   No
>
> C: "depending on where you stand." (lines 3–4, 1st paragraph)
>
> a   Yes
> b   No
>
> D: "hard on the heels of the European Constitutions' rejection by French and Dutch voters" (lines 8–9, 2nd paragraph)
>
> a   Yes
> b   No
>
> E: "as holders of the EU presidency" (line 5, 2nd paragraph)
>
> a   Yes
> b   No
>
> F: "A fractious and lengthy meeting strikes a budget deal" (subheading)
>
> c   Yes
> d   No

4 Training translators

A case for Arabic orthographic reforms

Maher Bahloul

4.1 Introduction

In the early 20th century, in 1917 in particular, the British Academy initiated transliterating projects related to Russian, Slavic, and Near Eastern languages, after which an Arabic transliteration system was recommended (Gorgis 2010). In 1923, Cambridge University Press published a book titled *System of Transliteration from Arabic into English*. The High Commissioner for Palestine appointed a committee of six members to produce a manuscript that would facilitate the writing of Arabic names and places in English in simple and uniform ways. Thus, a number of rules were suggested, especially for phonemes with no English counterparts such as the pharyngeal and uvular sounds, namely the voiceless uvular fricative /خ/, the voiceless uvular stop /ق/, the voiced uvular fricative /غ/, the voiceless pharyngeal stop /ع/, and the voiceless pharyngeal fricative /ح/. The project seems to have facilitated to a large extent the English writing of Arabic vocabulary items; it provided "a method for everyday use" governed by "simplicity" and "uniformity" (System of Transliteration 1923: 5).

While this project was relevant to Palestine, then under British rule, to facilitate written communication, the United States and the United Nations were similarly concerned with the writing of Romanized names in consistent ways across various languages, especially those with non-Roman alphabets. Thus, in 1947, the United States adopted a unified transliteration system with all government publications as per the US Board on Geographic Names (BGN). As for the United Nations, it has been very active with transliteration projects. Thus, it has created the Council of Orthography and Transcription of Geographical Names and passed several resolutions since its early conferences in the '60s and '70s relevant to each writing system, such as Bulgarian, Bengali, Hebrew, and Arabic, among others. With the latest advent in technology and computational schemes and systems (Habash et al. 2012, 2007, among others), new systems continue to appear, with the sole objective of reaching a unified system of Arabic to English transliteration that facilitates natural language processing and other artificial intelligence (AI) applications. The 2018 article of Alginabi, Al-Binali, and Dekkak in the *Arabian Journal for Science and Engineering* is yet another attempt to propose a homogeneous transliteration system and to develop a mobile-based application that is reliable and reversible.

In short, since the beginning of the 20th century, official and governmental institutions, in addition to the latest development within computational linguistics and natural language processing, have shown interest in Arabic to English transliteration. The fact that Arabic does not have a Roman alphabet and that several sounds do not have counterparts made the normalization highly challenging. Nevertheless, genuine research has been advancing the Arabic to English transliteration field. However, English to Arabic transliteration has not had similar interest; as such, issues relevant to the transliteration of such sounds as the voiceless bilabial stop /p/, the voiced velar stop /g/, and the voiced alveolar fricative /v/ to Arabic remain quite problematic.

Finally, involving translation programs within the effort of orthographic reforms through systematic training and research relevant to standardization will prove highly beneficial. As it is, we have to yet see such initiatives, and we hope to witness a degree of orthographic standardization and unification across the Arabic-speaking region.

4.2 English to Arabic transliteration

According to the transliteration.com website, "transliteration consists in representing the characters of a given script by the characters of another, while keeping the operation reversible". In other words, a word like 'Coca-Cola', for instance, may be written as pronounced in Arabic then read into English with no particular difficulty, as shown in (1a) and (1b) here:

1. a. Coca-Cola   ko#kə#kɔ#lə   (left to right)
      /kokəkɔlə/
   b. كوكاكولا   لا#كا#كو   (right to left)
      /kukakula/

The examples in (1a) and (1b) show two words written in English and in Arabic, respectively. Since the word in (1a) is a drink in English, the word in (1b) is a mere transliteration, written in Arabic as pronounced using the Roman alphabet. It is worth noting that similar to the English word, its Arabic counterpart includes four syllables, three of which start with voiceless velar fricatives /k/ onsets and one with a voiceless lateral liquid /l/ onset. While the vowel quality across the two languages differs, it remains minor and does not have an overall effect on the pronunciation similarity, clarity, or the meaning. In addition, the reading of the

Arabic transliterated word leads to its English counterpart, and vice versa; hence, the reversibility criterion is observed.

Examples like (1a) and (1b) are quite common nowadays and may be seen across all types of signs, either online or within the street signs in any one of the 22 Arabic speaking countries.[1] Table 4.1 shows a number of such cases:

Table 4.1 Sample of common transliterated English words

	Foreign Words	Arabic Transliteration	Sample Illustrations
a.	Halliday	هاليداي	هاليداي
b.	Facebook	فايسبوك	الدخول الى الفايسبوك
c.	Candy	كاندي	كاندي سوس
d.	McDonald's	ماكدونالدز	ماكدونالدز
e.	Cinema	سينما	سينما
f.	Colonel	كولونال	الكولونال
g.	Bush	بوش	بوش
h.	Cerelac	سيريلاك	سيريلاك
i.	My mommy	ماي مامي	ماي مامي
j.	London	لندن	لندن

The examples in Table 4.1 show a great deal of conformity to the definition of transliteration in terms of meaning and reversibility. As such, the reading of transliterated words in the Arabic script easily yields the corresponding form and meaning of the English word. Not only are the sounds very similar, but also the number of syllables is the same, and the meaning could only lead to its counterpart. Whether it is one syllable, as in the word 'Bush' (بوش), two syllables as in the word 'London' (لندن), or three syllables as in 'Hamburger' (همبرقر), the Arabic transliteration preserves the word's syllabic structure along with its general phonological properties.[2]

In fact, once we examine the English graphemes and sounds, we notice a much closer similarity with their Arabic counterparts. This is summarized in Table 4.2.[3]

Table 4.2 English vs. Arabic consonant graphemes and phonemes

	Gr.	Ex.	IPA	Arabic		Gr.	Ex.	IPA	Arabic
English Vs Arabic Consonant Graphemes & Phonemes	b	**b**oy	/b/	ب	English Vs Arabic Consonant Graphemes & Phonemes	h	**h**ere	/h/	ه
	d	**d**oll	/d/	د		k	**k**ilo	/k/	ك
	t	**t**all	/t/	ت		w	**w**ine	/w/	و
	f	**f**all	/f/	ف		l	**l**ine	/l/	ل
	n	**n**ame	/n/	ن		j	**j**am	/dʒ/	دج
	m	**m**ine	/m/	م		y	**y**ear	/j/	ي
	th	**th**in	/θ/	ث		g	**g**enre	/ʒ/	ج
	th	**th**is	/ð/	ذ		r	**r**oll	/r/	ر
	sh	**sh**ine	/ʃ/	ش		ng	ki**ng**	/ŋ/	---
	ch	**ch**air	/tʃ/	تش		p	**p**aul	/p/	---
	s	**s**un	/s/	س		v	**v**eal	/v/	---
	z	**z**ero	/z/	ز		g	**g**one	/g/	---

Table 4.2 shows, 20 out of the 23 English sound phonemes have their corresponding graphemes in Arabic; as such, English words with such sounds are easily transliterated in Arabic. However, the last four sounds of English in the table, namely the voiced labiodental fricative /v/, the voiced velar stops /g/ and /ng/, and the voiceless bilabial stop /p/, lack their Arabic correspondence, and their current transliteration constitutes a great deal of irregularity and confusion.

If we examine the vowels in both languages, without going into much detail, we notice a much simpler system of transliteration; this is summarized in Table 4.3:

Table 4.3 English vs. Arabic vowel sounds

English Vowel Sounds		Arabic Vowel Sounds & Graphemes	
		Short	Long
Front	[i], [ɪ], [ɛ], [æ]	/i/ (ِ)	(ـي)
Central	[ə], [3], [ʌ], [ɛ]	/a/ (َ)	(ـا)
Back	[o], [ɔ], [u], [ʊ]	/u/ (ُ)	(ـوُ)

As Table 4.3 shows, all English vowel phonemes fall within one of the three Arabic vowel system categories, the front vowel, the central vowel, and the back vowel: /i/, /a/, and /u/, respectively. The three Arabic vowels display graphemes in their short and long forms, resulting in six vowel graphemes total. Thus, the various vocalic subtleties in English get highly blurred when transliterated into Arabic, resulting in major difficulties and inconsistencies. This is not, however, the focus of this chapter, since the priority is given to consonants.

4.3 Current English to Arabic transliteration challenges

While most vowel subtleties may find ways of getting transliterated, the three major English consonant phonemes that lack their Arabic counterparts, as shown at the end of Table 4.2, mainly the consonant /g/, the consonant /v/, and the consonant /p/, remain highly problematic and display a considerable lack of uniformity when transliterated.[4] The example of the grapheme/phoneme /g/ in Table 4.4 explicates this phenomenon.

The case in Table 4.4 shows the voiced velar consonant /g/ in the English word 'hamburger' transliterated in five different ways in Arabic; thus, it is transcribed as a voiced uvular sound /ɣ, غ/ in (4a), a voiceless velar stop /k, ك/ in (4b), a voiceless uvular stop /q, ق/ in (4c), a voiced postalveolar fricative /ʒ, ج/ in (4d), and a voiced velar stop /g, ك/ in (4e). Most of these variants could be seen in one country and/or across all Arabic-speaking countries printed in such signs as restaurant menus, street signs, advertising texts, and regular and social media posts (see also Dasigi and Diab 2011). In addition, the transliteration in these examples is by no means representative of any rule or trend. This is especially true when one notices that the variation relates to the same word, 'hamburger'. In addition, this variation does not seem to be conditioned by any phonetic, phonological, or orthographic rule; it is quite random, reminiscent of the current chaotic state of the transcription and transliteration of the voiced velar stop /g/.

Table 4.4 Transliteration of the /g/ sound in 'hamburger'

/g/ hamburger	a. /ɣ/-/غ/	همبرغر	همبرغر الدجاج شام الأصيل
	b. /k/-/ك/	همبركر	طريقة عمل الهمبركر - أكلات عراقية **iraqi food**
	c. /ق/-/q/	برقر	برقر
	d. /ج/-/ʒ/	همبرجر	برجر اللحم (الهمبرجر) الهمبركر نفس المطاعم
	e. /ڨ/-/g/	برڨر	برڨر الأحلاااام

4.4 Transliteration issues of the English to Arabic voiced velar stop /g/

The above variation is not limited to the English word 'hamburger'. In fact, it is found in any Roman-based lexical item with the voiced velar stop /g/. Table 4.5 provides examples relevant to such variations:

As Table 4.5 shows, the voiced velar stop /g/ is transliterated in five different ways. The five different transcriptions, namely the voiced velar fricative /ɣ/-/غ/ as found in examples of 'Place Marburg' and 'Boeing Airplane' in (5a), the voiced velar stop /g/-/ڨ /, as seen in names such as 'Al-Ghamgi Perfumes' and 'Lotfi Gassara' in (5b), the voiced post-alveolar fricative /ʒ/-/ج/- as illustrated by 'Boeing Seats' and 'Google' in (5c), the voiceless uvular stop /q/-/ق/ as found in names such as '**G**abes' and '**G**argouri' in (5d), and the voiceless velar stop /k/-/ك/, as found in 'Hamburger' in (5e) are all variants of the transliteration of the English consonant /g/. Such graphological representations are found across the board within linguistic landscapes of Arab speaking countries. As such, the voiced velar fricative is found in the transliteration of foreign words such as names of places and airplanes (i.e., Marburg and Boeing); in names of Arab shop owners (i.e., Ghamgi and Gassara); in the transliteration of foreign names (i.e., Boeing and Google), in names of Arab cities and Arab last names (i.e., Gabes and Gargouri), and in the transliteration of food items in Roman script (i.e., Hamburger). However, the transcription and the transliteration of these examples are by no means representative of any rule or any trend. They are mere illustrations just to show such variation. The variation as illustrated in Table 4.5 does not seem to be conditioned by any phonetic, phonological, or orthographic rule; it is quite random,

64 Maher Bahloul

Table 4.5 Transliterations of the voiced velar stop sound /g/

Sounds	Sample Transliterations		Relevant Sample Visuals
Voiced Velar Stop /g/	a. Voiced Velar fricative /غ/-/ɣ/	ساحة ماربورغ Place Marburg	
		طائرة بوينغ Boing Airplane	
	b. Voiced velar stop /ڨ/-/g/	عطورات الڨمڨي Al-Ghamgi Perfumes	
		لطفي ڨصارة Lotfi Gassara	
	c. Voiced post-alveolar fricative /ج/-/ʒ/	مقاعد بوينج Boing Seats	
		جوجل Google	
	d. Voiceless uvular stop /ق/-/q/	قابس Gabes	
		قرقوري Gargouri	
	e. Voiceless Velar Stop /ك/-/k/	همبركر	طريقة عمل الهمبركر - أكلات عراقية iraqi food

reminiscent of the current chaotic state of the transcription and transliteration of the voiced velar stop /g/.

This conclusion is borne out when such lack of uniformity is observed within any one particular place, whereby the Arabic transliteration oscillates between two or three variants. The example in the Figure 4.1 illustrates such inconsistency:

Figure 4.1 is a screenshot taken from a YouTube link named 'Arabic Kitchen' (www.youtube.com/results?search_query=arabic+kitchen). As part of its marketing function, it includes a short descriptive summary of the culinary business. As the descriptive text in Figure 4.1 shows, while the third word of the first line includes the word 'hamburger' with the voiced velar fricative /غ,ɣ/ 'همبرغر', the same is written on the fourth word in the third line with the voiced post-alveolar fricative /ج,ʒ/ 'همبرجر'. In the last sentence of this short marketing paragraph, the

Arabic Kitchen المطبخ العربي
335K subscribers

جاءت تسمية الهمبرغر نسبة إلى مدينة هامبورغ الألمانية. والهمبرغر هو عبارة عن لحم داخل خبز, وقد وصلت هذه الاكلة الى امركا واصبحت من اشهر بلدان العالم بتقديم هذه الوجبات السريعة ومن اشهر المطاعم التي تقدم هذه الوجبات والتي انتشرت لها فروع في كافة دول العالم هي ماكدونالدز, برجر كنج كنتاكي. في هذا الفديو نقدم طريقة عمل همبرغر أو همبرجر اللحم البقري. ونتمنى ان ينال رضاكم

المقادير
‎——————

كيلوين لحم مفروم

اربع ملاعق كبيرة فتاة خبز

ملعقة ثوم مهروس

ملعقة كبيرة بصل مفروم ناعم

ملعقة كبيرة بقدونس مفروم ناعم

ملعقة كبيرة فلفل اسود

ملعقه كبيرة بابريكا

ملعقة كبيرة فلفل احمر حامي

ملعقة كبيرة قرفة

ملعقة كبيرة كبابة

ملعقتين كبيرة كاتشب

ملعقتين كبيرة خردل

Ingredients
‎——————

Figure 4.1 Transliteration of the voiced velar stop consonant /g/

author – clearly aware of the consonant /g/ variants – makes a statement about the video content and writes both variants with the conjunction 'or' in between, as shown in (2):

2. في هذا الفديو نقدم طريقة عمل <u>همبرغر</u> او <u>همبرجر</u> اللحم البقري

   In-this-video-show way-work-hamburɣer or hamburʒer-meat-beef
   'In this video, we show you the way a beef **hamburger or hamburger** is prepared'

Not only does the statement in (2) show mere variation, but it also illustrates some sort of hesitation and/or reluctance in choosing one variant over the other; thus, the decision was made to make use of both transliterations to accommodate customers' linguistic tastes and preferences. Such interpretation is born out when a careful sociolinguistic examination of such variation shows strong attitudes for or against the choice of a particular transliteration variant of the consonant /g/.[5]

66 *Maher Bahloul*

4.5 Transliteration issues of the voiceless bilabial stop /p/

A careful examination of the current English to Arabic transliteration of the consonant /p/ shows variation and inconsistencies. Examples of such variation are summarized in Table 4.6:

Table 4.6 English to Arabic transliterations of the voiceless bilabial stop /p/

Sounds	Sample Transliterations		Relevant Sample Visuals
Voiceless bilabial stop /p/	a. Voiced bilabial stop /b/-/ب/	كبا قهوة CUPA GAHWA	
		بليس Place	
	b. Voiceless bilabial stop /p/-/پ/	پودوس Peau Douce	

As Table 4.6 indicates, the voiceless bilabial stop /p/ is generally voiced when transliterated to Arabic; as such, it shows as a voiced bilabial stop /b/, as in 'CUPA, كبا', and 'PLACE, بليس', where the /p/ is replaced by its voiced counterpart /b/ in Arabic. In some other cases, it is transliterated with a grapheme that is foreign to the Arabic alphabet, a b-like grapheme with three dots underneath. While the first variant proves to be quite problematic, as we will see later, the second variant will be part of our proposal in order to unify the transliteration of the /p/ consonant and put an end to current irregularities.

4.6 English to Arabic transliteration issues of the voiced labiodental fricative /v/

Similar to the voiceless bilabial stop /p/ and the voiced velar stop /g/, the voiced labiodental fricative /v/ exhibits a variety of transliteration from English to Arabic and lacks consistency. This is summarized in Table 4.7:

As Table 4.7 clearly shows, the English voiced labiodental fricative consonant /v/ is transliterated in three different ways. The most common is its voiceless counterpart, since it exists in the Arabic alphabet, that is the voiceless labiodental fricative /f, ف/ as in (7a). Thus, English lexical items containing the consonant /v/

Table 4.7 Transliterations of the voiced labiodental fricative /v/

Sounds	Sample Transcriptions		Relevant Sample Visuals
Voiced labiodental fricative /v/	a. Voiceless labiodental fricative /f/-/ف/	هانوفر Hannover	
		فيديو Video	
	b. Voiced labiodental fricative /v/-/ ڥ /	نوڥيتا NOVITA	
		نوڤا NOVA	

are transliterated by /f/, as in the words 'Hannover' and 'video', which turn into 'Hannofer, هانوفر' and 'fideo, فيديو'. Two other variants are found with an f-like grapheme with three dots underneath, as in the word 'Novita, نوڥيتا', and three dots on top, as in the word 'Nova, نوڤا'. These two graphemes are not part of the Arabic graphemic system; however, they play a key role in shaping our unifying proposal.

Thus far, we have established that English to Arabic transliteration shows a great deal of inconsistencies with consonants such as the voiced velar stop /g/, the voiceless bilabial stop /p/, and the voiced labiodental fricative /v/. While the /g/ shows five different graphemic counterparts, the /p/ and the /v/ show three variants each, a total of 11 variants for three consonants. In addition, there do not seem to be any inherent or phonological conditions that would favor the choice of one variant over the other. However, in order to appreciate such variations, a closer examination of the current situation of the Arabic language within and across Arabic-speaking societies would provide informative input to elucidate such complexity. In other words, if orthographic variants are analyzed within one particular country (i.e., Egypt, etc.), the issue is much less disturbing because of regular transliteration practices. However, when such orthographic inconsistencies are assessed within the entire region, major systematic flaws, irregular practices, and semantic ambiguities start to surface, hence the call for a unifying approach that would empower both the language and its speakers.

4.7 Arabic in Arab speaking societies

Similar to the growth and widespread use of the French language spoken in Quebec, 'Québécois', where the oral medium differs qualitatively from the written medium, the Arabic language is characterized by a clear disconnect between the spoken language and the written one. While the written medium is typically and exclusively reserved for a learned language, namely Modern Standard Arabic (MSA), the spoken medium is exclusively reserved for the mother tongue, known as Dialectal Arabic (DA). Thus, the use of such labelling as Egyptian Arabic (EA), Moroccan Arabic (MA), Emirati Arabic (EA), Tunisian Arabic (TA), Palestinian Arabic (PA), and the like is meant to name and distinguish the mother tongue of each Arab country. Native speakers of Arabic in Egypt, for instance, are native to the dialectal language EA, not to MSA, since the latter is learned, and the same applies to all other Arabic speaking countries. We agree with Habash, Diab, and Rambow, who state that "DA differs from MSA on all levels of linguistic representation, from phonology and morphology to lexicon and syntax" (2012: 711).

As for intelligibility between the various Arabic dialects, the farther apart the countries are, the more difficult accessibility and intelligibility become. Such unintelligibility is also due to the fact that these languages grew too much apart, had separate histories, mixed with different other languages, and exhibit different linguistic characteristics.[6]

Thus, the local native Arabic languages continue to witness prevailing and preponderant use within their own societies. In other words, what used to be seen as a marginal form of language is being reassessed as a genuine native language. In Egypt, for instance, while Egyptian Arabic is observed across the board within Egyptian society, Modern Standard Arabic remains the language of instruction in schools and the language of official government written communication. This is the case for Moroccan Arabic, Tunisian Arabic (Tunsi), Emirati Arabic, Iraqi Arabic, etc.

I agree with Masmoudi (2018, 2015) and Bassiouney (2008), among several others, who clearly show that more and more Arabic speaking people make use of their local languages to communicate. This is especially true amongst the various users of social media; in fact, social media has affected to a great extent the incessant growth of Dialectal Arabic. However, this participation appears to face various challenges not only at the level of acceptability on the part of conservative academics and religious purists but also at the graphemic level, where Arabic shows a number of limitations.

Social media users from one of the major Tunisian cities called 'Gabes, قابس', for instance, find the Arabic script limited when writing the name of their city and the name of the city originator in its single and plural forms (i.e., Gabes, قابس; Gabsi, قابسي; Gwebsiya, قوابسية, respectively). The voiced velar stop /g/ does not exist in Arabic script; therefore, alternative solutions ought to be found and used instead. This is especially embarrassing in countries such as Egypt, Oman, and Yemen, to mention a few, where the voiced postalveolar fricative /ʒ, ج/ gets systematically replaced by the voiced velar stop /g/, a consonant with no corresponding Arabic grapheme. As such, a gap between the mother tongue and the written medium is quite apparent, which calls for urgent consideration and appropriate orthographic reform measures. This is yet another reason for translation programs to take transliteration issues into their own hands and initiate relevant orthographic reforms.

When current Arabic graphemes cannot accommodate people's names, people's cities, people's designations, and people's general and specific needs, a state of urgency, if not emergency, ought to be declared. Language policies within the Arabic-speaking societies where the Arabic script is used are more than ever jeopardized, and solutions to its shortcomings and flaws ought to be pondered and properly addressed.

In fact, a careful examination of language use and the linguistic landscape within the last couple decades shows an increasing use of Dialectal Arabic in spoken and written media. Bassiouney (2009: 4) writes: "Yes, increasingly these days, the characteristics of spoken and written language overlap"; this is true as people start reading messages on their digital devices every single day. From morning greetings to daily planning and discussions, it is easy to see that people are now writing the way they talk – hence the mere dumping of the official written language, that is, Modern Standard Arabic, in favor of their spoken Arabic dialects. This is further explained in the following section.

4.8 Modern standard Arabic (MSA) vs. Arabic dialects (AD)

Children born in an Arabic-speaking society whose parents are native speakers of an Arabic dialect acquire the language spoken by their parents, grandparents, siblings, and neighbors. From initial acquisition stages until Grade 1, that is, age 6, in general, children become fluent in their mother tongue. They can converse with ease, tell stories, quarrel, and even curse and fight using adult language. In addition, several teenagers are seen on social media chatting quite fluently and using their mother tongue, the Arabic dialect.

In Grade 1, children in Arab societies are introduced to a new language, commonly called 'Al-3arabiyya al-fushaa, العربية الفصحى' (Modern Standard Arabic). They begin a language-learning journey starting with its alphabet, its lexicon, its phrases, and its sentences. It is a language-learning process that begins in Grade 1 and continues until Grade 6, where it is expected of children to mature linguistically, and they are expected to read, write, and speak quite fluently. In addition, in monolingual educational systems, academic success is quite connected to a great deal of linguistic competence, hence the importance of Modern Standard Arabic in the life of any Arab child. Needless to mention, several Arab children fail school and end up working at early ages due to weak linguistic performance.

Local Arabic languages grew to become national languages. Thus, Tunsi, for example, is the language of Tunisians; Emirati is the language of Emiratis, and Egyptian is the language of Egyptians, and this is the case with each one of the 22

Arabic-speaking countries. Thus, most daily communication amongst Tunisians, for instance, makes use of Tunsi. Whether at home or outside, with friends or family members, in an office or in an administration, all spoken communication is done in Tunsi. In addition, radio stations, television channels, public advertising and marketing, popular and national songs, film and theater productions, and online social media chats and conversations are mostly communicated in Tunsi, the mother tongue.

In contrast, the use of Modern Standard Arabic is quite limited. In addition to academic writing, most people expect to hear the news broadcasted in MSA, and imams inside mosques use it, too, in addition to few official TV and radio programs. Such limitations may explain the reason for which fluency in MSA is not common among Arab speakers. However, the status of Modern Standard Arabic language as a second language has not been recognized as such, and several academics continue to assume that it is their native language. Such assumptions have left the native language, that is the so-called Arabic dialect, lagging behind, especially in official written communication.

The latest research, however, shows that the use of the native language in each Arab country is expanding and gaining momentum. In schools, for instance, several teachers are making use of the Arabic dialect (AD) in classrooms to explain lessons, analyze concepts, and communicate with students. In societies, various nongovernmental organizations are pushing forward with the local languages' agenda, calling for its official use in government circles and educational institutions (i.e., Darija & English Quotes,[7] Darija Dialect,[8] Derja La Langue Tunisienne,[9] etc.). In short, each Arabic speaking country is experiencing more and more use of their native languages and less and less of MSA, a language that seems to have thrived academically and politically for the past five to six decades (Masmoudi et al. 2018, 2015.)[10]

The current linguistic complexity, whereby the native language is assumed to be much less functional and much less academic than Modern Standard Arabic, a learned language, seems to have had negative consequences on the growth and development of the writing medium. In other words, the assumption that MSA and its alphabet, graphemes, and writing system are the 'official' form of communication has resulted, to a large extent, in an orthographic crisis whereby people are confused how to even write their own names (see Halimah 2016), let alone clearly and fluently writing thoughts and concepts without having to stop and ponder on orthographic complexities and puzzles.

Current challenges are clearly seen through studies done and research written about the translation or transliteration of the non-Arabic borrowed words, including names of newly discovered items related to technological advances such as televisions, telephones, computers, and all digital devices that are quite common and highly consumed worldwide in general and in the Arabic-speaking countries in particular, names of people, names of cars, names of places, names of food/drinks, names of clothes, names of furniture, names of professions, titles of films, titles of books, titles of newspapers, titles of magazines, titles of programs, and titles of artists, among various other general and specialized lexical items and day-to-day expressions; this is the reason behind the high level of frequency of transliteration within the Arab societies (see Table 4.8).

Transliteration discussions and debates could be seen through the various works of such academics and researchers as Bies et al. (2014); Saleh (2011), Mahjoub (2007), Fraiwan (2007), Al-Agha (2006), Obeidat (2005), AbdulJaleel and Larkey (2003), Al-Shehari (2001), Al-Saqqa (2001), and Stalls and Knight (1998).

Researchers in machine translation have also been facing a great deal of challenges and several phonetic, spelling, and orthographic issues. In addition, linear-combination models were designed to account for all sorts of transliteration issues (Al-Onaizan and Knight 2001; Arbabi et al. 1994.) Challenges arise from the acceptability of various different transliterating forms across the Arabic-speaking countries where the second or third European languages differ (i.e., French, Spanish, Italian, English, etc.), resulting in a variety of common transliterations.[11] In addition, the fast pace of incoming foreign words makes common translations and common transliterations a hard task, if not an impossible mission (Saadane et al. 2012, etc.)

In addition, the English language teaching (ELT) field in all Arabic-speaking societies faces enormous challenges, as students are found transliterating English words into Arabic using current limited orthography. As such, students tend to use different graphemes with different pronunciations to accommodate those non-existent graphemes in the Arabic writing system. Students would, for instance, use the grapheme /b, ب/ to write the consonant /p/, the grapheme /f,ف/ to write the consonant /v/, and the grapheme /q,ق/, /k,ك/, or /gh,غ/ to write the grapheme /g/ (Bahloul 2007a, 2007b). Such misleading orthographic transcription results in false pronunciation and false mental representations, aggravating the learning process and delaying effective learning of adequate spelling and accurate writing, in addition to speaking and writing in general.

The Arabic as a Foreign Language (AFL) teaching and learning field has also been facing challenges related to the lack of systematic rendering of the European names into Arabic. AFL students are constantly uncertain about the common rendering of lexical items into Arabic despite the teachers' tendency to minimize the effect of such issues. The adoption of one grapheme variant in Egypt is not the same in some other Arabic-speaking countries such as Morocco, Saudi Arabia, or Syria (Alsalman et al. 2007; Saadane et al. 2018). While there is a general tendency to keep the writing system as it is, it is much more beneficial to seek improvement and betterment of the current state. Students of Arabic would find it much more reader friendly to have a writing system that manages to maximize accurate readings of foreign words and minimize lexical ambiguities and inaccuracies. When the student's name 'Paul' is rendered as 'Baul' (بول),

which has a direct denotational reference to urine with the letter /b/, it becomes highly undesirable. This is so simply because the current writing system refuses to make such graphemes as /p/ (پ) available within the general orthographic system of Arabic.

Although there are several different ways of rendering an English lexeme into Arabic, transliteration remains the most common one; hence, the orthographic challenge appears at the core of such daily tasks. Saleh, for instance, mentions seven different ways through which an English word is rendered into Arabic. In addition to transliteration and literal translation, there is adaptation, omission, and translation using either general or specific terms (Saleh 2011: 59). This is summarized in Table 4.8:

Despite the limited sample of this study ($n = 241$), the results are very likely to be generalized for transliteration across the board. If, within a sample of 241 words a decade ago, almost 43% of translations are mere transliteration, it is a clear indication of the salience of this strategy of rendering foreign words in the Arabic-speaking societies.

4.9 Translation and transliteration

Apart from current Arab governments who attempt to impose the use of Modern Standard Arabic as the language of official written communication through all incoming and outgoing documents, the educational system tends to oscillate between the use of Modern Standard Arabic and other foreign languages (i.e., English, French) as a primary, concurrent, or second medium of instruction. Thus, most Arab children grow to becoming trilingual by the end of their primary and secondary education. In addition to their mother tongue, they learn Modern Standard Arabic as a second language and another foreign language as a third language. A Tunisian child, for instance, would grow up speaking Tunisian Arabic (Tunsi) as a mother tongue, MSA as a second learned language, and French as a third learned language. With English being slowly and surely integrated into various school curricula (Haj Mabrouk forthcoming), Tunisian children end up speaking four languages by the time they go to college.[12] While this richness ought to be celebrated, several critics note the dilution of language proficiency and linguistic competence. They raised, for instance, issues relevant to language and identity, language and linguistic competence, and language and academic policies. While each one of these issues is of a paramount importance, dealing with them goes beyond the scope of this chapter.[13]

This linguistic richness has resulted in various types of language and linguistic diversities. However, with the sharp rise of globalization and constant interaction among countries, communities, nearby and faraway languages and language families, a need for a level of unification, especially with the

Table 4.8 Frequency and percentage of translation strategies/techniques

Translation Strategies	Frequency (times)	Percentage
Transliteration (borrowing)	103	42.738%
Literal translation	82	34.024%
Adaptation	15	6.224%
Addition	23	9.543%
Omission	8	3.319%
Translation by more than one world (superordinate)	5	2.074%
Translation by a more specific word (hyponym)	5	2.074%
Total	241	100%

transliteration of foreign words using the common Arabic script, is becoming a pressing matter.

While linguistic diversity caters to the need of different communities and should be cherished, transliteration diversity is more a case of inconsistency for the confusion it creates and the hesitation it promotes within various communicative contexts. Whether in the field of foreign language learning, business communication, or the medical field, especially the acronyms, transliteration remains a major obstacle to clarity, simplicity, uniformity, and smooth communication.

When examining translation programs within most Arabic-speaking countries, issues of transliteration and standardization, especially from English to Arabic, tend to be overlooked and not addressed. In part, this is due to traditional and conservative curricula that focus on common translation and interpreting topics and themes. Transliteration, however, has no place in any single department's curricula. From Syria to Morocco, passing by Saudi Arabia and Egypt, amongst others, no single translation program includes transliteration and the 'Art of Transliteration' as a course in its own right. This lack of attention from the academic community on the one hand and from the government official policies on the other hand has resulted in a situation where inconsistencies, confusion, and lack of uniformity are common features of the general Arabic linguistic landscape.

The current difficulties facing Arabic transliteration of the sounds /g/, /v/, and /p/ are even greater when general and specific acronyms get transliterated. Let us examine the examples in Table 4.9:

Table 4.9 Transliteration of acronyms containing the voiceless bilabial stop /p/

Acronyms	Meanings	Transliteration
RP	Republican Party	آر بي
UP	United Press	يو بي
NPR	National Public Radio	آن بي آر
AFP	Agence France Presse	آي آف بي

Table 4.9 shows four acronyms with two and three syllables: RP, UP, and NPR, AFP, respectively. Each syllable is a full letter which represents the initial sound of each word within the compound, as in 'R' of 'Republican' and

Training translators 75

'P' of 'Party' – hence the acronym 'RP'. When transliterated in Arabic, while the first letter 'R' has its Arabic counterpart, the letter 'P' does not. Thus, it gets replaced by the nearest letter/sound in Arabic that is the voiced version of the sound 'P', that is 'B'. As a result, the acronym 'RP' turns into 'RB', and so do 'UP', 'NPR', and 'AFP', for they become 'UB', 'NBR', and 'AFB', respectively.

One may argue that the difference is negligent since the meaning is preserved and the voicing of the sound 'p' does not result in major misunderstandings. This conclusion is not borne out when we examine the cases in Table 4.10:

Table 4.10 Transliteration of acronym pairs

Acronyms	Meanings	Transliteration
ABC	American Broadcasting Company	آي بي سي
APC	American Peace Corps	
BC	Before Christ	بي سي
PC	Personal Computer	
BBC	British Broadcasting Company	بي بي سي
PPC	Pet Population Control	
BBA	Bachelor of Business Administration	بي بي آي
PPA	Pakistan Press Association	
FBI	Federal Bureau of Investigation	أف بي آي
FPI	Federal Prison Industries	

In addition, latest studies of acronym disambiguation within natural language modeling frameworks highlight the challenges that acronyms present (Ahmed et al. 2015; Ammar et al. 2011; Stevenson et al. 2009). First, acronyms are quite frequent in language, especially in English. Ammar et al. (2011) clearly show that almost one in ten (9.7) words in Wikipedia is an acronym. Second, acronyms are characterized by expansions or multiple semantic interpretations, hence the salience of immediate and larger context to select the most appropriate interpretation. The acronyms ATM and AAC, according to Ahmed et al. (2015) for instance, exhibit 23 to 46 possible references, respectively. Examples in (3a) and (3b) show such semantic variations:

3. a. AAC Atlanta Athletic Club

    "The AAC has hosted many non-Gulf events including the first two South-eastern Conference men's basketball tournaments in 1933 and 1934."

    b. AAC American Aeronautical Corporation

    "With a factory already in place in Port Washington, on Long Island, the AAC sponsored the construction of a sea-plane base in the town."

As the examples in (3a) and (3b) show, the same acronym may have two completely unrelated references, a typical case of polysemy, where similarly pronounced lexical items exhibit different and unrelated meanings.

When English acronyms are transliterated to Arabic, as illustrated in Table 4.10, an additional level of ambiguity gets added. Apart from cases of polysemy, readers ought to wonder about the original orthographic and phonological nature of the acronym. In other words, since the Arabic acronym 'آي بي سي' may refer to either ABC or APC, two completely different constructs, clarity and intended meanings get minimized, and the entire communicative aspect of language gets jeopardized. This situation gets aggravated when acronyms include more sounds for which Arabic does not provide counterparts. Such examples are shown in Table 4.11:

When such acronyms are carefully examined, it is clear to note that conditions of clarity and reversibility in transliteration are violated. When 'Pay Per View' and 'Broadband Forum' are similarly transliterated in Arabic as 'بي بي في' with voiced bilabial stops /b/ and a voiceless labiodental fricative /f/, it simply shows a great deal of deficiency. This is apparent with each one of the five pairs of acronyms in Table 4.11. Thus, the obvious difference between each pair member gets neutralized by the Arabic transliteration, since Arabic lacks the corresponding graphemes, namely the voiced labiodental fricative /v/, the voiced velar stop /g/, and the voiceless bilabial stop /p/. Transliterating the acronym 'VG' as 'في جي' and the other acronym 'FJ' as 'في جي' in Arabic is a highly erratic practice considering the great deal of confusion it incurs. In other words, when the compound expressions 'Virtual Pro Gaming', shortened as 'VPG', is transliterated in Arabic in a similar way to 'FBG' of the 'French Business Group', it constitutes a major source of miscommunication and a sign of language shortcoming, a condition

Table 4.11 Transliteration of challenging acronyms

Acronyms	Meanings	Transliteration
PPV	Pay Per View	بي بي في
BBF	Broadband Forum	
VG	Verdens Gang	في جي
FJ	FJ Land Cruiser	
VPB	Ventricle Premature Beats	في بي بي
FBP	FBP International	
VPG	Virtual Pro Gaming	في بي جي
FBG	French Business Group	
BG	BG Group	بي جي
PJ	PJ Masks	

that, in our opinion, is a result of linguistic conservatism, not linguistic shortcoming. The Arabic writing system is capable of accommodating such differences when its graphemic system, and resources are carefully considered.

4.10 Conclusions and recommendations

The chapter has thus far established that English to Arabic transliteration suffers from a huge lack of systematicity, consistency, clarity, and converseness. In order to overcome current challenges relevant to acronym ambiguities, the graphological aspect ought to be addressed so that the multiplicity of meanings inherent to acronyms does not get aggravated by the graphological complexity, which leads not only to inaccuracies but also to severe misinterpretations. In fields such as medicine and aviation, mistakes and misunderstandings could be highly undesirable, fatal, and life threatening. Table 4.12 shows a proposal of three graphemes for each one of the consonants that current written Arabic does not accommodate.

Table 4.12 shows the three consonants /p/, /g/, and /v/ along with their suggested Arabic graphemes /پ/, /ڨ/, and /ڤ/. Examples are also provided to explicate the

Table 4.12 Graphemes for /p/, /g/, and /v/

English Grapheme	Suggested Arabic Grapheme	Examples	
/p/	/پ/	پودوس	Peau Douce
/g/	/ڨ/	ڨوڨل	Google
/v/	/ڤ/	نوڤيتا	Novita

use of such graphemes. Thus, the /پ,p/ grapheme will be used in the transliteration of words such as the diaper brand 'Peau Douce, پودوس'; the /ڨ,g/ grapheme will be used to transliterate words such as the search engine 'ڨوڨل, Google', and the 'ڤ,v' grapheme will transliterate the voiced labiodental fricative. While these graphemes are found within the Arabic-speaking countries, they are by no means incorporated within the writing system of any official or unofficial Arabic within such countries. As such, their use remains sporadic, inconsistent, and at best highly limited.

If the proposed graphemes get adopted, the examples in Tables, 4.9, 4.10, and 4.11 get smoothly differentiated, since the new set of Arabic graphemes will accurately transliterate the English consonants /p/, /g/, and /v/. This is shown in Table 4.13:

It is clear to see that each English acronym in Table 4.13 gets transliterated in a unique and systematic way without any graphemic ambiguity. Thanks to the unique graphemic representation of the English consonants /p/, /g/, and /v/, acronyms of various types that contain any one of such consonants get a much clearer interpretation.

While the three graphemes /p/, /g/, and /v/ constitute a graphemic challenge for Arabic writing for the lack of their presence, the writing system with bases and diacritics may easily generate new graphemes. The 'B'-base, for instance, '‬ـبـ‬' generates a variety of consonants when diacritics are added, as shown in Table 4.14:

As Table 4.14 shows, dot diacritics are added to the flat base to generate a number of different consonants. While adding one dot to the top of the base results in the consonant /n/, adding it to the bottom of the base yields the consonant /b/. The two dots result in consonants /t/ and /y/ when added on top and underneath, respectively. However, adding three dots on top results in the consonant /θ/. We propose adding three dots underneath to transcribe the consonant /p/. As such, the single, the double, and the triple dot mechanism[14] on top of the base and

Table 4.13 Acronyms with /p/, /g/, and /v/ graphemes

Acronyms	Meanings	Transliteration
RP	Republican Party	آر پي
UP	United Press	يو پي
NPR	National Public Radio	آن پي آر
AFP	Agence France Presse	آي آف پي
ABC	American Broadcasting Company	آي بي سي
APC	American Peace Corps	آي پي سي
BC	Before Christ	بي سي
PC	Personal Computer	پي سي
BBC	British Broadcasting Company	بي بي سي
PPC	Pet Population Control	پي پي سي
BBA	Bachelor of Business Administration	بي بي آي
PPA	Pakistan Press Association	پي پي آي
FBI	Federal Bureau of Investigation	آف بي آي
FPI	Federal Prison Industries	آف پي آي
PPV	Pay Per View	پي پي ڤي
BBF	Broadband Forum	بي بي ڤي
VG	Verdens Gang	ڤي جي
FJ	FJ Land Cruiser	آف جاي
VPB	Ventricle Premature Beats	ڤي پي بي
FBP	FBP International	آف بي پي
VPG	Virtual Pro Gaming	ڤي پي جي
FBG	French Business Group	آف بي جي
BG	BG Group	بي جي
PJ	PJ Masks	پي جاي

underneath it exhibits much more coherence. In other words, adding the grapheme /p/ to the current writing system is even desirable for the level of binarism and wholeness it adds to the Arabic writing system.

In addition to the /p/ grapheme, both /g/ and /v/ could easily and similarly be accommodated by the Arabic orthographic system. This is shown in Table 4.15:

80 *Maher Bahloul*

Table 4.14 Arabic script base and diacritics for /p/

Script Base	Diacritics	Consonantal Outcome
ب	• one dot underneath • one dot on top • two dots on top • two dots underneath • three dots on top • three dots underneath	• /b, ب/ • /n, ن/ • /t, ت/ • /y, ي/ • /th, ث/ • /p, پ/

Table 4.15 Arabic base and diacritics for /g/ and /v/

Script Base	Diacritics	Consonantal Outcome
ف	• one dot on top • two dots on top • three dots on top • three dots underneath	• /f, ف/ • /q, ق/ • /g, ڨ/ • /v, ڤ/

As Table 4.15 explicates, the ف base allows for the production of the grapheme /f, ف/ and the grapheme /q, ق/ when one dot and two dots are added to the top, respectively. We suggest adding three dots on the top to produce the /g, ڨ/ grapheme and three dots at the bottom to produce the /v, ڤ/ grapheme.

The addition of the three graphemes to the current Arabic writing system will not only participate in accommodating the transliteration of foreign words in their long and short forms, resulting in a much more stable linguistic landscape within Arabic-speaking countries and across all 22 of them, but it will also equally benefit the local Arabic dialects, especially those that make use of the voiced velar stop /g/, for instance, as part of their daily communication (Bahloul 2011). As such, the /g/ sound is used as part of family names (i.e., Gahtani, قصحاني; Gargouri, قرڤوري; etc.), names of cities (i.e., Gabes, ڤابس, etc.), and professional occupations, among various other day-to-day communications. Once recognized within the Arabic orthographic system, it will lessen current sociolinguistic tensions and streamline official and unofficial uses of such graphemes in daily life.

When Arabic is learned as an additional language, the three graphemes /p/, /g/, and /v/ play a positive role in lessening graphemic tensions and facilitating the accurate pronunciation of words containing such consonants. This is especially true when Arabic dialects are systematically offered in Arabic and Middle Eastern departments within several universities worldwide. Thus, students will no longer have to write the name 'Paul/پول' with a voiced bilabial stop 'Baul/ بول'; instead, the voiceless bilabial stop grapheme /p,پ/ is used.

Ironically, departments of Arabic language and translation are present in each one of the 22 Arabic speaking countries. Had they addressed transliteration issues and attempted unifying current transliteration practices, various research fields that rely on transliteration and seek consistency would have welcomed such systematicity. In other words, if attention had been given to transliteration, some genuine resolutions could have promoted standardization and unification of graphemes such as /p/, /g/, and /v/. If a genuine effort started a century ago to simplify and systematize the transcription of Arabic phonemes to English graphemes (P2G), why is it that the reverse is lagging? In other words, while the Arabic P2G has been addressed and simplified, the English P2G continues to lack uniformity and to display a great deal of variation.

In the face of all sorts of conservatism that bleeds any type of developments of any writing system (Borgwaldt and Joyce 2013), the academic community should take such tasks seriously, incorporate orthographic studies within their programs, and be at the forefront of recommending changes as per the required communicative contexts. Departments of Arabic and translation are unquestionably concerned with this field, since transliteration is one way of rendering foreign languages into native ears. Not having incorporated transliteration and the art of transliterating for so long doesn't mean they should be excluded. In our view, the curriculum of translation programs should address such graphological issues and be the first to promote some unifying and systematic system to make research easier and life of second language learners simpler.

From a pedagogical perspective, with these orthographic changes, Arab children get introduced to an accommodating writing system in their early years of elementary education. As such, they get exposed to foreign words transliterated with their corresponding graphemes. They also learn to appreciate the phoneme to grapheme systematicity and an Arabic writing system that accurately represents foreign sounds. It is high time the Arabic language overcame pertinent orthographic challenges, especially in an era where social media has turned national and international, cultural and intercultural, translation and transliteration communication and practices to constant, fast-paced changes. Academics, especially translators, throughout the Arabic-speaking countries are called more than ever to step in and initiate urgent orthographic reforms to put an end to current transliteration inconsistencies.

Notes

1. As per the Arab League, an official institution which represents Arabic speaking countries, also known as the 'Arab world' (العالم العربي), there are 22 such countries: Algeria, Bahrain, Comoros, Djibouti, Egypt, Iraq, Jordan, Kuwait, Lebanon, Libya, Mauritania, Morocco, Oman, Palestine, Qatar, Saudi Arabic, Somalia, Sudan, Syria, and Tunisia (see Appendix A for a relevant map and more details).
2. While the consonants may have general phonetic similarities (i.e. voiced/voiceless onset sounds, voiceless/voiced syllable codas, etc.) the vowel quality in each language differs a great deal; see Table 2.3.
3. Ex. is for 'Example', Gr. Is for 'Grapheme', and IPA is for 'International Phonetic Alphabet', a standard way of transcribing sounds of languages.
4. Since /ŋ/ may be argued to be an allophone of the voiced velar nasal phoneme /n/, we will limit the discussion to the sound /g/.
5. See Bahloul (2011), where a sociolinguistic analysis explores the consonant /q/ pronounced differently within the Arabic speaking countries, showing strong attitudes vis-à-vis its variants.
6. See Bassiouney (2009) for a detailed discussion and explanation of the current situation of Arabic across the Arabic speaking countries. See in particular Chapters 1 and 5 (9–27 and 198–272, respectively; this is also explained in Appendix B, where languages spoken in each Arabic speaking country are highlighted.
7. See the relevant Facebook page for more information (www.facebook.com/Darija EnglishQuotes/).
8. See the relevant Facebook page for more information (www.facebook.com/DarijaDialect/).
9. See more information relevant to Tunisian language (www.facebook.com/derja.association/).
10. This linguistic complexity would have been very similar to that of the state of Québec had Québec become a separate independent state, a desire they expressed and voted on a few times now without overwhelming success.
11. See Appendix B for the current mixture of languages within each Arab country, a mixture that has affected the transliteration norms and practice and contributed to the diversity of forms.
12. It is worth noting that other European languages such as Italian, Spanish, and German are generally made available to students as additional languages they may choose should they decide to do so.
13. For relevant readings, you may check Holes (2018), Albirini (2015), Suleiman (1999).
14. See Rüdiger (2013) for a thorough discussion of writing systems and the concept of transparency.

References

AbdulJaleel, Nasreen, and Leah Larkey. 2003. "Statistical Transliteration for English-Arabic Cross Language Information Retrieval". In *Proceedings of the Twelfth ACM*

International Conference on Information and Knowledge Management, New Orleans, LA, 3–8 November, 139–146. New York, ACM.

Ahmed, Akram Gaballah, Mohamed Farouk Abdel Hady, Emad Nabil, and Amr Badr. 2015. "A Language Modeling Approach for Acronym Expansion Disambiguation". In *CICLing 2015, Part I, LINCS 9041*, ed. by Alexander Gelbukh, 264–278. Switzerland: Springer. https://doi.org/10.1007/978-3-319-18111-0_21.

Albirini, Abdulkafi. 2015. *Modern Arabic Sociolinguistics: Diglossia, Variation, Codeswitching, attitudes and Identity*. London: Routledge, 438 pages.

Alginabi, Yasser, Abdullah M. Al-Binali, Mohammed Dekkak, and Abdulkarim Kushk. 2018. "A Computerized Reversible Arabic Transliteration System". *Arabian Journal for Science and Engineering* 43: 759–776.

Al-Agha, Basem Abbas. 2006. *The Translation of Fast-Food Advertising Texts from English to Arabic*. Unpublished M.A. Thesis. Pretoria: University of South Africa.

Al-Onaizan, Yaser, and Kevin Knight. 2001. "Machine Transliteration of Names in Arabic Texts". In *SEMITIC '02: Proceedings of the ACL-02 Workshop on Computational Approaches to Semitic Languages*, 1–13. https://doi.org/10.3115/1118637.1118642

Alsalman, Abdulmalik, Mansour Alghamdi, Khalid Alhuqayl, and S. Alsubai. 2007. "Romanization System for Arabic Names". In *Proceedings of The First International Symposium on Computer and Arabic Language (ISCAL – 07)*, 214–227. Riyadh, Kingdom of Saudi Arabia, King Abdulaziz City for Science and Technology (KACST).

Al-Saqqa, Samar. 2001. *English Loan Words in the Language of Arabic Advertising in Jordan 1998–2000*. Unpublished M.A. Thesis. Amman: University of Jordan.

Al-Shehari, Khaled. 2001. *The Semiotics and Translation of Advertising Text Conventions, Constraints and Translation Strategies with a Particular Reference to English and Arabic*. Unpublished Ph.D. Dissertation. Manchester: Manchester University.

Ammar, Waleed, Kareem Darwish, Ali El Kahki, and Khaled Hafez. 2011. "ICE-TEA: In-context Expansion and Translation of English Abbreviations". In *CICLing, Part II. LNCS, (6609)*, ed. by Alexander Gelbukh, 41–54. Heidelberg: Springer.

Arbabi, Mansur, Scott Fischthal, Vincent Cheng, and Elisabeth Bart. 1994. "Algorithms for Arabic Names Transliteration". *IBM Journal of Research and Development*, 38(2): 183–194.

Bahloul, Maher. 2007a. "Spelling Errors of Arab Learners: Evidence for Intergraphemic Mapping". In *Language Teacher Research in the Middle East*, ed. by Christine Coomb and Lisa Barlow, 41–51. Alexandria, VA, USA: TESOL. ISBN: 978-1-93118-541-7.

Bahloul, Maher. 2007b. "Linguistic Diversity: The Qaf Across Arabic Dialects". In *Current Issues in Linguistic Theory*, ed. by Elabbes Benmamoun, 247–256. Amsterdam: John Benjamin's Publishing Company. ISBN 978-9-02724-804-6.

Bahloul, Maher. 2011. "Variation and Attitudes: A Sociolinguistic Analysis of the Qaaf". In *Modern Trends in Arabic Dialectology*, ed. by Mohamed Embarki and Hamma Ennaji, 69–96. Trenton: The Red Sea Press. ISBN 978-1-56902-346-4.

Bassiouney, Reem. 2009. *Arabic Sociolinguistics*. Edinburgh: Edinburgh University Press, 336 pages.

Bies, Ann, Zhiya Song, Mohamed Maamouri, Stephen Grimes, Haejoong Lee, H. Jonathan Wright, Stephanie Strassel, Habash Nizar, Ramy Eskander, and Owen Rambow. 2014. "Transliteration of Arabizi into Arabic Orthography: Developing a Parallel Annotated Arabizi-Arabic Script SMS/Chat Corpus". In *Proceedings of the EMNLP 2014 Workshop on Arabic Natural Language Processing*, 93–103. Doha, Qatar: Association for Computational Linguistics. https://doi.org/10.3115/v1/W14–3612

Borgwaldt, Suzanne, and Terry Joyce (eds.). 2013. *Typology of Writing Systems*. Amsterdam: John Benjamins Publishing Company.

British Academy. 1917. *Transliteration of Arabic and Persian*. London: Oxford University Press. www.archive.org/details/br00itishacademytrbritrich (accessed February 10, 2020).

Dasigi, Pradeep, and Mona Diab. 2011. "Codact: Towards Identifying Orthographic Variants in Dialectal Arabic". In *Proceedings of the International Joint Conference on Natural Language Processing*. Chiang Mai, Thailand, Asian Federation of Natural Language Processing (AFNLP).

Fraiwan, R.A. 2007. *English-Arabic Translation of TV Advertisements Targeting Woman*. Unpublished M.A. Thesis. Irbid: Yarmouk University.

Gorgis, Dinha. 2010. "Transliterating Arabic: The Nuisances of Conversion between Romanization and Transcription Schemes". In *Romanization of Arabic Names*, ed. by Sattar Izwaini, 19–31. Abu Dhabi, United Arab Emirates, Ministry of Culture, Youth and Community Development.

Habash, Nizar, Mona Diab, and Owen Rambow. 2012. "Conventional Orthography for Dialectal Arabic". In *Proceedings of the Eight International Conference on Language Resources and Evaluations* (LREC), 711–718. Center for computational Learning Systems. New York: Columbia University.

Habash, Nizar, Abdelhadi Soudi, and Timothy Buckwalter. 2007. "On Arabic Transliteration". In *Arabic Computational Morphology: Knowledge-based and Empirical Methods*, ed. by Soudi Abdelhadi, Van den Bosch, and G. Neumann, 15–22. New York and Berlin: Springer.

Haj Mabrouk, Maaouia. Forthcoming. *The Effect of Arts-Integration on Tunisian EFL Learners' Oral Performance*. PhD Dissertation. Tunisia: University of Sfax.

Halimah, Ahmad. 2016. "Translating Arabic Proper Names: A Foreignizing Approach". *International Journal of English Language and Linguistics Research* 4(2): 1–16.

Holes, Clive. 2018. *Arabic Historical Dialectology: Linguistic and Sociolinguistic Approaches*. London: Oxford University Press, 448 pages.

Izwaini, Sattar. 2010. "Romanization of Arabic Names". In *Proceedings of the International Symposium on Arabic Transliteration Standard: Challenges and Solutions*. Abu Dhabi: United Arab Emirates. ISBN 978-9948-15-988-9.

Mahjoub, A. 2007. *At-ta3liim bil-lugha al-3arabiyya fi t-ta3liim al-jaami3ii* (The Use of Arabic in Tertiary Education). www.dahsha.com (accessed December 10, 2019).

Masmoudi, Abir, Fethi Bougares, Mariem Ellouze, Yannick Esteve, and Lamia Belghuith. 2018. "Automatic Speech Recognition System for Tunisian Dialect". *Lang Resources & Evaluation* 52: 249–267.

Masmoudi, Abir, Nizar Habash, Mariem Ellouze, Yannick Esteve, and Lamia Hadrich Belguith. 2015. "Arabic Transliteration of Romanized Tunisian Dialect Text: A Preliminary Investigation". In *CICLing 2015, Part I, LNCS 9041*, ed. by Alexander Gelbukh, 608–619. New York: Springer.

Obeidat, Eshraq. 2005. *Problems in Arabic–English Translation of Tourist Brochures in Jordan*. Unpublished M.A. Thesis. Jordan: Yarmouk University.

Palestine, Government. 1923. *System of Transliteration from Arabic into English*. Cambridge: University Press.

Rüdiger, Weingarten. 2013. "Comparative Graphematics". In *Typology of Writing Systems*, ed. by Suzanne R. Borgwaldt and Terry Joyce (Benjamins Current Topics 51), 13–40. Amsterdam: John Benjamins Publishing Company.

Saadane, Houda, Seffih Hosni, Fluhr Christian, Choukri Khaled, and Semmar Nasredine. 2018. "Automatic Identification of Maghreb Dialects Using a Dictionary-based Approach". In *Paper presented at the Eleventh International Conference on Language Resources and Evaluation (LREC)*, 3638–3644. Miyazaki, Japan.

Saadane, Houda, Alessandra Rossi, Christian Fluhr, and Mathieu Guidere. 2012. "Transcription of Arabic names into English". In *Sciences of Electronics, Technologies of Information and Telecommunications (SETIT), March 21–24, Sousse, Tunisia*. Institute of Electrical and Electronics Engineers (IEEE).

Saleh, Kefaya Adeeb Hafeth. 2011. *Translating restaurants' menus from English into Arabic: problems and strategies*. Unpublished M.A. Dissertation. Nablus, Palestine: Al-Najah National University.

Stalls, Bonnie, and Kevin Knight. 1998. "Translating Names and Technical Terms in Arabic Text". In *Proceedings of the COLING/ACL Workshop on Computational Approaches to Semitic Languages*, 34–41. Montreal, Quebec. Amsterdam: IOS Press.

Steven, Moran and Michael Cysouw. 2018. *The Unicode Cookbook for Linguists: Managing Writing Systems Using Orthography Profiles* (Translation and Multilingual Natural Language Processing 10). Berlin: Language Science Press.

Stevenson, Mark, Yikun Guo, Abdulaziz Amri, and Robert Gaizauskas. 2009. "Disambiguation of Biomedical Abbreviations". In *BioNLP Workshop, HLT*, 71–79. Boulder, Colorado: Association for Computational Linguistics.

Suleiman, Yasir. 1999. *Language and Society in the Middle East and North Africa*. London: RoutledgeCurzon, 304 pages.

Turki, Houcemeddine, Adel Emad, Tariq Daouda, and Nassim Regragui. 2016. *A Conventional Orthography for Maghrebi Arabic*. www.researchgate.net/profile/Houcemeddine_Turki/publication/311589181_A_Conventional_Orthography_for_Maghrebi_Arabic/links/584fd40608ae4bc8993b35ae.pdf (accessed February 22, 2020).

Websites www.translitteration.com/what-is-transliteration/en/.

Appendix A

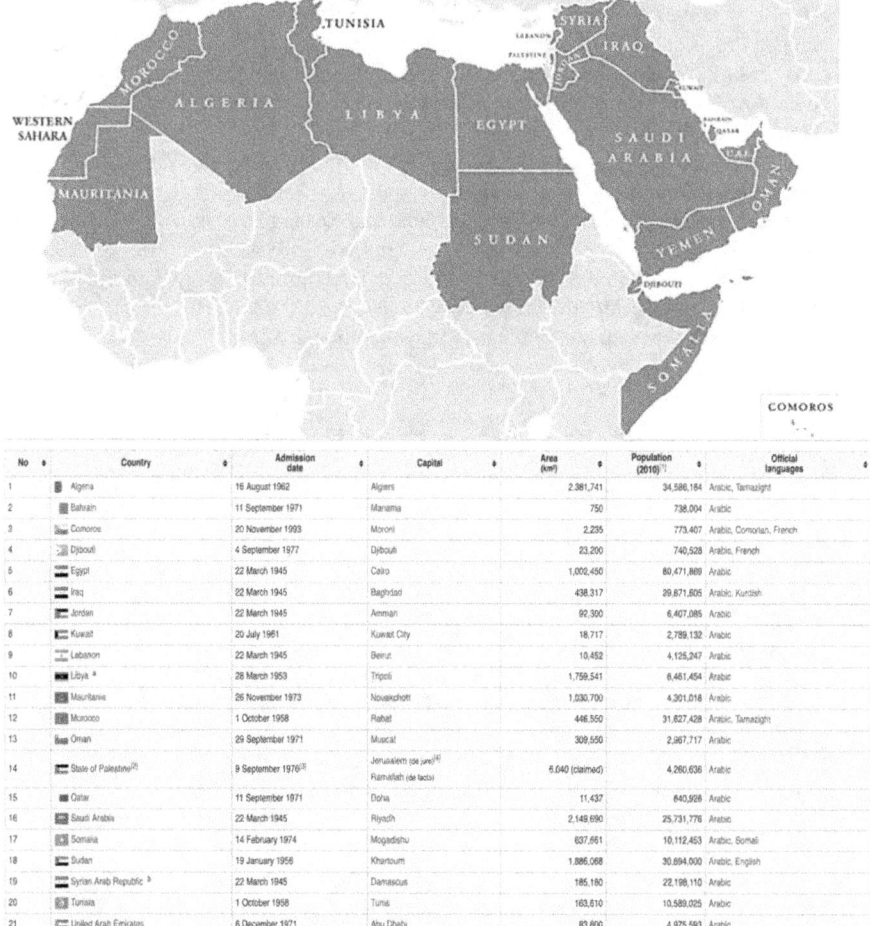

Figure 4.2 Map of the Arab-speaking countries
https://www.worldatlas.com/articles/arabic-speaking-countries.html

Appendix B

Country	Official language[a]	Languages used[b]
Algeria	Arabic	Arabic, Chaouia, French, Kabyle, Tachelhit, Tamazight, Taznatit
Bahrain	Arabic	Arabic, English, Farsi, Urdu
Chad[c]	French, Arabic	Arabic, Daza, French, Gulay, Kanuri, Maba, Sara, Zaghawa
Comoros	Shikomor, Arabic, French[d]	Arabic, French, Shikomor
Djibouti	Arabic, French	Afar, Arabic, French, Somali
Egypt	Arabic	Arabic, Armenian, Domari, Greek, Nubian
Iraq	Arabic	Arabic, Azeri, Farsi, Kurdish, Turkmen
Jordan	Arabic	Arabic, Armenian, Chechen, Circassian
Kuwait	Arabic	Arabic, English
Lebanon	Arabic	Arabic, Armenian, English, French, Kurdish
Libya	Arabic	Arabic, Nefusi, Tamashek, Zuara
Mauritania	Arabic	Arabic, Fulfulde, Soninke, Tamashek, Wolof
Morocco	Arabic	Arabic, Draa, French, Spanish, Tachelhit, Tamazight, Tarifit,
Oman	Arabic	Arabic, Baluchi, English, Farsi, Swahili
Palestinian Territories	Arabic	Arabic, Domari
Qatar	Arabic	Arabic, English, Farsi
Saudi Arabia	Arabic	Arabic, English
Somalia	Somali, Arabic	Arabic, Gabre, Jiddu, Maay, Mushungulu, Somali, Swahili,
Sudan	Arabic	Arabic, Bedawi, Beja, Dinka, English, Fur, Nuer
Syria	Arabic	Arabic, Armenian, Assyrian, Azeri, Kurdish
Tunisia	Arabic	Arabic, Berber languages/dialects, French
United Arab Emirates	Arabic	Arabic, Baluchi, English, Farsi, Pashto, Somali
Yemen	Arabic	Arabic, Mehri, Somali

Notes:
(a) UNESCO, (unless otherwise indicated), http://portal.unesco.org/education/en/ev.php-URL_ID=20183&URL_DO_TOPIC&URL_SECTION=201.html; last accessed 18 April 2009.
(b) UNESCO (ibid; Versteegh et al. (2006–70); Moseley and Asher (1994). This list should be treated as a rough guide.
(c) Chad, although not a member of the Arab League, is a partly Arabic-speaking country.
(d) Source: Constitution of the Comoros Islands: http://www.beit-salam.km/article.php3?id_article=34; last accessed 20 October 2008.

Figure 4.3 Arabic languages and their linguistic environment

Appendix C

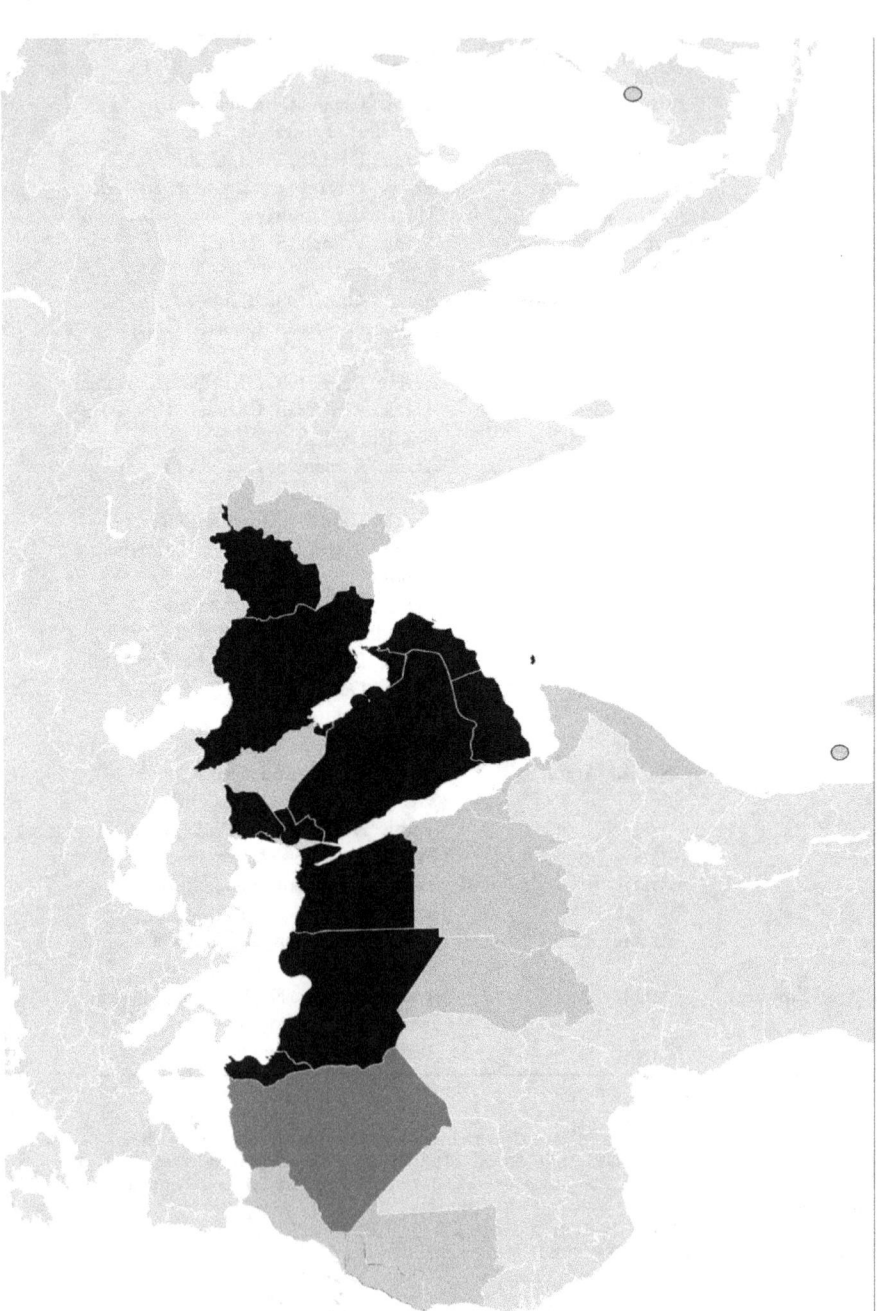

Figure 4.4 Worldwide use of the Arabic script

Note: The darkest shading in this table represents most frequent use of Arabic script and the lightest shading for where the use of Arabic script is less common.

Source: https://upload.wikimedia.org/wikipedia/commons/e/e8/Arabic_alphabet_world_distribution_-_four_shades.png

5 Analytical translation quality assessment

Insights for translators' training

Heidi Verplaetse and An Lambrechts

5.1 Introduction

Adequacy and acceptability are well-known notions in translation quality definition as well as in translation quality assessment. In translation quality assessment, adequacy (also known as accuracy) refers to the relationship between the source text and the target text. Acceptability (also labelled fluency) refers to the quality of the target text only (Daems et al. 2013, 2014). Translation quality can be assessed by humans or with automatic means. For human translation quality assessment, the following methods can be distinguished: holistic, analytical and calibration methods. The current chapter focuses on analytical translation quality assessment methods. These translation assessment methods offer the popular advantage of a systematic analysis based on concrete parameters, so translation quality is often quantified on that basis in academic contexts (cf. Conde 2012: 67). However, in translation training contexts a potentially negative pedagogical implication may result from a one-sided focus on error assessment. But the same parameters may equally form the basis to annotate and reward particularly good translation decisions. Analytical translation quality assessment includes error typologies which are often based on the notions of adequacy and acceptability. Six error typologies, viz. the Canadian Language Quality Measurement System (Sical), the SAE J 2450 quality metric, MeLLANGE, the Multidimensional Quality Metrics (MQM) framework, the Smart Computer-Aided Translation Environment (SCATE) error taxonomy and the ATA Framework for Standardized Error Marking, are discussed briefly.

Error analyses executed with error taxonomies may apply in different ways depending on the aids used in translation, viz. no aids (human translation), machine translation (MT) and translation memories (TMs). Five different studies involving error typology-based comparisons of human translation, (post-edited) MT and TM-based translation are described (Guerberof 2009; Daems et al. 2013, 2014; Costa et al. 2015; Tezcan et al. 2018). A sample of frequently occurring errors per translation aid drawn from these studies shows that language errors in the target text are frequently included in all studies regardless of the translation aid used. This attests that (academic) translation education literature devotes considerable attention not only to transfer from the source text and language into the target text and language but also to (independent) target text and target language quality.

When we consider the various error types in the different error typologies discussed here, we see that the MQM framework and the SCATE taxonomy provide the most complete typologies (cf. section 5.3.2). Both these typologies are suitable for any text type (Lommel et al. 2014: 456; Daems et al. 2013: 63). Apart from target text language (acceptability), other common categories in all error typologies discussed here are the adequacy-related categories of terminology and omission.[1] Thus we may derive that these categories also deserve particular attention in translation teaching and training.

Before embarking on the discussion of different translation error typologies as a basis to assess translation product quality, we should ask ourselves what constitutes translation quality; we will begin our chapter with a definition of this concept in section 5.2. In sections 5.3 and 5.4 we will proceed with a description of human translation quality and automatic translation quality assessment methods. The question is which error typology we should use. This depends on various aspects, including text type or register and whether the typology needs to be language dependent or language independent. Other aspects which lie at the basis of this decision include the context and main aim of the error analyses. Are these mainly didactic, or rather geared towards (professional) certification purposes and recruitment? Another question concerns how discriminating power can be calculated or achieved. If discriminating power is a relevant criterion for your purposes, how does it relate to the questions of translation difficulty and, if needed, ranking of candidate translators? Or perhaps specific concrete didactic or professional translation quality criteria and translator profiles need to be achieved, rather than norm-referenced ranking of candidates. Which models offer methods to achieve these specific test aspects? With the comparative descriptions of the translation quality assessment methods presented in this chapter, we hope to offer a gateway to the decisions you need to make for your assessment purposes. A major criterion in this respect is the impact of different translation methods and aids on translation quality; these are discussed in section 5.5.

In addition to the question which translation quality assessment model fits your professional or didactic purposes, one other problem remains for researchers and readers of (academic) translation quality studies in various contexts: how can results from different studies based on different assessment methods be compared and interpreted with relation to one another, so as to accommodate further research purposes? Section 5.6 presents an overview of common error categories in the different models described in the chapter in order to contribute to a solution to that problem. The main culminating aim of the chapter is to provide a starting point for a benchmarking of different error typologies so as to allow clearer

5.2 What is translation quality?

Defining translation quality is not an easy feat. Considering translation quality from a broad perspective, Koby et al. (2014) define a quality translation as follows:

> A quality translation demonstrates accuracy and fluency required for the audience and purpose and complies with all other specifications negotiated between the requester and provider, taking into account end-user needs.
>
> (Koby et al. 2014: 416)

With regard to translation quality, requesters (clients) focus on the "acceptability and suitability to their needs" (Nerudová 2012: 59), whereas translation service providers (e.g. translation agencies) perceive translation quality as the "linguistic and situational correctness of the text" (Nerudová 2012: 58–59). For translators a quality translation should contain no linguistic mistakes, the instructions of the translation service provider must be followed and the deadline needs to be respected (Nerudová 2012: 59). This implies that, depending on the role in the translation process (requester, provider, translator), the notion of translation quality may differ.

Taking into account the end-user needs, a translation may have information quality, viz. when the translation will be read by a small number of people for information purposes only and the translation will be discarded afterwards. At the other end of the spectrum is publication quality, where the translation is read by many external readers over a longer period of time (Mossop 2001: 22). Therefore, publication-quality translations achieve higher quality standards than information-quality translations. In a narrow definition of translation quality by Koby et al. (2014), a high-quality translation is defined as follows:

> A high-quality translation is one in which the message embodied in the source text is transferred completely into the target text, including denotation, connotation, nuance, and style, and the target text is written in the target language using correct grammar and word order, to produce a culturally appropriate text that, in most cases, reads as if originally written by a native speaker of the target language for readers in the target culture.
>
> (Koby et al. 2014: 416–417)[2]

We may add other aspects of target text quality, such as register-specific terminology, idiomatic grammatical language use and word choice. The definition also implies that the naturalness of a translation contributes to translation quality; in other words, the ideal target text seems to be written originally by a native speaker of the target language.³

5.3 Human translation quality assessment

Translation quality assessment mostly focuses on the translation product (target text), particularly on translation errors, but may also take the translation process from source to target text into account (cf. Thelen 2018: 9). Translation quality can be assessed by human evaluators through holistic or analytical assessment methods (Waddington 2001). Other human translation quality assessment methods are the so-called calibration translation quality assessment methods. The latter will be discussed only briefly, as we focus on analytical translation quality assessment methods for the current chapter.

5.3.1 Holistic translation quality assessment

In the holistic translation quality assessment method, the translation product is considered as a whole (Thelen 2018: 9; van Egdom et al. 2018: 54). Evaluators base their value judgments on an overall impression and ratings. No detailed analysis of the translation is carried out (Moreno and Valero-Garcés 2017: 13). Holistic translation quality assessment methods have been described as subjective and derive from the evaluator's intuition (Akbari and Segers, 2017a: 15, 2017b: 412). A well-known example of holistic quality assessment is Skopos theory. The starting point in Skopos theory is a text in source language A which needs to be translated into target language B. The target text is intended to fulfill a particular function, and this function determines the skopos (or purpose) of the translation (Nord 2005: 27). The definition of translation skopos may differ per translation and determines whether a particular expression or utterance is considered an error or not. For example, if the translation skopos requires that the whole text content is reproduced, the smallest omission is considered an error. However, if only a rough summary of the information in the text is needed, this particular omission is not seen as an error (Nord 2005: 186–187).

5.3.2 Analytical translation quality assessment methods

Analytical translation assessment methods mostly use linguistic criteria (Thelen 2018: 9). They identify specific errors in translation and quantify them (Lommel et al. 2014: 460; Akbari and Segers 2017a: 16; Akbari and Segers 2017b: 414), for instance through error taxonomies. Error taxonomies often distinguish acceptability and adequacy errors (Daems et al. 2013, 2014). An acceptability-oriented translation adheres "to norms which originate and act in the target culture itself" (Toury 2012: 79). Thus, acceptability errors relate to the target text only (Daems et al. 2014: 62). If a translation leans heavily on the original, it is an adequacy-oriented translation (Toury 2012: 79). Similarly, for the identification of adequacy errors both the source text and its translation are considered. Adequacy errors are true translation errors, as they relate to the relationship between source and target texts (Hansen 2010: 386), whereas acceptability errors are independent of the source text. Examples of error taxonomies include the Canadian Language Quality Measurement System (Sical), the SAE J 2450 quality metric, the MeLLANGE error typology, the Multidimensional Quality Metrics (MQM) framework and the Smart Computer-Aided Translation Environment (SCATE) error taxonomy. These taxonomies are discussed in the following sections.

5.3.2.1 Canadian Language Quality Measurement System (Sical)

Sical was developed by the Canadian government's translation agency. It focuses on the number and the type of errors (Lavault-Olléon and Allignol 2014: 9), for example, transfer versus language errors, as well as on error severity (minor versus major errors) (Secară 2005: 39). It distinguishes errors in the translation process, composition errors and criteria affecting both the source language text and the target language text (Campbell 2014: 170). One disadvantage of the Sical system is its limitation to errors at the syntactic and semantic levels without taking sentence relations into account. In addition, the system is hard to use because of its high number of error types (Secară 2005: 40). The system thus indicates the need for a quality measurement system with a more limited set of well-defined error types, while still allowing a fine-grained analysis.

5.3.2.2 SAE J 2450 quality metric

SAE (Society of Automotive Engineers) International developed the SAE J 2450 quality metric for the translation of service manuals in the automotive industry (Lommel et al. 2014: 457). It can be used for translation from any source language into any target language and regardless of the translation method used, viz. human or MT (Vandepitte 2017: 24). Currently, the last revised edition of the SAE J 2450 quality metric dates from August 2016 and provides the stabilized version.[4] It contains the following seven error categories: *Wrong Term, Syntactic Error, Omission, Word Structure and Agreement Error, Misspelling, Punctuation Error, Miscellaneous Error* (Secară 2005: 40). In this quality metric, style is disregarded (Secară 2005; Vandepitte 2017). This is also one of the points of criticism related to this evaluation method: it is criticized for focusing too much on terminological evaluation, allocating the highest error weight to the category Wrong Term (Secară 2005: 40). Terminology will be assigned a higher error weight depending on text type, for example, in technical texts (Daems et al. 2014: 62), but some sectors may be equally interested in other aspects such as grammar, spelling and style (Secară 2005: 40). If needed, this should lead to an adjustment of the error weights. The advantages of the SAE J 2450 quality metric are its user-friendliness and, similarly to the Sical system described earlier, it can be applied for any source or target language (Secară 2005: 40).

5.3.2.3 MeLLANGE error typology

The MeLLANGE error typology was designed as part of the MeLLANGE project, which collected student and professional translations. These translations were annotated on the basis of this typology. However, quality judgment is not its primary purpose: it focuses "on describing and studying specific translation phenomena rather than giving any quality judgment" (Castagnoli et al. 2011: 5). The initial MeLLANGE error typology contains more than 30 types of issues, distinguishing *Transfer* and *Language* issues (cf. adequacy versus acceptability errors), with further subdivisions, such as *source language intrusion* and *target language intrusion* in *Content Transfer*, *Inflection and Agreement*, *Terminology and Lexis* in *Language*, *Hygiene*, *Register and Style* (Kübler et al. 2016: 734).

5.3.2.4 Multidimensional Quality Metrics (MQM) framework

The Multidimensional Quality Metrics (MQM) framework can be applied to both human and machine translated texts, regardless of text type (Lommel et al. 2014: 456) or language pair (Lommel et al. 2014: 459). Within the current MQM framework (version 1.0), error categories are presented at a hierarchical level, with *Accuracy* (Adequacy), *Design*, *Fluency* (Acceptability), *Internationalization*, *Locale convention*, *Style*, *Terminology*, *Verity* and *Other* as the major dimensions.[5] Verity focuses "on the suitability of the text for a given audience and context" (Lommel et al. 2014: 459), for example, the translation of an employment contract from US English into Spanish for an audience in Spain (a civil-law jurisdiction) versus the translation of the same contract for a Spanish audience in the US, with the latter having a common-law jurisdiction (Lommel et al. 2014: 459). Some of the major dimensions are divided into sub-dimensions, for example, the dimension *Accuracy*, which is subdivided into, among other things, *Addition*, *Mistranslation*, *Omission* and *Untranslated*. For every major dimension as well as its sub-dimensions a definition is provided. These definitions can help to determine which error category applies, as the MQM framework contains quite an extensive set of categories and subcategories. The MQM framework, a text type-independent error typology, contains more categories and subcategories than a text type-dependent error typology such as the SAE J 2450 quality metric, described earlier.

5.3.2.5 Smart Computer-Aided Translation Environment (SCATE) error taxonomy

The SCATE MT error taxonomy is a "hierarchical error taxonomy with error categories based on linguistic notions" (Tezcan et al. 2018: 224). Within the SCATE project, which aimed at an improved translation environment, the error taxonomy was applied to build an annotated corpus of MT errors. The taxonomy is accompanied by detailed annotation guidelines (cf. also Daems and Macken 2013; Tezcan et al. 2015), which are needed to achieve a quality annotation task (Tezcan et al. 2018: 221). By allowing users to define their own error categories and by applying error weights, the SCATE error taxonomy increases the objectivity of value judgments (Daems et al. 2013: 65–66). The error taxonomy can be applied to different translation methods and not only to MT. It is also text type independent (Daems et al. 2013: 63).

5.3.2.6 ATA Framework for Standardized Error Marking

The Framework for Standardized Error Marking of the American Translators Association (ATA) is an analytical error annotation framework which was originally designed for professional certification purposes. The framework contains three main error categories and a set of subcategories (ATA 2017). Apart from a category which focuses on the form of the test, the two other categories are those of (i) "Meaning transfer or strategic errors" which entail a "Negative impact on clarity or usefulness of target text" and (ii) "Mechanical errors" which have a "Negative impact on overall quality of target text". Category (i) contains the following subcategories: *Addition, Ambiguity, Cohesion, Faithfulness, Faux ami, Literalness, Misinterpretation of source text, Omission, Terminology and word choice, Text type* (incl. register and style), *Verb tense*, and *Other*. Category (ii) contains separate subcategories for *Grammar, Syntax, Word form/part of speech, Punctuation, Spelling, Character, Diacritical marks/Accents, Capitalization, Usage*, and *Other*.

A flowchart for error grading systematizes the framework (ATA 2009). The flowchart functions as a guideline on error severity for evaluators. "Overall questions to guide decisions" are "Can target text be used for intended purpose? Is it intelligible to the intended target reader? Does it transfer the meaning of the source text?" (ATA 2009). But the flowchart contains many more detailed questions to guide the evaluator, such as "Is disruption limited in scope?" Each of the questions entails a specific number of points to be added to the score. Adding all points for error weights as well as subtracting points for exceptionally good translation solutions yields a score which enables a decision to certify translators (or not) for numerous language combinations with English. Although this method was designed for professional certification purposes, it can also be used to assess the frequency of the errors students make for several target languages (cf. Doyle 2003: 25) and has been adapted to some extent for translation training purposes (cf. Doyle 2003; Koby and Baer 2005).

5.3.3 Calibration translation quality assessment methods

In calibration translation quality assessment methods, "the accuracy of the measuring instrument is checked and adjusted". Furthermore, these methods distinguish correct and wrong translations without taking error severity into account (Kockaert and Segers 2017: 150–151). Examples of calibration translation quality assessment methods include the Calibration of Dichotomous Items (CDI) method and the Preselected Items Evaluation (PIE) method.

5.3.3.1 Calibration of Dichotomous Items (CDI)

The Calibration of Dichotomous Items (CDI) method (Eyckmans, Anckaert and Segers 2009) is norm-referenced. In norm-referenced translation assessment the results of the entire tested population set the norm. An individual's translation score will then depend on the norm set by the tested group. Thus, a weak translation will receive a higher score in a weak group than the same translation if it is assessed as part of a strong group (Segers and van Egdom 2018: 72). Norm-referenced methods produce rankings and are commonly used for entrance exams in schools where there is a limit to the number of accepted students or in translation testing environments (Mariana et al. 2015: 156–157), for instance to recruit language professionals. The CDI method involves a pretest procedure in which an entire source text is translated by all members of the tested group. Next, the evaluators analyze all translated target text items of all source text items. The evaluators decide which target text solutions are correct and which are incorrect. They then determine the difficulty of the items; this is the p-value. The evaluators also determine the discriminatory power of the items; this is the d-index (Segers and van Egdom 2018: 21). Discriminating power is defined as "text segments [which] are translated correctly by test-takers who demonstrate good translation competence and incorrectly by test-takers who are not competent translators" (Eyckmans and Anckaert 2017: 43). These text segments are called 'calibrated items' or 'items'. The sample of participants in the pretest procedure has to represent the population of the participants in the actual test which is performed after the pretest (Eyckmans and Anckaert 2017: 43–44). To calculate the scores, only items with good p-values and d-indices will be used. Scoring is dichotomous, viz. a target text solution is considered as either correct or incorrect and error severity is not weighted. The score is calculated in function of the number of items with good p-values and d-indices related to the number of incorrect solutions for the items with good p-values and d-indices (adapted from Segers and van Egdom 2018: 30). This is a very labour-intensive assessment method. In order to alleviate the labour-intensive character, the PIE method was developed by Kockaert and Segers (2014).

5.3.3.2 Preselected Items Evaluation (PIE)

Like CDI, the PIE method is a norm-referenced method. But it is also a criterion-based assessment method. The latter implies that specific criteria are established prior to analysis (Segers and van Egdom 2018: 72, 29). Thus, this method also relates to analytical translation assessment methods, but it is used for the evaluation of translation products based on *specific* items in the source text. The selection of these items is based on the expertise of the evaluator, the translation brief, and the test requirements (Van Egdom et al. 2018: 54). Unlike the CDI method, the PIE method does not involve a full text translation pretest phase. The evaluator(s) decide prior to the translation test which source text items will be tested. Obviously, item selection is of great importance and can be established in function of learning targets and/or course contents in a didactic context. In a professional context, *Preselected items* may be decided as a function of the candidate's targeted profile (Segers and van Egdom 2018: 79–80). In this manner it may be established "whether or not [a translator] can perform at a certain level or has passed a certain threshold of competency" (Mariana et al. 2015: 157).

As with CDI, scoring is dichotomous; the evaluator decides which target text solutions are correct and which are incorrect. She or he then calculates p-values and d-indices of the target text solutions respectively for level of difficulty and discriminatory power. Only items with good p-values and d-indices between specific threshold values are used to calculate the scores (cf. Eyckmans and Anckaert 2017: 44). Those items represent the *Selected items*. The scores are calculated as the number of incorrect solutions for the Selected items in function of the number of Selected items. (Segers and van Egdom 2018: 79).

Like analytical quality assessment methods, the Preselected Items Evaluation (PIE) is a criterion-referenced translation quality evaluation method which measures "how well each individual meets set reference standards" (Koby and Lacruz 2017: 6).

5.4 Automatic translation quality assessment

Next to human translation quality assessment, translation quality can also be assessed automatically, for instance through automatic metrics, such as BLEU and METEOR, which are common instruments in assessing MT quality (cf. Costa et al. 2015). When calculating BLEU scores, translated segments are compared with reference translations (cf. also reference translations for preselected items in the PIE method). In order to estimate the overall translation quality, the average of those scores over the whole corpus is taken. The METEOR metric also compares between MT translations and human reference translations, but in addition it takes linguistic resources such as paraphrases into account (Costa et al. 2015: 131). Popović and Burchardt (2011) proposed a method for automatic error classification, concluding that the results of the automatic evaluation method correlated well with the human evaluation results; the errors detected by human evaluators were also found by the automatic method.

5.5 The impact of translation method on translation quality

Analytical translation quality assessment methods based on error typologies are popular in translation evaluation (Conde 2012: 67) and are also frequently used in studies examining the impact of different translation methods on translation quality (e.g., Guerberof 2009; Daems et al. 2013, 2014; O'Curran 2014). The errors made by humans are not necessarily the same as those made by MT systems and vice versa (Costa et al. 2015; Tezcan et al. 2018). The use of TM matches (Guerberof 2009) as well as post-editing (PE) and text type also have an influence on the type of errors (Daems et al. 2013, 2014).

5.5.1 Error analysis in human translation, machine translation and post-editing

Fine-grained categorizations in the form of annotation guidelines are needed to execute thorough comparisons between translation methods (Daems et al. 2013: 64). Such guidelines also help to reach increased inter-annotator agreement if several annotators (error-)annotate a translation, so that this will lead to an improved error analysis (Stymne and Ahrenberg 2012: 1789).

Daems et al. (2013) state that because of "the well-known distinction between adequacy and acceptability and universal concepts such as 'grammar' and 'lexicon'" in their annotation guidelines for the English–Dutch language pair, this "categorization can easily be tailored to suit language-specific problems" (Daems et al. 2013: 65), making it fit for different languages as well.

In addition, both the translation situation and the context should be taken into account when assessing translation quality, and value judgment needs to be more objective, which is achieved by allowing for user-defined categories and error weights (Daems et al. 2013: 65–66). In order to check whether these annotation guidelines, which later accompanied the SCATE error typology (cf. section 5.3.2.5), were detailed enough and whether they were suitable "for a comparative analysis of translation problems for different methods of translation" (Daems et al. 2013: 66), 16 master students taking a general translation course were given a translation and a PE task of an MT originating from Google Translate, at the time a statistical machine translation (SMT) engine (Daems et al. 2013: 66). The aim was to make comparisons between human translation (HT) and post-edited MT (MT+PE). The corpus consisted of four newspaper articles.

In a later pilot study Daems et al. (2014) used the same corpus to compare the PE output from the translation students with MT originating from Google Translate. Two annotators were responsible for the error annotation. Table 5.1 provides an overview of the most common error types in general from the first pilot study (Daems et al. 2013) and specific acceptability- versus adequacy-related errors.

Meaning shifts (deletion and other) commonly occur in HT as opposed to MT+PE. In MT+PE, *wrong collocation* and *word sense disambiguation* are common error types (Daems et al. 2013: 69). Taking into account the distinction between acceptability versus adequacy errors, the majority of errors in both HT and MT+PE are acceptability errors: in comparison to HT, mostly *grammar, syntax*

Table 5.1 Error analysis HT versus MT+PE (based on Daems et al. 2013)

	HT	MT+PE
most common error types	meaning shifts (deletion / other)	– wrong collocation – word sense disambiguation*
acceptability versus adequacy	mostly acceptability errors (style and register)	mostly acceptability errors (grammar, syntax, lexical problems)
	more adequacy errors than in MT+PE (addition, deletion, meaning shifts - other)	fewer adequacy errors than in HT (word sense disambiguation, misplaced word)

* Word sense disambiguation: "the Dutch word is a possible translation of the word in the ST [source text] but not of the meaning the word has in this context" (Daems & Macken 2013:26)

and lexical problems occur in MT+PE as opposed to *style and register problems* in HT. Adequacy-related errors occur more in HT, where *additions, deletions* and *other meaning shifts* are more common. MT+PE adequacy-related errors include *word sense disambiguation* and *misplaced word* (Daems et al. 2013: 70). Concluding with regard to translation quality, Daems et al.'s (2013) study shows that the average of the total error scores was lower in MT+PE. This means that MT+PE yielded higher quality translation than HT without any translation aids (Daems et al. 2013: 69), a finding which is also confirmed by O'Curran (2014).

Table 5.2 presents an overview of the most common error types from the second pilot study by Daems et al. (2014), comparing MT and MT+PE. *Grammatical errors* seem to be most common in MT, compared to MT+PE (Daems et al. 2014: 64). Problematic cases in MT+PE include *wrong collocation* and *word sense disambiguation* (Daems et al. 2013, 2014) along with *spelling errors* in MT+PE compared to MT (Daems et al. 2014: 64). As *wrong collocation* and *word sense disambiguation* are two of the error types which mostly seem to be caused by MT errors, special attention should be paid to recognizing such errors in student post-editor training (Daems et al. 2014: 65). Similar to the previous pilot study using the same corpus (Daems et al. 2013) in which MT+PE achieved higher-quality translations than HT, this pilot study also shows that MT+PE

Table 5.2 Error analysis MT versus MT+PE (based on Daems et al. 2014)

	MT	MT+PE
most common error types	−grammar −wrong collocation −word sense disambiguation	−wrong collocation −word sense disambiguation −spelling
acceptability versus adequacy	more acceptability and adequacy errors than in MT+PE	

achieves an increased translation quality in comparison to MT (Daems et al. 2014), as may be expected. This demonstrates the importance of a proper post-editing procedure when applying MT. More importantly, under all circumstances, PE is faster than HT (cf. the notion of PE effort), but a productivity increase is only positive if higher speed does not negatively influence translation quality (Daems et al. 2013: 68). We should also remember that in professional translation environments, different types of quality may be required, viz. information quality versus publication quality (Mossop 2001: 22, cf. section 5.2, this volume: What is translation quality?)

5.5.2 Error analysis in statistical and rule-based machine translation

Costa et al. (2015) performed a detailed linguistic error analysis involving the language pair English–European Portuguese (EP) with texts translated by Google Translate (SMT), with Systran, a rule-based machine translation (RBMT) system, and by two MT systems based on Moses technology (SMT), viz. the phrase-based and the hierarchical phrase-based models. The MT systems were trained using corpora containing speech transcriptions of technology entertainment design (TED) Talks (including translations in EP of the subtitles), touristic magazine texts and evaluation questions translated into EP (Costa et al. 2015: 129). The Moses-based MT systems were also trained, using data from Europarl (Costa et al. 2015: 144). Seven hundred and fifty sentences taken from the TED Talk corpus, the touristic magazine corpus and the evaluation question corpus were translated by the four MT engines and then error-analyzed (Costa et al. 2015: 142).

For this study, both a human analysis and an automatic error analysis were carried out. Human error analysis was undertaken by two annotators (Costa et al. 2015: 145). They used an error typology distinguishing language-dependent errors and language-independent errors (Costa et al. 2015: 140–141). A distinction was made between *orthographic* (punctuation, capitalization and spelling), *lexical* (omission, addition, untranslated), *grammatical* (misselection, misordering), *semantic* (confusion of senses, wrong choice, collocational error, idioms) and *discourse* (style, variety, should not be translated) *errors* (Costa et al. 2015: 139). The automatic error analysis was performed using the BLEU and METEOR metrics (Costa et al. 2015: 152). Table 5.3 provides a brief overview of the most common error types.

At the lexical level, the two Moses-based systems performed considerably worse with regard to *untranslated words*, viz. words they were not trained for (Costa et al. 2015: 147). This shows that the amount of training data in traditional MT plays an important role in limiting errors. Regarding grammatical errors, *misordering errors* (word order) occur rather seldom, as English and EP often share the same subject-verb-object structure (Costa et al. 2015: 148). This implies that in traditional MT engines such interlingual similarities were useful in order to limit certain errors. However, interlingual differences may at the same time increase the occurrence of other error types, such as *misselection errors*. These can be further subdivided into *errors affecting verbs*, *agreements* and *contractions* (Costa et al. 2015: 148). *Agreement errors* rank first for all traditional MT engines due to structural interlingual differences, for example, number and gender agreement in EP in contrast to English (Costa et al. 2015: 150). At the semantic level, the most frequent error type for all MT engines was *confusion of senses* (Costa et al. 2015: 151), viz. the given translation represents one of the meanings of the word or phrase but does not fit the context (Costa et al. 2015: 137; cp. *word sense disambiguation* in Daems et al. 2013).

Concerning error gravity, in this study mostly errors with regard to *confusion of senses*, *wrong choice* (viz. when a wrong word, lacking an apparent relation, is used as the translation of another word) (Costa et al. 2015: 137), and *misordering*

Table 5.3 Error analysis in SMT and RBMT (based on Costa et al. 2015)

	Google (SMT)	Systran (RBMT)	Moses (SMT)
most common error types			untranslated words/expressions
	agreement errors	agreement errors	agreement errors
	confusion of senses	confusion of senses	confusion of senses

have a major impact on translation quality. It must be noted, however, that this conclusion was drawn by means of a subjective translation ranking (Costa et al. 2015: 158–159). *Confusion of senses* is a context-related problem. The frequent occurrence of this error type may indicate that traditional MT engines had difficulties coping with contexts, a problem which can also be related to the *wrong choice* error type: as the word chosen lacks a relation at text level, it can be assumed that the context is not understood.

In this study, *misordering errors* were fairly limited due to similar structures of the languages in question (English versus EP) (Costa et al. 2015: 148), but when interlingual differences occur, word order may pose a challenge. This implies that traditional MT translation quality was language dependent, that is, translation pairs with more structural interlingual differences might be expected to yield worse syntactic results, unless the MT systems were trained for such systemic structural differences.

Tezcan et al. (2018) compared the Dutch output of Google Translate (SMT) with the output of Systran (RBMT). The source sentences in the SMT error corpus originated from the Dutch Parallel Corpus (text types: external communication, non-fiction literature and journalistic texts). For the Systran error corpus, a subset of the data from the SMT corpus (Dutch Parallel Corpus) was used. The output was annotated by two pairs of annotators (Tezcan et al. 2018: 229–230) with the SCATE error taxonomy (cf. section 5.3.2.5). Table 5.4 is a brief overview of the most common error types and acceptability-versus adequacy-related errors.

Table 5.4 Error analysis in SMT and RBMT (based on Tezcan et al. 2018)

	Google (SMT)	Systran (RBMT)
most common error types	–grammar –omission –untranslated	–grammar –do not translate
adequacy versus acceptability	adequacy: mistranslation, viz. word sense disambiguation	adequacy: mistranslation, viz. word sense disambiguation more acceptability errors than SMT: lexical choice

Most errors were found in the RBMT corpus, with an increased number of errors in the category *Do not translate* (in other studies also referred to as the category *should not be translated*). As for adequacy errors, mostly *mistranslation* errors were made in both the RBMT corpus and the SMT corpus (Tezcan et al. 2018: 237), with *word sense disambiguation* as the largest category of mistranslation errors (Tezcan et al. 2018: 239). In the SMT corpus, more *omission* and *untranslated* errors occurred (Tezcan et al. 2018: 237). In the study by Costa et al. (2015), the Moses-based (SMT) systems also performed considerably worse with regard to untranslated words, which could be due to the amount of data the corpus was trained with. The RBMT corpus contained more acceptability errors than the SMT corpus, viz. *lexical choice errors*. Lexical choice errors occur when a word is used that belongs to the (target language) Dutch lexicon but other words are needed to produce a correct sentence (Tezcan et al. 2018: 247). This could be due to the RBMT system heavily relying on bilingual dictionaries without taking the context into account (Tezcan et al. 2018: 240–241). The majority of errors in both the RBMT and the SMT were *grammatical errors*, but the number of grammatical errors was lower in RBMT. However, proportionally fewer *word order errors* (a subcategory of *grammar errors*) were made in the word order category in SMT (Tezcan et al. 2018: 241). This is in line with the findings from Costa et al. (2015), where the lowest number of *misordering errors* could also be found in SMT (Google Translate). Just like EP and English, Dutch and English (the languages of the corpus under examination) also often share the same subject-verb-object structure. This could explain the low number of *misordering errors* in SMT in these cases.

Also, the more recent development of MT as neural MT (NMT) has been studied very recently in terms of its effect on translation quality. We refer to Wu et al. (2016) and Shterionov et al. (2018), for instance, who have studied the effect of early NMT on translation quality. The correspondence of NMT translation products with reference translations is applied to measure NMT translation quality (Thelen 2018: 7).

5.5.3 Error analysis in TM-based translation

Guerberof (2009: 2) examined whether there is a difference in final quality between target segments translated with MT and 'new' or TM segments. Eight professional translators carried out a pilot study in which they translated/post-edited text content originating from a help system from English into Spanish. The translators were offered three types of segments which they needed to translate/post-edit: MT-based, TM-based (80–90% fuzzy matches) and new segments. For the new segments, no translation was provided. In order to avoid bias, the translators also did not know the origin (MT/TM) of the segments (Guerberof 2009: 2). The translations were error-annotated using the standards developed by the Localization Industry Standards Association, or LISA standards, distinguishing the

Table 5.5 Most common error categories in TM-based, MT-based, and new translation segments (based on Guerberof 2009)

	TM	MT	New
most common error types	1. *accuracy* 2. *language* 3. *terminology*	1. *accuracy* 2. *terminology* 3. *language*	1. *mistranslation* 2. *accuracy* 3. *language*

following categories: *Mistranslation, Accuracy, Terminology, Language, Style, Country, Consistency* and *Format* (Guerberof 2009: 4). Table 5.5 contains the top three most frequent errors per category (TM, MT, New).

The majority of the errors (44%) were accuracy-related (Guerberof 2009: 7), with accuracy referring to "omissions, additions, cross-references, headers and footers and not reflecting the source text properly" (Guerberof 2009: 4) (cp. adequacy). The TM category showed consistently higher error rates for all eight test subjects (65 errors in total), followed by MT (34) and new segments (27). The errors in the post-edited MT and the new category showed variation among the subjects (Guerberof 2009: 5). The high number of errors in TM segments could be due to "the fact that translators possibly consulted the source text less than they would have if they had been translating a new text with no aid", Guerberof states (2009: 5). With a focus on the target text in TM translations, translators do not consult the source text, while in traditional MT translation errors were obvious and therefore easier to detect without consulting the source text. However, also with MT, translators apparently do not consult the source text sufficiently, as MT contains many errors related to the relationship between source and target text as well (Guerberof 2009: 7).

Errors in TM sequences were overlooked more frequently than errors in MT segments, possibly because translators do not question the text correctness if they "are provided with a text that flows naturally" (Guerberof 2009: 5).[6] The post-edited MT segments contain few mistranslations, viz. "incorrect understanding of the source text" (Guerberof 2009: 4), which may indicate that MT "helps translators clarify possibly difficult aspects of the source texts" (Guerberof 2009: 6). The latter may be identified as one of the advantages of MT, notably for translators working with Language for Specific Purposes (LSP). When translating previously untranslated (new) text segments, translators appear to consult glossaries more, whereas the terminology offered in TM and MT translations appears to be questioned less often (ibid: 6). The latter may have implications for terminology guidelines in translation supported by different aids.

With respect to the differences in final quality between post-edited MT, TM and new segments, a TM with 80 to 90 % fuzzy matches in Guerberof's study yielded more final errors than MT translations or human translations (new segments) (Guerberof 2009: 8). This implies that TMs as translation aids do not always positively impact translation quality. Obviously, TM quality itself impacts transfer and target text quality, and TMs exist in different sizes and qualities. Exactly for this reason translators and translation students should remain vigilant and critical of specific TM input, either created by themselves or provided externally. This also includes TM maintenance over time, especially in collaborative contexts with multiple users.

In addition to the use of TMs to aid the translation process, monolingual corpora in the target language may also impact target text quality positively, notably in LSP context (cf. Bowker 1998, 1999). Verplaetse and Lambrechts (2019, forthcoming) conducted several experiments with mixed method translation support and conditions, including the use of specialized TMs, as well as monolingual corpora in the target language for English to Dutch translation tasks among third-year general applied linguistics bachelor's students and master's in translation students of specialized legal and medical translation workshops. A limited positive effect of monolingual corpora in the target language was found in these small-scale studies, where translation quality was measured in terms of analytical assessment methods (Daems and Macken 2013; Daems et al. 2013; Kübler et al. 2016).

5.5.4 Summary: error analysis in HT, MT, PE and TM-based translation

Different translation aids (or the lack thereof, viz. HT) generate different error types. Summarizing the studies discussed in sections 5.5.1, 5.5.2 and 5.5.3, Table 5.6 presents a sample of common error types identified in these studies per translation method. The categories HT and new, discussed earlier, are considered as one category (*No Aids*), as no translation aids such as TMs or MT are used in both these translation conditions. Further, in the sample presented in Table 5.6. *Word sense disambiguation* is considered a subcategory of *mistranslation* (Tezcan et al. 2018) and is therefore not added as a separate category.

The common error categories for all studies described here are (target text) *language* and *mistranslation*. This confirms that translation training under different translation conditions should pay due attention both to the transfer from source text and language to target text and language (cf. adequacy – *mistranslation*) and to thorough knowledge of the target language and textual requirements of the target culture (cf. acceptability – *language*). It also underlines the importance of the distinction between adequacy and acceptability as separate aspects of translation which should be brought to translation students' attention in terms of competences which deserve learners' efforts, each in their own right.

Style and register errors occur only frequently when no aids are used (new and/or human translation) in the studies referenced here. As mentioned previously,

Table 5.6 Sample of common error types per translation method (based on Guerberof 2009; Daems et al. 2013, 2014; Costa et al. 2015; Tezcan et al. 2018)

	No Aids	TM	(S/RB) MT	SMT+PE
adequacy errors				
additions	x	x		
deletions (omission)	x	x	x	
terminology		x		
mistranslation	x	x	x	x
Untranslated			x	
meaning shifts – other	x			x
acceptability errors				
language*	x	x	x	x
style and register	x			
wrong collocation			x	X

* The category *language* refers to target text "grammar, semantics, spelling, punctuation" (Guerberof 2009: 4)

however, different text types were analyzed in the various studies, for example, newspaper articles for HT (no aids), MT and MT+PE (Daems et al. 2013, 2014) and help system files for the categories new (no aids) and TM (Guerberof 2009). The differences in text type may perhaps partly explain why style and register errors do not occur for other translation methods. For instance, in the 80 to 90 % of TM matches no apparent style and register errors occur, possibly because the TM content proposed was already register- and style-specific, depending on the TM used. Proper TM quality has an impact on various levels besides terminology and includes style as well.

A thorough comparison of source text and target text will limit or even avoid common (HT) errors such as *additions* and *deletions*. Problems such as *wrong collocation* and *word sense disambiguation* could be remedied by making proper use of translation resources, e.g. (collocation) dictionaries, corpora, etc. Adequate use of such resources is an integral part of translation education.

5.6 Error taxonomies: which error categories in common?

When we compare the frequently occurring error categories in the various studies described (Guerberof 2009; Daems et al. 2013, 2014; Costa et al. 2015; Tezcan et al. 2018) with the existing analytical error taxonomies described in sections 5.3.2.1 through 5.3.2.5, we see that all five typologies, apart from the SAE J 2450 error categorization, distinguish adequacy (accuracy) and acceptability (fluency). The MeLLANGE error typology refers to content transfer and language respectively. Also, the broad definition of translation quality by Koby et al. (2014: 416) refers literally to accuracy (adequacy) and fluency (acceptability): "quality translation demonstrates accuracy and fluency required for the audience and purpose". The narrow definition equally includes a reference to accuracy (adequacy) ("a high quality translation is one in which the message embodied in the source text is transferred completely into the target text", Koby et al. 2014: 416–417; cf. *equivalence* of source and target text in Thelen 2018: 3), and a reference to fluency (acceptability) ("the target text is written in the target language using correct grammar and word order, to produce a culturally appropriate text", Koby et al. 2014: 416–417). These definitions of translation quality, the error typologies discussed and the different (adequacy- and acceptability-related) error categories frequently occurring in the studies described here show that adequacy/accuracy and acceptability/fluency are inextricably linked to translation quality. Table 5.7 presents an overview of the error typologies discussed, and their common error categories are organized as adequacy errors or acceptability errors.

The most complete error typologies in terms of *common* error categories based on the studies described in the current chapter is the MQM typology, followed by the SCATE and the MeLLANGE error typologies. The SAE J 2450 is the most incomplete typology for the error categories described in the current chapter, but it is also the only text-type specific error typology. This may explain the limited number of error categories.

Regarding adequacy, all error typologies contain a *terminological* (sub-) category, as well as a *deletions* (*omission*) category. Concerning acceptability, *language-related errors* are present in all typologies discussed in the current chapter. As *language errors* are also included under all translation conditions in the studies discussed here, a linguistic category may be considered a prerequisite for an efficient error typology.

5.7 Conclusion

In this chapter, we discussed how different translation conditions yield different error types. This confirms the usefulness of error typologies which are suitable for specific or several different translation conditions. A number of existing error taxonomies are already adequate for both HT and MT, e.g., MQM (Lommel et al. 2014) and the SCATE error taxonomy, with its annotation guidelines (Daems and Macken

Table 5.7 Overview of error typologies and common error categories

	Sical	SAE J 2450	MeLLANGE	MQM	SCATE
adequacy errors					
additions	x	x	x	x	x
deletions (omission)	x	x	x	x	x
terminology	x	x	x	x	x
mistranslation	x		x	x	x
untranslated			x	x	x
meaning shifts	x			x	x
acceptability errors					
language	x	x	x	x	x
style and register	x		x	x	
wrong collocation			x	x	x

2013; Daems et al. 2014; Tezcan et al. 2018). Such concrete annotation guidelines contribute to the increase of inter-annotator reliability and an improvement of error analyses (Stymne and Ahrenberg 2012: 1789). But the myriad of error typologies requires benchmarking means which can aid comparison or – if required – uniformization of such typologies. In this manner, a clearer comparison of different error annotations under different translation conditions and for different text types and registers may be achieved. And this may also apply when users require their own tailored additional error categories, when these can be similarly benchmarked. We hope that the current chapter has contributed a step in that direction.

In its turn, enhanced insight in and comparison (or uniformization) of different error typologies will benefit translator trainers and hence student translators, as well as professional translators. Translator trainers and trainees specifically will benefit from applying analytical error typologies, notably when concrete guidelines are provided to distinguish error types. Such concrete annotation guidelines will then not only promote inter-annotator reliability, and hence research purposes, but – even more importantly – didactic translation contexts. One concrete didactic situation which may be promoted and enhanced by this is the application of analytical error typology for guided student peer review of their fellow students' translations. In addition to peer review, of course, students will gain insight into their own translation performance. In this respect, and at a first (but very important) level, students may learn whether they need to focus more on the adequacy-related related aspects in source text to target text transfer or whether acceptability in the target language and target text writing deserve extra attention and training in their overall translation performance.

Also, professional translators could make additional efforts in order to decrease their error rates, leading to better-quality translations, namely by focusing on revision more as part of their translation task (Heine 2018: 338). We believe such professional translation revision may also be enhanced relevantly if it is error-typology informed.

Notes

1 In this chapter the error category of terminology refers to non-adherence to predefined terminological requirements (cf. Tezcan et al. 2015: 15), e.g. glossary lists.
2 In a somewhat broader, applied definition, a high-quality translation may be defined as one in which the message embodied in the source text is transferred adequately, rather than completely, into the target text (cf. Daems & Macken's concept of "adequacy").
3 Translation quality is a topic which deserves due attention. For more elaborate discussions of translation quality, see Gouadec (2010), House (2014) and van Egdom et al. (2018).
4 www.sae.org/standards/content/j2450_201608/ (accessed 24–12–2019)
5 www.qt21.eu/mqm-definition/definition-2015-12-30.html (accessed 24–12–2019)
6 In this respect we should also note the sometimes-misleading syntactic fluency resulting from the latest generation of MT, viz. NMT.

References

Akbari, A., and Segers, W. 2017a. "Translation Difficulty: How to Measure and What to Measure." *Lebende Sprachen*, 62(1), 3–29.
Akbari, A., and Segers, W. 2017b. "Evaluation of Translation through the Proposal of Error Typology: An Explanatory Attempt." *Lebende Sprachen*, 62(2), 408–430.
American Translators Association (ATA). 2009. *Flowchart for Error Point Decisions*. www.atanet.org/certification/aboutexams_flowchart.pdf (accessed 24 December 2019).
American Translators Association (ATA). 2017. *ATA Certification Program Framework for Standardized Error Marking*. https://atanet.org/certification/Framework_2017.pdf (accessed 24 December 2019).
Bowker, L. 1998. "Using Specialized Monolingual Native-language Corpora as a Translation Resource: A Pilot Study." *Meta: Journal des traducteurs/Meta: Translators' Journal* 43(4), 631–651.

Bowker, L. 1999. "Exploring the Potential of Corpora for Raising Language Awareness in Student Translators." *Language Awareness* 8(3–4), 160–173.
Campbell, S. 2014. *Translation into the Second Language*. London/New York: Routledge.
Castagnoli, S., Ciobanu, D., Kübler N., Kunz, K., and Volanschi, A. 2011. *Designing a Learner Translator Corpus for Training Purposes*. https://s3.amazonaws.com/academia.edu.documents/44403804/castagnoli_et_al.pdf?AWSAccessKeyId=AKIAIWOWYYGZ2Y53UL3A&Expires=1523353681&Signature =kwiz7XU6XxYBZcmWS%2FslTC9QUdE%3D&response-content-disposition=inline%3B%20filename%3DDesigning_a_Learner_Translator_Corpus_fo.pdf (accessed 13 October 2016).
Conde, T. 2012. "Quality and Quantity in Translation Evaluation: A Starting Point." *Across Languages and Cultures*, 13(1), 67–80.
Costa, Â., Ling, W., Luís, T., Correia, R., and Coheur, L. 2015. "A Linguistically Motivated Taxonomy for Machine Translation Error Analysis." *Machine Translation*, 29(2), 127–161.
Daems, J., and Macken, L. 2013. *Annotation Guidelines for English-Dutch Translation Quality Assessment, version 1.0. LT3 Technical Report-LT3 13.02*. www.lt3.ugent.be/media/uploads/publications/2013/Technical%20Report%20TQA%20Annotation.pdf (accessed 27 October 2017).
Daems, J., Macken, L., and Vandepitte, S. 2013. "Quality as the Sum of its Parts: A Two-step Approach for the Identification of Translation Problems and Translation Quality Assessment for HT and MT+ PE." In *Proceedings of MT Summit XIV Workshop on Post-Editing Technology and Practice*. Nice, France, 2 September 2013, Vol. 2, 63–71. Geneva: European Association for Machine Translation (EAMT).
Daems, J., Macken, L., and Vandepitte, S. 2014. "On the Origin of Errors: A Fine-grained Analysis of MT and PE Errors and their Relationship." In *Proceedings of the Ninth International Conference on Language Resources and Evaluation*. Reykjavik, Iceland, 26–31 May 2014, 62–66. Luxembourg: European Language Resources Association (ELRA).
Doyle, M. 2003. "Translation Pedagogy and Assessment: Adopting ATA's Framework for Standard Error Marking." *ATA Chronicle* 32(11), 21–28.
Eyckmans, J., Anckaert, Ph. and Segers, W. 2009. "The perks of norm-referenced translation evaluation." In *Testing and assessment in translation and interpreting*, ed. by C. Angelelli and H. Jacobson, 73–93. Amsterdam: John Benjamins.
Eyckmans, J., and Anckaert, P. 2017. "Chimera of Objectivity versus Prospect of Reliable Measurement." *Linguistica Antverpiensia, New Series: Themes in Translation Studies*, 16, 40–56.
Gouadec, D. 2010. "Quality in Translation." In *Handbook of Translation Studies*, Vol. 1, ed. by Y. Gambier and L. van Doorslaer, 270–275. Amsterdam/Philadelphia: John Benjamins.
Guerberof, A. 2009. "Productivity and Quality in MT Post-editing." In *Proceedings of MT Summit XII – Workshop: Beyond Translation Memories: New Tools for Translators MT*. Ottawa, Canada, 29 August 2009. http://citeseerx.ist.psu.edu/viewdoc/download?doi=10.1.1.575.5398&rep=rep1&type=pdf (accessed 26 February 2018).
Hansen, G. 2010. "Translation Errors." In *Handbook of Translation Studies*, Vol. 1. ed. by Y. Gambier and L. van Doorslaer, 385–388. Amsterdam/Philadelphia: John Benjamins.
Heine, C. 2018. "Student Peer-feedback in a Translation Task: Experiences with Social Science Research Methods." In *Quality Assurance and Assessment Practices in Translation and Interpreting*, ed. by E. Huertas-Barros, S. Vandepitte, and E. Iglesias-Fernández, 337–357. Hershey, PA: IGI Global.
House, J. 2014. *Translation Quality Assessment: Past and Present*. London/New York: Routledge.
Koby, G. S., and Baer, B. J. 2005. "From Professional Certification to the Translator Training Classroom: Adapting the ATA Error Marking Scale." *Translation Watch Quarterly* 1(1), 33–45.

Koby, G. S., and Lacruz, I. 2017. "The Thorny Problem of Translation and Interpreting Quality." *Linguistica Antverpiensia, New Series: Themes in Translation Studies*, 16, 1–12.

Koby, G. S., Melby, A., Fields, P., Lommel, A., and Hague, D. 2014. "Defining Translation Quality." *Tradumàtica*, 12, 413–420.

Kockaert, H. J., and Segers, W. 2014. "Evaluation de la traduction: la méthode PIE (Preselected Items Evaluation)." *Turjuman*, 23(2), 232–250.

Kockaert, H. J., and Segers, W. 2017. "Evaluation of Legal Translation: PIE Method (Preselected Items Evaluation)." *Journal of Specialised Translation*, 27, 148–163.

Kübler, N., Mestivier, A., Pecman, M., and Zimina, M. 2016. "Exploitation quantitative de corpus de traductions annotés selon la typologie d'erreurs pour améliorer les méthodes d'enseignement de la traduction spécialisée." In *Actes des 13èmes Journées internationales d'analyse statistique des données textuelles (JADT 2016)*. Nice, France, 7–10 June 2016, 731–741. Paris: Lexicometrica.

Lavault-Olléon, É., and Allignol, C. 2014. "La notion d'acceptabilité en traduction professionnelle: où placer le curseur?" *ILCEA. Revue de l'Institut des langues et cultures d'Europe, Amérique, Afrique, Asie et Australie*, 19. http://ilcea.revues.org/2455 (accessed 8 November 2017).

Lommel, A., Uszkoreit, H., and Burchardt, A. 2014. "Multidimensional Quality Metrics (MQM)." *Tradumàtica*, 12, 455–463.

Mariana, V. R., Cox, T., and Melby, A. 2015. "The Multidimensional Quality Metric (MQM) Framework: A New Framework for Translation Quality Assessment." *The Journal of Specialised Translation*, 23, 137–161.

Moreno, F. J. V., and Valero-Garcés, C. 2017. "Shedding Light on the Grey Area of Assessment in Legal Translation: A Case Study Based on a Holistic Method." *ITISPos International Journal*, 4, 11–27.

Mossop, B. 2001. *Revising and Editing for Translators*. Manchester, UK: St. Jerome Publishing.

Nerudová, L. 2012. *Quality of Translation: Approaches and a Field Survey* (Unpublished master thesis). Masarykova Univerzita, Brno, Czech Republic.

Nord, C. 2005. *Text Analysis in Translation: Theory, Methodology, and Didactic Application of a Model for Translation-oriented Text Analysis*. Amsterdam/New York: Rodopi.

O'Curran, E. 2014. "Translation Quality in Post-edited versus Human-translated Segments: A Case Study." In *Proceedings of the Third Workshop on Post-Editing Technology and Practice (WPTP-3)*, ed. by S. O'Brien, M. Simard, and L. Specia. Vancouver, Canada, 22–26 October 2014, 113–118. District of Columbia: Association for Machine Translation in the Americas.

Popović, M., and Burchardt, A. 2011. "From Human to Automatic Error Classification for Machine Translation Output." In *Proceedings of the 15th Annual Conference of the European Association for Machine Translation (EAMT 11)*. Leuven, Belgium, 30–31 May 2011, 265–272. Geneva: European Association for Machine Translation (EAMT).

Secară, A. 2005. "Translation Evaluation – A State of the Art Survey." In *Proceedings of the eCoLoRe/MeLLANGE Workshop*. Leeds, United Kingdom, 21–23 March 2005, 39–44. Leeds, UK: Centre for Translation Studies, University of Leeds.

Segers, W., and van Egdom, G. 2018. *De kwaliteit van vertalingen. Een terminologie van de vertaalevaluatie*. Kalmthout: Pelckmans Pro.

Shterionov, D., Superbo, R., Nagle, P., Casanellas, L., O'Dowd, T., and Way, A. 2018. "Human versus Automatic Quality Evaluation of NMT and PBSMT." *Machine Translation*, 1–19.

Stymne, S., and Ahrenberg, L. 2012. "On the Practice of Error Analysis for Machine Translation Evaluation." In *Proceedings of the Eight International Conference on Language Resources and Evaluation*, 1785–1790. Paris: European Language Resources Association.

Tezcan, A., Daems, J., Macken, L., and Van Brussel, L. 2015. *Annotation Guidelines for English-Dutch Machine Translation Quality Assessment, version 1.3.2 LT3 Technical Report-LT3 13.02*. www.lt3.ugent.be/media/uploads/publications/2013/Technical%20Report%20TQA%20Annotation.pdf (accessed 7 February 2018).

Tezcan, A., Hoste, V., and Macken, L. 2018. "SCATE Taxonomy and Corpus of Machine Translation Errors." In *Trends in E-tools and Resources for Translators and Interpreters*, ed. by G. Corpas Pastor and I. Durán-Muñoz, 219–248. Leiden: Brill/Rodopi.

Thelen, M. 2018. "Quality and Quality Assessment in Translation." In *Quality Assurance and Assessment Practices in Translation and Interpreting*, ed. by E. Huertas-Barros, S. Vandepitte, and E. Iglesias-Fernández, 1–25. Hershey, PA: IGI Global.

Toury, G. 2012. *Descriptive Translation Studies and Beyond*. Amsterdam/Philadelphia: John Benjamins.

van Egdom, G., Verplaetse, H., Schrijver, I., Kockaert, H., Segers, W., Pauwels, J., Bloemen, H., and Wylin, B. 2018. "How to Put the Translation Test to the Test? On Preselected Items Evaluation and Perturbation." In *Quality Assurance and Assessment Practices in Translation and Interpreting*, ed. by E. Huertas-Barros, S. Vandepitte, and E. Iglesias-Fernández, 26–56. Hershey, PA: IGI Global.

Vandepitte, S. 2017. "Translation Product Quality: A Conceptual Analysis." In *Quality aspects in institutional translation*, Vol. 8, ed. by T. Svoboda, L. Biel, and K. Łoboda, 15–29. Berlin: Language Science Press.

Verplaetse, H., and Lambrechts, A. 2019. "Translation Error Type in Medical and Legal Student Translations: Impact of Dictionary, CAT Tool and Corpus Use." *Dragoman – Journal of Translation Studies*, 8(9), 62–76.

Verplaetse, H., and Lambrechts, A. Forthcoming. "Dictionary, Corpus and CAT tool Use in Legal and Business Translation: A Comparative Pilot Study." *Papers of the Linguistic Society of Belgium*, 22 pp.

Waddington, C. 2001. "Different Methods of Evaluating Student Translations: The Question of Validity." *Meta*, 46(2), 311–332.

Wu, Y., Schuster, M., Chen, Z., Le, Q. V., Norouzi, M., Macherey, W., and Dean, J. 2016. *Google's Neural Machine Translation System: Bridging the Gap between Human and Machine Translation*. https://arxiv.org/pdf/1609.08144.pdf%20(7.pdf (accessed 13 August 2018).

6 Toward training terminologists on promoting and marketing terms from a language planning perspective

Fawwaz M. Al-Abed Al-Haq, Abdel-Rahman H. Abu-Melhim and Suhaib F. Al-Abed Al-Haq

6.1 Introduction

This chapter offers a proposed model for training terminologists on managing, promoting and marketing terms and evaluating and accepting these terms from a language planning perspective. The model shows how to plan coinage and Arabicizing terms through different processes and strategies. The chapter opens with an introduction to term planning, followed by a survey of related studies. Methods of analyzing data and results then are presented. The chapter concludes with discussing conclusions and recommendations for future studies.

Terminology planning is a discipline that can benefit from language planning theories, models and practices. Inspired by Cooper (1989), term planning can be defined as deliberate efforts to influence the behaviors of others with respect to the acquisition and coinage of terms, the status of the coined terms and the corpus of terms. This definition is inadequate (insufficient) because it does not restrict the term planners to authoritative agencies, does not restrict the type of the target group and fails to specify an ideal form of term planning. Further, it is stated in behavioral rather than problem-solving terms. It employs the term "influence" rather than "change" because the former includes the maintenance or preservation of current behavior, a plausible goal of term planning, as well as the change of current behavior. Because there are no generally accepted frameworks for the study of terminology planning, it may be useful to look at frameworks proposed by other fields of inquiry not only to understand term planning better but also to enhance the development of a framework specifically suited for term planning. Thus, we turn to models proposed for the diffusion of innovation, marketing, politics and decision making and apply them to term planning. The selection of these four models for language planning was because they offer concise accounts of language planning cases with defining examples of language planning at different places and in various times:

A   The management of coined terms.
B   A case of marketing.

C   A tool in the acquisition and maintenance of power.
D   An example of decision making.

6.1.1 Term planning as management of innovation

A newly coined term is a case of communicative innovation, by which we mean changes in term use, term status and term acquisition, which of course are non-material and have been largely ignored by scholars of diffusion. We can apply the diffusionist approach to the study of term planning by attempting to answer the following questions: Who adopts what, when, where, why and how? (Cooper 1989). Adoption includes the following: Awareness, evaluation, proficiency and usage.

6.1.2 Term planning as marketing

The marketing of terms is defined as developing the right product backed by the right promotion and put in the right place at the right price used by the right people (Kotler and Zaltman 1971). Marketing of products of Arabization involve promoting them as business managers promote their products (Cooper 1989).

6.1.3 Term Auger planning as pursuit and maintenance of power

Cooper states that if politics is the field of influence and influential, who are the influential people in term planning? According to Laswell, cited in Cooper (1989), those who get the most are the elite, and the rest are the masses. Thus, politics determines who gets what, when, how, why and where.

6.1.4 Term planning as decision making

In decision making, term planners are concerned with who makes what decisions, why, how, under what conditions and with what effects.

In this chapter, we are concerned with the application of the management of term planning. Students of translation and interpretation were surveyed to determine the level of acceptability of translated terms in two well-known dictionaries of sociolinguistics, namely: *A Dictionary of Sociolinguistics* (Swan et al. 2004) and *A Dictionary of Sociolinguistics* (Translated from English into Arabic) by (Al-Abed Al-Haq and Abu-Melhim 2019).

The goal of this study was to investigate the attitudes and usage of localized (i.e., Arabicized) sociolinguistic terms by university students in Jordan. For this purpose, a questionnaire was developed and distributed to 186 students of English language and translation at Yarmouk University in Jordan. The questionnaire included 35 sociolinguistic terms that were assessed by the participants in terms of Cooper's (1989) assessment criteria (knowledge, evaluation, usage, adoption and proficiency). Moreover, the instrument included 11 attitudinal statements and two open questions for the students to provide their feedback about the Arabicization process in Jordan.

6.2 Literature review

Sociolinguistics is concerned with the interrelationship between language and society. The discipline covers a wide range of topics that includes language maintenance and shift, language planning, language attitude, language varieties and multilingual nations, national languages and language policies, regional and social dialects, gender and age, ethnicity and social networks, language change, style, context and register, speech functions, politeness and cross-cultural communication Holmes (2013). It goes without saying that these domains of sociolinguistics are conveyed through terms and concepts. and these terms need to be coined and defined, used and accepted. There are two seminal works that tackled sociolinguistic terms: *The Handbook of Sociolinguistics* by Coulmas (1997) and *A Dictionary of Sociolinguistics* by Swan et al. (2004), which was recently translated into Arabic by Al-Abed Al-Haq and Abu-Melhim (2019).

Currently, researchers and stakeholders are interested in translating terms in different fields in general and linguistics and sociolinguistics to serve the needs of communities and societies due to the spread of social media in the Arab world. Language and terminology planners have realized the need to achieve comprehensive and understandable communicative innovation. Translating and coining new terms can be classified under these communicative functions (Cooper 1989). Equivalence has always been an interest among translation scholars such as Catford and Newmark, among others.

Finding an equivalent term in the target language, as Catford (1965: 27) suggests, is "an empirical phenomenon which can be discovered by comparing the SLT [source language text] with the TLT [target language text]".

Following Catford (1965), Newmark (1988) classifies equivalence into three types: cultural equivalence, where a SL cultural word is translated by a TL cultural word, functional equivalence, which requires the use of a culture-free word, and descriptive equivalence. Likewise, Shunnaq and Farghal (1999) suggest three kinds of equivalence: formal, which seeks the form of the SL expression, functional, which seeks to capture the function of the SL expression, and ideational, which seeks to convey the communicative sense of the SL expression far from the function and the form.

Based on the discussion of the different types of equivalence, it can be argued that translation is not a mere linguistic process in which translators replace one word of the source language (SL) with another in the target language (TL). Translation is not restricted to literal translation; rather, it provides translators with a variety of strategies to convey the intended meaning and to overcome the two main types of translation problems: the linguistic problem and the cultural problem, especially when it comes to two remote languages like English and Arabic (Hassan 2014).

Some of these distinctions have been reformed in the theoretical contrast between formal equivalence and dynamic equivalence. According to Nida (1964), the former type of equivalence places the "attention on the message itself, in both form and content", while the latter attempts to assure that "the relationship between reception and message should be substantially the same as that which existed between the original receptors and the message" (Nida 1964: 159). In other words, dynamic equivalence is concerned with the acceptability and endorsement of the localized terms by the target audience. Equivalence is pivotal but is also a debatable issue in translation studies. Term equivalence is urgently needed in translating sociolinguistic terms at dynamic ideational, linguistic, conceptional and motivational levels. Since Al-Didawi (2007) considers translation into Arabic the same as Arabicization, he combines Arabicization and translation in one term, namely *Arabicized translation*. He defines Arabicized translation as rendering ideas into Arabic by summarizing the original text in the target language and simplifying it for the readers, having the right to change it without affecting its meaning. Summarizing foreign scientific research in Arabic is an example (Al-Didawi 2007).

It is worth mentioning that Arabicization is an adequate and an independent form of translation from English into Arabic. Both concepts (Arabicization and translation) are often used in literature interchangeably. It seems that a non-organized translation activity may add ambiguity to translated terms, which may confuse the term users when they encounter the floods of terms produced (i.e., localized) for the same foreign (English in this case) term. Therefore, standardizing Arabicized terms is a basic requirement for the success of translation planning activities. Doing so may also help solve the problem of synonymy in the Arabic language, which emerges from inaccurate choices of non-organized Arabicized terms.

Arabicization is not a simple, one-step process but rather a multilayered one. As Al-Abed Al-Haq (1998b) suggests Arabicization planning has three stages: linguistic, regulatory and operational. The first stage is a linguistic one, which he labels as *corpus Arabicization*. It includes coining new terms and adopting new scientific symbols. It also refers to issues related to the spelling conventions of the Arabic language. The second stage, *status Arabicization*, is concerned with the authorization of Arabicized terms by bodies and agencies that have power over the users, such as governments. Moreover, Al-Abed Al-Haq (1998b) labels the last stage as *acquisition planning of Arabicization*, referring to the activities of teaching Arabicized terms on the part of teachers and learning them on the part of students and users. In addition, this stage includes the spread and diffusion of

Arabic language and accepting the idea of Arabicization and endorsing Arabicized terms.

Abo Abdo (1984) suggests many recommendations to ensure proper Arabicization. He proposes procedures such as combating illiteracy and teaching Arabs the standard Arabic variety, standardizing Arabicized terms across all fields and areas, passing a law to enhance Arabicization and raising public awareness among Arabs regarding the importance of Arabicization. The previous points reflect the last two processes of Arabicization suggested by Al-Abed Al-Haq (1998b), namely status Arabicization and acquisition planning.

Abo Abdo (1984) does not encourage translating foreign phrases literally. He provides other recommendations: avoiding colloquial words, trying not to use archaic words that aim at showing off but trying to utilize common ones. These points are examples of the corpus Arabicization approach suggested by Al-Abed Al-Haq (1998b).

Al-Smadi (1997) followed a language planning approach in his investigation of the Arabicization of military terms, as performed by the Jordan Academy of Arabic. The results of his study revealed lack of correspondence between Arabicized military terms provided by the Jordan Academy of Arabic and the actual terms used by the Jordanian army. He attributed this lack of correspondence to the fact that soldiers were more motivated to learn English than Arabic. Al-Smadi (1997) explained that the terms used by the soldiers were more acceptable and effective than the equivalent terms set by the academy. However, he explained that the soldiers had a positive attitude when it comes to the process of Arabicization of military terms.

Diknash (1998) tackled another side of the problem in her study, which examined the Arabicization of nursing terms from a language planning perspective. Similar to Al-Smadi (1997), she found that there was a mismatch between the terms proposed by the Jordan Academy of Arabic and the terms that were often used by specialists and students in the field of nursing. Again, most students revealed positive attitudes toward the Arabicization of nursing terms. However, most of the participants in the study preferred English to Arabic as a medium of instruction.

Taking a language planning perspective, Al-Oliemat (1998) examined the attitudes of Jordanian parliament members toward Arabicization. The results of his study showed that PMs had a favorable and supportive attitude toward the Arabicization process, taking pride in that as a means of reviving the Pan-Arab identity. This supportive attitude was echoed in a procedural manner in the form of passing a law that promotes and organizes Arabicization.

Following this line of research from a language and term planning perspective, Halloush (2000) addressed the issue of Arabicization of medical terms, eliciting her data from a sample of 100 physicians in Jordan. The results of her study showed that most physicians did not approve or endorse Arabicized medical terms. Moreover, the doctors even thought that the Arabicization of medical terms was useless and did not see any point in this effort. In addition, they believed that the performance of the Jordan Academy of Arabic was poor and unsystematic.

Mahasneh (2002) assessed the localization of internet terms taking language and term planning perspectives. She found that students majoring in computer science did not accept Arabicized equivalent terms of English internet terms. Moreover, students' attitude toward Arabicization was overall negative and unsupportive, indicating that they were not willing to support and endorse the Arabicization process. Additionally, students also believed that there was a need to reform and promote the work of the Jordan Academy of Arabic because the academy did not provide Arabicized equivalents for internet terms at the time the study was conducted.

Al-Abed Al-Haq and Al-Essa (2016b)[1] examined the perception of Arabicized business terms among 200 business students at the University of Jordan and Yarmouk University, highlighting and emphasizing the importance of the acceptability criteria in the Arabicization process in order to produce acceptable and adequate business terms. In addition, Al-Abed Al-Haq and Al-Essa investigated the correlation among these different acceptability criteria, while focusing on the roles of sociolinguistic factors such as gender, affiliation and major in the Arabicization process of business terms. The results of their study revealed that the investigated Arabicized business terms were moderately accepted by the participating students. The attitudes of the participants toward Arabicized business terms were overall relatively positive. The results indicated that students' responses were affected by their gender and university affiliation (University of Jordan vs. Yarmouk University). As such, females and University of Jordan students held more positive attitudes toward Arabicized terms, believing that Arabicized terms would work better in the Arab world, reflecting a strong Pan-Arab identity and nationalism.

Al Sakran's study (2004) examined the extent of acceptability of Arabicized agricultural terms. It was found that "the extent of acceptability of Arabicized agricultural terms is moderate as evidenced by the 2.56 overall averages on the 5-point scale". It also showed the challenges the terms faced and presented several pieces of advice and solutions. Also, agricultural students in Jordan asked for rephrasing and improving some Arabicized agricultural terms and a fundamental change in the new mechanism. In contrast, in the study by Halloush (2000), the extent of acceptability of Arabicized medical terms was very low: "The extent of Arabicized medical terms is very low as evidenced by the 1.54 overall average on the 5-point scale". It was also found that physicians are not ready to accept and adopt Arabicized medical terms and that it would take a lot of effort and time.

6.3 Purpose of the study

The purpose of this study is to determine the degree of acceptability of some problematic Arabicized sociolinguistic terms based on these criteria of acceptability:

Knowledge, evaluation, usage, adoption and proficiency, which were suggested by Cooper (1989). This study is the first attempt to publish a separate pamphlet for Arabicized sociolinguistic terms. Efforts have been oriented toward scientific and medical terms. This study thus aims to offer Arabic linguists with acceptable and unified sociolinguistic terms that would help translators and Arabic sociolinguists in rendering texts and resources in Arabic.

6.4 Methods and procedures

This section presents the reader with the sample of the study, the instruments for collecting data, the procedures and the method of data analysis.

6.4.1 Sample of the study

This study consists of 182 students from Yarmouk University, 96 of whom are enrolled in the Department of English Language and Literature, while 86 are enrolled in the Department of Translation. The researchers opted for this sample size because it was believed to be sufficient for statistical analysis to get reliable and meaningful results. Among these 182 students, 150 of them were female and 32 participants were male. In terms of the number of sociolinguistic courses taken by the participants, 118 students (65%) had never enrolled in a sociolinguistic course, 51 students (28%) had enrolled in one course, 11 students (6%) had enrolled in two courses and only 2 students (1%) had enrolled in three courses.

6.4.2 Instruments

The data collection instrument in this study was based on a revised version developed by Halloush (2000) and Al-Abed Al-Haq and Al-Essa (2016a). This revised instrument was chosen because it is one of the most feasible ways to get valid and reliable results. The instrument is in the form of a questionnaire consisting of four parts. The first part serves as a tool to elicit demographic and background information about the respondents (gender, age, and familiarity with sociolinguistics). The second part of the questionnaire examines the acceptability of 35 Arabicized terms that were selected at the discretion of the researchers, such as creole, pidgin, standardization and diglossia. The participants were asked to evaluate these terms, depending on the criteria of acceptability suggested and defined by Cooper (1989: 61–62):

1 Knowledge: Indicates whether the respondent knows Arabicized term or not. It also reveals whether the respondent has heard it before.
2 Evaluation: Is the extent of accepting Arabicized equivalent of the English term by the respondent. In addition, it is concerned with the extent of considering this Arabicized equivalent as a good one.

3   Usage: Refers to the frequency of using the Arabicized term by the respondent.
4   Proficiency: Shows the ability of the respondent to utilize Arabicized terms within the correct context accurately.
5   Adoption: Is the use of an Arabicized term consistently, repetitively and acceptably.

Each criterion of acceptability was tested using a 5-point Likert scale. The minimum point on this scale was 1, while 5 was the maximum, where 1 stood for strongly disagree and 5 represented strongly agree.

The third part includes 11 statements that elicit responses along a 5-point Likert scale, examining the attitudes of English and translation students toward Arabicization. The fourth section consisted of four open-ended questions. The first was intended to investigate the respondent's evaluation of the work of the Jordan Academy of Arabic in the Arabicization of sociolinguistic terms. The aim of the second question was to elicit the participants' recommended procedures to promote Arabicization of English sociolinguistic terms by the Academy. Finally, the last two questions were concerned with the participants' degree of understandability of the questionnaire content and the degree of accuracy of their responses in the questionnaire.

6.4.3 Procedures

Copies of the questionnaire were distributed by the researchers to 182 English and Translation students at Yarmouk University. Then the copies of the questionnaire were collected and codified in terms of the elicited demographic information before the data were analyzed.

6.4.4 Methods of data analysis

The collected data were entered into an Excel sheet, where the participants' responses were marked as dependent variables and the background data (e.g., gender and age) were marked as independent. Subsequently, data were analyzed for frequency and patterns of responses. Finally, data were statistically analyzed using the SPSS statistical package for significant results.

6.5 Rationale of the study

The Jordan Academy of Arabic has not published a separate pamphlet for Arabicized sociolinguistic terms. Efforts have been oriented toward scientific and medical terms. This study is the first step toward providing Arabic with acceptable and unified sociolinguistic terms that would help translators and Arabic sociolinguists in rendering texts and resources in Arabic.

6.5.1 Significance of the study

This study brings into focus the criteria for measuring the acceptability of translated sociolinguistic terms; hence, it paves the way for Arabic language academies in Jordan and the Arab world to produce acceptable terminology. It is important in term translation and Arabicization to take into consideration the attitude and the ideology held by the consumers or users in determining the primary climate for accepting and determining the acceptability of the translated sociolinguistic terms. In this regard, it is worth paraphrasing Pool (1974), who states that theorists of language planning have recognized the need for popular support if government language policies are to be implemented. Mass attitudes can be viewed as playing crucial roles in implementation of language planning. Furthermore, the study promotes awareness among translators, linguists, and sociolinguists, Arabization specialists, curriculum designers and authors. The significance of this study lies in its attempt to refresh and revitalize the literature of term planning in general and sociolinguistic terms in particular as well as translators not only in Jordan but also in the Arab world by presenting the acceptable sociolinguistic terms to the academies and potential users.

Sager (1990) defines terminology as a field of study that examines how terms are compiled, described, processed and presented as lexical items that belong to jargons in one or more languages. He argues that the objective of studying terminology is twofold:

> Combining the goal of collecting data about the lexicon of a language while providing an informative, and sometime even an advisory, service to language users. The justification of considering it a traditionally assembled, the different background of people involved in the work, and to some extent in the different methods used.
>
> (p. 2)

Moreover, Sager distinguishes three meanings of the word "terminology": the set of practice and methods, for the collection, description and presentation; the set of premises, arguments and conclusions required for explaining the relationships between concepts and terms; and a vocabulary of the special subject field.

Following Cooper (1989), the concept of terminology planning refers to activities and deliberate efforts to plan for corpus, status and acquisition of terms. Thus, corpus term planning refers to purely linguistic issues such as coining new terms, reforming their spellings and adopting them. It refers to the creation of new forms by word coinage processes, the modification of old ones or the selection from alternative forms in a spoken or written code. Terms such as cultivation, reform, standardization, selection, codification, elaboration and modernization represent instances of corpus term planning. Status term planning is mainly concerned with how the significance or position of terms in all aspects of life is recognized by government, government-authorized agencies, authoritative bodies and individuals. Therefore, it refers to the allocation of terms to a given function. Term allocation is defined as authoritative decisions to maintain, extend or restrict the range of uses (functional range) of a term in a setting. Thus, status term planning refers to deliberate efforts to influence the allocation of term functions among speech communities. Therefore, coining specialized terms in different functions is a target for status term planning. Jahr (1992: 12–13) states that language planning involves organized activity (private or official)

> which attempts to solve language problems within a given society, usually at the national level. Through language planning, attempts are made to direct, change, or preserve the linguistic norm or the social status (and communicative function) of a given written or spoken language variety of a language. Language planning is usually conducted according to a declared program or a defined set of criteria, and with a deliberate goal by officially appointed committees or bodies, by private organizations, or by prescriptive linguists working on behalf of official authorities. Its object is to establish norms (primarily written) which are validated by high social status; oral norms connected with their written standards to follow.

According to Al-Abed Al-Haq and Al-Essa (2016a), terms cannot be set arbitrarily. There must be coordination between language academies, translators, planners, linguists and scientists to coin new terms in different fields on a linguistic basis. Since every language has its own nature, which is different from other languages, what is acceptable in one language could not be adequate in another. Accordingly, terminology planning is an organized activity that revives languages and provides planners with new scientific terms to protect languages from death. This also applies to translating sociolinguistic expressions.

Moreover, Al-Abed Al-Haq (2015) suggests that Arabicization and terminology planning in translation have received much attention over the last two decades. Terminology planning will inescapably be one of the critical issues in translation due to ongoing developments in all fields of science and the continuing need for coining new terms. There are numerous studies on the translation and Arabicization of terms and terminology planning in different disciplines such as Al-Smadi (1997), Al-Sakran (2004), El-Fadni (2004) and El-Khafaifi (1985). But there is no single study on the acceptability of sociolinguistic terms and attitudes of consumers and stakeholders toward these newly translated and Arabicized sociolinguistic terms.

Like Jaied (2010), Farghal (2012) regards Arabicization as a strategy of translation. Farghal argues that whenever the translator comes across new terms, he may borrow terms from other languages, making them suitable morphologically and phonologically to the Arabic language. In addition, Al-Abed Al-Haq (1998b:

59–60) suggests that Arabicization planning has three stages. As noted previously in section 6.2, the first stage is a linguistic one which Al-Abed Al-Haq calls *corpus Arabicization*. The second stage is concerned with the authorization of Arabicized terms by bodies that have power over the users, such as governments. This stage is called *status Arabicization*. Al-Abed Al-Haq (1998b: 59) calls the last stage *acquisition planning of Arabicization*. It refers to the activities of teaching Arabicized terms and learning them.

Language planning can be defined as deliberate efforts to influence the behavior of others with respect to the status, corpus and the acquisition of language (Cooper 1989). This definition can be extended to planning Arabicization as an activity of translation or localization from English into Arabic. By the same token, this is applicable to planning the translation of terms (i.e., terminology planning) in different fields and disciplines where the status, corpus and acquisition of terms and their translation are involved. Moreover, Jernudd (1977: 18) states that

> language planning is a branch of sociolinguistics. It is a developing field that sees language as a social resource. As such, language requires planned action if it is to be used to its full potential. Language planning is done through the cooperative efforts of political, educational, economic, and linguistic authorities.

Al-Abed Al-Haq (1998a), citing Cooper (1989), comments on this definition, stating that it does not limit the planning mission to authoritative agencies, leaving the door open for possibilities in terms of the target group and the ideal form of planning. Jahr (1992), cited in Al-Abed Al-Haq (1998a: 3), argues that language planning involves

> Organized activity (private or official) which attempts to solve language problems within a given society, usually at the national level. Through language planning, attempts are made to direct, change, or preserve the linguistic norm or the social status (and communicative function) of a given, written, or spoken language variety of a language. Language planning is usually conducted according to a declared program or a defined set of criteria, and with a deliberate goal by officially appointed committees or bodies, by private organizations, or by prescriptive linguists working on behalf of official authorities. Its object is to establish norms (primarily written) which are validated by high social status; oral norms connected with their written standards to follow.

Emran (1993) defines terminology as "a scientific and technical discipline which is concerned with the profound study of scientific terms in specific scientific and technical fields regarding the concepts, naming these concepts, standardizing and unifying them" (cited in Al-Abed Al-Haq and Al-Essa 2016a: 151).

6.5.2 Research questions

The primary questions to be dealt with are as follows:

1 To what extent are the translated sociolinguistic terms acceptable?
2 To what extent are the five criteria of acceptability (knowledge, usage, evaluation, adoption and proficiency) influenced by gender?[1]
3 What are the prevailing attitudes toward the translated sociolinguistic terms as perceived by students of the Department of English at Yarmouk University?

6.5.3 Criteria of acceptability of a translated term

The International Organization for Standardization (ISO) has set global guidelines for word formation that are applicable across all human languages. These guidelines are explained in ISO document R704 (called Naming Principles). Sager (1990: 89) summarized such guidelines as follows:

1 Terms should not be created arbitrarily. They should conform to the language in which they are created morphologically, syntactically, semantically, and pragmatically.
2 Terms should follow the phonological and morphological characteristics of the language in which they are created. They should also follow its spelling conventions.
3 When the terms become widely accepted by their users, they should not be changed without persuasive reasons and strong certainty that the new terms will be fully accepted as alternatives.
4 In case that a term becomes a partial substitute of an old one, a new term should be cooked to avoid terminological consistency and confusion.

Al-Sayadi (1980) addresses the accuracy of the term to be approved and adopted by users. Likewise, Al-Abed Al-Haq (1998a) focuses on the conciseness of the term to be accepted. Khalifah (1978) believes that the factors that control the diffusion or the death of a term are the endorsement of a term by the speakers, the spread of it and the time span. Sager (1990: 89) summarizes that the requirements that should be met for a term to be endorsed by users as follows:

1 There should be a logical relationship between the term and the concept it refers to.
2 The term should conform to an existing lexical system and follow the transcription system of the language in which it is created.
3 The rules of word-formation of the language should be followed when coining a new term.

4   The term should be derivative.
5   The term should not constitute redundant repetition by having within the same term a foreign word with a native one in which both have the same meaning.
6   The term should be precise and concise.
7   The term should not have synonyms, homonyms, or morphological variants.

According to Sager (1990), the theory of terminology has three vital areas to consider; these are cognitive, linguistic and communicative dimensions. Sager (1990: 13) elaborates on these dimensions. The cognitive dimension examines the relationship between the linguistic structure of the terminologies and their intangible contents. The linguistic dimension investigates the representation of these abstract contents in language. Finally, the communicative dimension studies the usage of these terminologies and the way they are organized. The translation of terms should relate to these criteria and echo the essence of their meaning.

6.6 Results

In this section, the results of this study are presented in the form of frequency and percentages (raw results). Moreover, the results of statistical analyses (t-test and ANOVA) are presented and discussed in terms of the effect of the independent variables on each of the dependent variables. Before presenting the results, it is worth noting that participants' average response to the question "Did you understand the questionnaire?" was 3.32 out of 5 and to the question "Is your answer considered precise?" was 3.28 out of 5.

6.6.1 Assessment of the selected terminology

In this section, the participants' assessment of the selected terminology will be presented (Tables 6.1–6.5) in terms of each of the five criteria (knowledge, evaluation, usage, proficiency and adoption). For each term, the data will be presented as a mean (out of 5) of the participants' responses.

6.6.1.1 Knowledge

In this section, knowledge is defined as the participant's familiarity with the Arabicized term and whether s(he) has heard it before. Table 6.1 shows the ranking of the target terms in relation to knowledge in a descending order. Thus, 5 means "extremely knowledgeable", 4 "very knowledgeable", 3 "knowledgeable", 2 "not knowledgeable" and 1 "not knowledgeable at all". While terms that received a score of 3 or above reflect knowledge, terms that received a score below 3 reflect a lack of knowledge. The latter group of terms (i.e., terms that show a low level of

Table 6.1 Knowledge

No.	Item	Mean	Std. Deviation
24	Globalization (know)	4.21	1.231
34	Setting (know)	4.18	1.258
33	Race (know)	4.11	1.273
32	Power (know)	4.04	1.218
22	Face (know)	3.99	1.455
31	Politeness (know)	3.98	1.352
2	Casual speech (know)	3.86	1.373
23	Feminism (know)	3.82	1.423
28	Language diversity (know)	3.77	1.375
27	Language choice (know)	3.69	1.459
35	Sexism (know)	3.66	1.514
8	Sociolect (know)	3.62	1.447
26	Language attitude (know)	3.60	1.317
14	Gender (know)	3.59	1.487
21	Ethnicity (know)	3.45	1.561
18	Language death (know)	3.43	1.480
7	Codification (know)	3.40	1.417
20	Elite (know)	3.31	1.579
10	Linguistic revival (know)	3.30	1.491
30	Mock language (know)	3.29	1.533
9	Idiolect (know)	3.26	1.443
29	Lingua franca (know)	3.26	1.492
17	Language shift (know)	3.25	1.491
19	Language reform (know)	3.24	1.481
11	Code-mixing (know)	3.02	1.529
4	Diglossia (know)	3.01	1.500
15	Community of practice (know)	3.00	1.593
	Knowledge	2.80	.865
6	Jargon (know)	2.73	1.478
5	Immersion (know)	2.68	1.428
25	Honorific (know)	2.48	1.504
16	Linguistic imperialism (know)	2.40	1.556
1	Code-switching (know)	2.25	1.391
3	Pidgin (know)	2.25	1.414
12	Corpus planning (know)	2.19	1.357
13	Acrolect (know)	2.14	1.356

knowledge) includes jargon, immersion, honorific, linguistic imperialism, code-switching, pidgin, corpus planning and acrolect.

6.6.1.2 *Evaluation*

In this section, evaluation is defined as the extent of accepting the Arabicized term as a good equivalent for the English one. Table 6.2 shows the ranking of the target terms in relation to evaluation in a descending order. While terms that received a

Table 6.2 Evaluation

No.	Item	Mean	Std. Deviation
33	Race (eval)	4.07	1.241
31	Politeness (eval)	4.05	1.262
22	Face (eval)	4.03	1.420
24	Globalization (eval)	4.03	1.230
34	Setting (eval)	4.03	1.273
32	Power (eval)	3.94	1.258
2	Casual speech (eval)	3.91	1.193
28	Language diversity (eval)	3.84	1.272
23	Feminism (eval)	3.80	1.335
27	Language choice (eval)	3.64	1.325
26	Language attitude (eval)	3.62	1.259
7	Codification (eval)	3.60	1.273
8	Sociolect (eval)	3.58	1.240
35	Sexism (eval)	3.58	1.430
21	Ethnicity (eval)	3.53	1.337
29	Lingua franca (eval)	3.45	1.332
14	Gender (eval)	3.44	1.439
19	Language reform (eval)	3.43	1.280
10	Linguistic revival (eval)	3.40	1.398
20	Elite (eval)	3.39	1.504
9	Idiolect (eval)	3.38	1.283
18	Language death (eval)	3.38	1.435
30	Mock language (eval)	3.28	1.457
17	Language shift (eval)	3.23	1.430
4	Diglossia (eval)	3.22	1.311
11	Code-mixing (eval)	3.15	1.418
-	Evaluation	3.13	.783
5	Immersion (eval)	3.10	1.229
15	Community of practice (eval)	3.09	1.503
1	Code-switching (eval)	2.99	1.242
6	Jargon (eval)	2.91	1.357
25	Honorific (eval)	2.73	1.414
16	Linguistic imperialism (eval)	2.66	1.445
3	Pidgin (eval)	2.62	1.291
12	Corpus planning (eval)	2.49	1.275
13	Acrolect (eval)	2.47	1.182

score of 3 or above reflect evaluation, terms that received a score below 3 reflect a lack of evaluation. The latter group of terms (i.e., terms that show a low level of evaluation) includes code-switching, jargon, honorific, linguistic imperialism, pidgin, corpus planning and acrolect.

6.6.1.3 Usage

In this section, usage is defined as the frequency of the use of the Arabicized term. Table 6.3 shows the ranking of the target terms in relation to usage in a descending order. While terms that received a score of 3 or above reflect usage, terms

Table 6.3 Usage

No.	Item	Mean	Std. Deviation
34	Setting (usage)	3.86	1.334
22	Face (usage)	3.81	1.453
32	Power (usage)	3.79	1.344
31	Politeness (usage)	3.76	1.339
33	Race (usage)	3.69	1.360
24	Globalization (usage)	3.67	1.426
23	Feminism (usage)	3.50	1.440
2	Casual speech (usage)	3.41	1.277
28	Language diversity (usage)	3.41	1.330
8	Sociolect (usage)	3.37	1.415
27	Language choice (usage)	3.35	1.432
14	Gender (usage)	3.27	1.527
21	Ethnicity (usage)	3.21	1.347
26	Language attitude (usage)	3.18	1.389
35	Sexism (usage)	3.06	1.557
17	Language shift (usage)	2.99	1.436
29	Lingua franca (usage)	2.96	1.372
19	Language reform (usage)	2.95	1.397
10	Linguistic revival (usage)	2.94	1.467
18	Language death (usage)	2.93	1.459
7	Codification (usage)	2.91	1.379
20	Elite (usage)	2.91	1.562
9	Idiolect (usage)	2.90	1.416
30	Mock language (usage)	2.89	1.487
11	Code-mixing (usage)	2.80	1.471
15	Community of practice (usage)	2.74	1.489
4	Diglossia (usage)	2.56	1.309
-	Usage	2.51	.843
5	Immersion (usage)	2.41	1.310
25	Honorific (usage)	2.37	1.367
6	Jargon (usage)	2.29	1.314
13	Acrolect (usage)	2.21	1.341
16	Linguistic imperialism (usage)	2.21	1.425
12	Corpus planning (usage)	2.12	1.229
1	Code-switching (usage)	2.08	1.297
3	Pidgin (usage)	1.99	1.287

that received a score below 3 reflect a lack of usage. The latter group of terms (i.e. terms that show a low level of usage) includes language shift, lingua franca, language reform, linguistic revival, language death, codification, elite, idiolect, mock language, code-mixing, community of practice, diglossia, usage, immersion, honorific, jargon, acrolect, linguistic imperialism, corpus planning, code-switching and pidgin.

6.6.1.4 Proficiency

In this section, proficiency is defined as the participant's ability to use the Arabicized term within correct contexts. Table 6.4 shows the ranking of the target terms in relation to proficiency in a descending order. While terms that received

Table 6.4 Proficiency

No.	Item	Mean	Std. Deviation
34	Setting (prof)	3.89	1.316
22	Face (prof)	3.81	1.482
31	Politeness (prof)	3.78	1.293
24	Globalization (prof)	3.73	1.411
33	Race (prof)	3.72	1.322
32	Power (prof)	3.71	1.288
2	Casual speech (prof)	3.60	1.238
23	Feminism (prof)	3.49	1.444
28	Language diversity (prof)	3.46	1.365
8	Sociolect (prof)	3.31	1.353
27	Language choice (prof)	3.31	1.455
26	Language attitude (prof)	3.30	1.342
14	Gender (prof)	3.26	1.474
21	Ethnicity (prof)	3.20	1.413
35	Sexism (prof)	3.17	1.538
9	Idiolect (prof)	3.14	1.353
18	Language death (prof)	3.07	1.453
29	Lingua franca (prof)	3.06	1.423
10	Linguistic revival (prof)	3.05	1.382
17	Language shift (prof)	2.99	1.394
19	Language reform (prof)	2.99	1.383
20	Elite (prof)	2.96	1.576
7	Codification (prof)	2.95	1.355
30	Mock language (prof)	2.94	1.527
11	Code-mixing (prof)	2.93	1.418
15	Community of practice (prof)	2.75	1.465
-	Proficiency	2.73	.937
4	Diglossia (prof)	2.70	1.253
25	Honorific (prof)	2.52	1.327
5	Immersion (prof)	2.49	1.335
6	Jargon (prof)	2.44	1.322
1	Code-switching (prof)	2.41	1.289
12	Corpus planning (prof)	2.21	1.306
16	Linguistic imperialism (prof)	2.19	1.374
13	Acrolect (prof)	2.17	1.299
3	Pidgin (prof)	2.16	1.272

a score of 3 or above reflect proficiency, terms that received a score below 3 reflect a lack of proficiency. The latter group of terms (i.e., terms that show a low level of proficiency) includes language shift, language reform, elite, codification, mock language, code-mixing, community of practice, proficiency, diglossia, honorific, immersion, jargon, code-switching, corpus planning, linguistic imperialism, acrolect and pidgin.

6.6.1.5 Adoption

In this section, adoption refers to the usage of the Arabicized term repetitively, consistently and acceptably among other alternatives. Table 6.5 shows the ranking of the target terms in relation to adoption in a descending order. While terms that received a score of 3 or above reflect adoption, terms that received a score below 3 reflect a lack of adoption. The latter group of terms (i.e. terms that show a low level of adoption) includes mock language, linguistic revival, language shift, elite, language reform, code-mixing, community of practice, linguistic imperialism, acrolect, pidgin and corpus planning.

6.6.2 Terminology assessment criteria

Each of the 35 terms in this study was assessed by the participants in terms of the five assessment criteria: knowledge, evaluation, usage, proficiency and adoption. In this section, the mean value for each criterion is presented and the effect of major (English vs. Translation) and gender are presented and discussed.

As provided by the survey respondents, the mean value for knowledge was 2.80 (out of 5), meaning that the respondents showed overall a low level of familiarity (56%) with the complete list of target terms. In other words, many of the participants had hardly heard of most of the target terms dealt with in this study. In terms of major, English language students (2.96 out of 5) were significantly more familiar with the target terms than the translation students (2.62 out of 5), as revealed by a t-test ($a < 0.05$). As for gender, there were no statistically significant differences between males and females in terms of their knowledge of the selected localized terms ($a < 0.859$).

The mean value for evaluation was 3.13 (out of 5), meaning the participants accepted Arabicized terms as good equivalents of the English terms almost two-thirds of the time. In terms of major, there was no statistically significant difference between the English language students (3.14 out of 5) and the translation students (3.11 out of 5), as revealed by the t-test ($a = 0.764$). As for gender, there were no statistically significant differences between males and females in terms of their evaluation of the selected localized terms ($a < 0.479$).

Table 6.5 Adoption

No.	Item	Mean	Std. Deviation
22	Face (adopt)	3.88	1.515
34	Setting (adopt)	3.85	1.396
33	Race (adopt)	3.78	1.340
31	Politeness (adopt)	3.71	1.420
24	Globalization (adopt)	3.68	1.471
32	Power (adopt)	3.66	1.412
23	Feminism (adopt)	3.57	1.480
2	Casual speech (adopt)	3.37	1.376
28	Language diversity (adopt)	3.36	1.387
8	Sociolect (adopt)	3.31	1.484
21	Ethnicity (adopt)	3.26	1.451
27	Language choice (adopt)	3.25	1.491
35	Sexism (adopt)	3.20	1.537
7	Codification (adopt)	3.15	1.428
26	Language attitude (adopt)	3.13	1.412
29	Lingua franca (adopt)	3.11	1.414
14	Gender (adopt)	3.07	1.515
18	Language death (adopt)	3.04	1.539
9	Idiolect (adopt)	3.03	1.460
30	Mock language (adopt)	2.99	1.474
10	Linguistic revival (adopt)	2.97	1.482
17	Language shift (adopt)	2.94	1.476
20	Elite (adopt)	2.94	1.577
19	Language reform (adopt)	2.86	1.465
11	Code-mixing (adopt)	2.85	1.385
15	Community of practice (adopt)	2.83	1.460
4	Diglossia (adopt)	2.70	1.419
-	Adoption	2.67	.971
6	Jargon (adopt)	2.59	1.449
25	Honorific (adopt)	2.59	1.460
5	Immersion (adopt)	2.52	1.343
1	Code-switching (adopt)	2.46	1.416
16	Linguistic imperialism (adopt)	2.41	1.441
13	Acrolect (adopt)	2.27	1.362
3	Pidgin (adopt)	2.11	1.290
12	Corpus planning (adopt)	2.10	1.272

As provided by the survey respondents, the mean value for usage was 2.51 (out of 5), meaning that the respondents demonstrated a low frequency of use (50%) of the complete list of target terms. In other words, many of the participants had hardly used most of the target terms discussed in this study. In terms of major, English language students (2.73 out of 5) more frequently used the target terms than the translation students (2.27 out of 5) did, as revealed by a t-test ($\alpha < 0.05$). As for gender, there were no statistically significant differences between males and females in terms of their usage of the selected localized terms ($\alpha < 0.315$).

The results indicate that the mean value for proficiency was 2.73 (out of 5), meaning that the respondents showed overall a low level of proficiency (55%) with the complete list of target terms. In other words, many of the participants were only partially able to use Arabicized term within correct contexts. In terms of major, English language students (2.86 out of 5) were significantly more able to use the target terms in an informed way than the translation students (2.58 out of 5), as revealed by a t-test ($\alpha < 0.05$). As for gender, there were no statistically significant differences between males and females in terms of their proficiency of the selected localized terms ($\alpha < 0.120$).

The mean value for adoption was 2.67 (out of 5), meaning that the respondents showed overall a low level of adoption (53%) of the complete list of target terms. In other words, many of the participants could hardly use Arabicized terms repetitively, consistently and acceptably among other localized alternatives. In terms of major, English language students (2.84 out of 5) were significantly more endorsing of the target terms than the translation students (2.47 out of 5), as revealed by a t-test statistical test ($\alpha < 0.05$). As for gender, there were no statistically significant differences between males and females in terms of their adoption of the target localized terms ($\alpha < 0.242$.).

6.6.3 Correlation among the assessment criteria

In this section, the correlation among the assessment criteria (knowledge, evaluation, usage, proficiency and adoption) is presented and discussed to reveal how each assessment criterion interplays with the other four criteria in regard to the participants' assessment of Arabicized terms.

As shown in Table 6.6, there are statistically significant positive correlations at ($\alpha = 0.01$) between the five variables (i.e., criteria). In other words, the more familiar students are with a particular term, the more positive an evaluation (i.e., acceptance) they hold toward the term, the more frequently they use the term, the more informed they are about the contextual use of the term and the more adopting they are of the term, in the sense that students use the Arabicized term consistently, repetitively and acceptably.

Breaking down the results by major (English vs. translation), the findings still reveal a statistically significant correlation among the five variables for both major groups, as evident in Table 6.7 and Table 6.8. However, the correlation between these variables was mainly higher for English language students than for the translation students.

Table 6.6 Correlations (all students)

		Knowledge	Evaluation	Usage	Proficiency	Adoption
Knowledge	Pearson Correlation	1	.582(**)	.647(**)	.406(**)	.401(**)
	Sig. (2-tailed)	.	.000	.000	.000	.000
	N	182	182	181	182	182
Evaluation	Pearson Correlation	.582(**)	1	.485(**)	.525(**)	.554(**)
	Sig. (2-tailed)	.000	.	.000	.000	.000
	N	182	182	181	182	182
Usage	Pearson Correlation	.647(**)	.485(**)	1	.570(**)	.577(**)
	Sig. (2-tailed)	.000	.000	.	.000	.000
	N	181	181	181	181	181
Proficiency	Pearson Correlation	.406(**)	.525(**)	.570(**)	1	.607(**)
	Sig. (2-tailed)	.000	.000	.000	.	.000
	N	182	182	181	182	182
Adoption	Pearson Correlation	.401(**)	.554(**)	.577(**)	.607(**)	1
	Sig. (2-tailed)	.000	.000	.000	.000	.
	N	182	182	181	182	182

** Correlation is significant at the 0.01 level (2-tailed).

Table 6.7 Correlations (Translation students)

		Knowledge	Evaluation	Usage	Proficiency	Adoption
Knowledge	Pearson Correlation	1	.579(**)	.562(**)	.255(*)	.341(**)
	Sig. (2-tailed)	.	.000	.000	.018	.001
	N	86	86	85	86	86
Evaluation	Pearson Correlation	.579(**)	1	.307(**)	.277(**)	.353(**)
	Sig. (2-tailed)	.000	.	.004	.010	.001
	N	86	86	85	86	86
Usage	Pearson Correlation	.562(**)	.307(**)	1	.314(**)	.361(**)
	Sig. (2-tailed)	.000	.004	.	.003	.001
	N	85	85	85	85	85
Proficiency	Pearson Correlation	.255(*)	.277(**)	.314(**)	1	.337(**)
	Sig. (2-tailed)	.018	.010	.003	.	.002
	N	86	86	85	86	86
Adoption	Pearson Correlation	.341(**)	.353(**)	.361(**)	.337(**)	1
	Sig. (2-tailed)	.001	.001	.001	.002	.
	N	86	86	85	86	86

** Correlation is significant at the 0.01 level (2-tailed).

6.6.4 Attitudes toward the Arabicization of sociolinguistic terms

The results indicate that the students had a moderately positive attitude toward the localization of sociolinguistic terms and the Arabicization process in general. As evident in the first two statements in Table 6.9, the participants demonstrated a sentimental attachment to Arabicized terms and associated their use with Pan-Arabism or Arab nationalism. Moreover, the participants demonstrated an instrumental attachment to these localized terms in the academic domain, stating that Arabicized sociolinguistic terms facilitate the interactive communication with their colleagues and professors at the department.

Table 6.8 Correlations (English language students)

		Knowledge	Evaluation	Usage	Proficiency	Adoption
Knowledge	Pearson Correlation	1	.594(**)	.658(**)	.459(**)	.395(**)
	Sig. (2-tailed)		.000	.000	.000	.000
	N	96	96	96	96	96
Evaluation	Pearson Correlation	.594(**)	1	.580(**)	.653(**)	.649(**)
	Sig. (2-tailed)	.000		.000	.000	.000
	N	96	96	96	96	96
Usage	Pearson Correlation	.658(**)	.580(**)	1	.670(**)	.634(**)
	Sig. (2-tailed)	.000	.000		.000	.000
	N	96	96	96	96	96
Proficiency	Pearson Correlation	.459(**)	.653(**)	.670(**)	1	.715(**)
	Sig. (2-tailed)	.000	.000	.000		.000
	N	96	96	96	96	96
Adoption	Pearson Correlation	.395(**)	.649(**)	.634(**)	.715(**)	1
	Sig. (2-tailed)	.000	.000	.000	.000	
	N	96	96	96	96	96

** Correlation is significant at the 0.01 level (2-tailed).

Although the students believed that Arabicized sociolinguistic terms are clear and precise, they felt that these terms need to be developed and rephrased. The participants strongly believed that Arabicized sociolinguistic terms help the Arabic language to cope with developments in contemporary life. Despite the students' feelings of enthusiasm about Arabicized sociolinguistic terms, the participants' responses to Statements 10 and 11 reflect low actual use of these terms. The participating students do not use Arabicized sociolinguistic terms frequently in their discussions with their friends, nor do they seek to spread and develop these terms. These results indicate a separation between beliefs and actual use.

6.7 Conclusion and recommendations

6.7.1 Conclusion

In this section, results of this study were discussed in light of related literature in an attempt to come up with sound conclusions and a set of recommendations for future researchers and decision makers (e.g., the Jordan Academy of Arabic).

Table 6.9 Attitudes toward the Arabicization of sociolinguistic terms

No.	Statement	Estimation
1	My self-confidence increases when using Arabicized sociolinguistic terms.	3.83
2	My belonging to the Arabic language is the motive to accept Arabicized sociolinguistic terms.	3.78
3	I think that Arabicized sociolinguistic terms facilitate interactive communication with my colleagues and professors at the department.	3.93
4	I think that unifying Arabicized sociolinguistic terms helps in distributing them in the Arab World.	4.06
5	I think that the shorter the syllables are for Arabicized sociolinguistic terms, the more they become distributed.	4.07
6	I think that Arabicized sociolinguistic terms are clear and precise.	3.33
7	I think that some Arabicized sociolinguistic terms need to be developed and rephrased.	3.62
8	My colleagues respect me when I use Arabicized sociolinguistic terms.	3.36
9	I think that Arabicized sociolinguistic terms help the Arabic language cope with the developments in contemporary life.	4.00
10	In my discussions with my friends, I frequently use Arabicized sociolinguistic terms.	2.98
11	I am seeking to spread and develop Arabicized sociolinguistic terms.	3.23

This study aimed at assessing the familiarity, adequacy and use of a selected set of Arabicized sociolinguistic terms in light of Cooper's (1989) assessment criteria: knowledge, evaluation, usage, adoption and proficiency.

Overall, results revealed moderately low levels of knowledge (mean = 3.3/5; 66%), evaluation (mean = 3.4/5; 68%), usage (mean = 3/5; 60%), proficiency (mean = 3/5; 60%) and adoption (mean = 3/5; 60%) for the examined Arabicized sociolinguistic terms. In terms of this overall pattern, results of this study are in line with results of previous studies (Al-Smadi 1997; Diknash 1998; Al-Oliemat 1998; Halloush 2000; Mahasneh 2002; Al Sakran 2004; Al-Abed Al-Haq and

AL-Essa 2016b). Generally speaking, low responses in the domains of knowledge, usage, proficiency and adoption suggest inadequacy in terms of the Arabicization initiatives on the part of researchers, sociolinguistics course offerings and institutional efforts to localize sociolinguistic terms and promote them.

However, looking deeper into the response differences among these components, the highest score was for the evaluation criterion, compared with the other criteria. Unlike Al-Smadi (1997), Halloush (2000) and Mahasneh (2002), the selected Arabicized sociolinguistic terms were accepted by participants as good equivalents for the English terms. In other words, the idea of Arabicization was positively evaluated and perceived as adequate by the students, reflecting good lexical correspondence.

Recalling that the participating students believed that Arabicized sociolinguistic terms are clear and precise, it may be reasonable to say that the main problem with Arabicization is not with attitude (i.e., evaluation) but with lack of familiarity (i.e., knowledge), which leads to weak usage, proficiency and adoption. These observations are supported by the students' responses to the attitude statements, where they expressed a sentimental attachment to Arabic and an overall positive attitude toward the localization of sociolinguistic terms and the Arabicization process as whole. This places a burden on researchers, professors of linguistics and relevant institutions to raise awareness regarding these terms and enhance proficiency leading to adoption.

Results of this study and previous studies (e.g., Al-Smadi 1997; Diknash 1998; Al-Abed Al-Haq and Al-Essa 2016a) reveal a contradiction between beliefs and attitudes on the one hand and practices and usage on the other hand. While most of the respondents expressed positive attitudes toward Arabicized terms and the Arabicization process in general, they preferred using the English terms. This contradiction may reflect a conflict between the sentimental attachment that users hold toward their mother tongue (i.e., Arabic) and their culture and the instrumental value of the English terms. However, in some studies (e.g., Halloush (2000) and Mahasneh (2002)), the attitudes toward Arabicized terms were clearly negative and the Arabicization process was considered unnecessary and useless. The negative attitudes reported in Halloush (2000) and Mahasneh (2002) may be attributed to the fact that these studies investigated highly technical terms (medical terms and IT terms, respectively) for which English language is the main medium of instruction at the university level and for which English is the dominant language.

Although students believed that Arabicized sociolinguistic terms are clear and precise, they felt that these terms need to be developed and rephrased. The participants strongly believed that Arabicized sociolinguistic terms help the Arabic language to cope with developments in contemporary life. Despite students' feelings of enthusiasm about Arabicized sociolinguistic terms, the participants' responses to Statements 11 and 12 reflect low use of these terms. The participating students do not use Arabicized sociolinguistic terms frequently in their discussions with their friends, nor do they seek to spread and develop these terms. These results indicate a separation between beliefs and actual use.

As for the reasons why the Jordan Academy of Arabic has not yet localized and published the sociolinguistic terms, participants provided several explanations including the absence of actual usage in real life, the weak attention at both university and community levels and the lack of sponsoring agencies for these terms. As for the means and methods suggested for Arabicization of sociolinguistic terms by the Jordan Academy of Arabic, participants mentioned promoting the recurrent use of these terms at the personal level, increasing the attention to these terms through offering university specialized courses in sociolinguistics, attempting to promote these terms and spreading them throughout the community and relating these terms to daily life.

6.7.2 Recommendations

In light of the results of this study, the following recommendations are provided to specialists (i.e., professors of linguistics and researchers) as well as relevant institutions, including the academies of Arabic language:

1. More efforts need to be exerted in raising awareness with existing Arabicized sociolinguistic terms among students, particularly linguistics and translation students.
2. The current sociolinguistic terms need to be improved to attract attention in order to sound appealing to users, especially students.
3. Feedback should be elicited from students and users in general in the process of localizing sociolinguistic terms to ensure their adoption and endorsement. This could be implemented at university campuses or through workshops coordinated by the Jordan Academy of Arabic. Alternatively, written surveys and questionnaires may be distributed to stakeholders (i.e., students, professors and researchers) to elicit their feedback.
4. Decision makers should capitalize on the positive attitudes that students have toward Arabicization and should exert an effort to create positive attitudes when not evident in the first place (in technical domains in particular). In technical domains, researchers and linguists should emphasize the fact that Arabic is as adequate as English in terms of conveying and communicating the specialized message.
5. As results revealed lower levels of sociolinguistic terminology mastery for translation students compared with English language students, it is recommended that departments of translation include sociolinguistics in their course offerings.
6. Sociolinguistics, as a subfield of linguistics, is believed to be essential in helping translation students in placing language in its cultural context.

To conclude, the following framework is proposed as an exemplary model for term planning, as adopted from Cooper (1989) and further modified to suit the field of terminology planning and term translation and Arabicization:

1 What actors, for example, formal elites, the influential, counter-elites and non-elite policy implementers?
2 Attempt to influence what behaviors?
3 Of which people?
4 For what ends?
5 Under what conditions?
6 By what means?
7 Through what decision-making process?
8 With what effects?

Note

1 Based on Al-Abed Al-Haq and Al-Essa's (2016b) conclusion that the perception of Arabized business terms was affected by their gender, the current study aims to find out how the five criteria of acceptability (knowledge, usage, evaluation, adoption and proficiency) are influenced by gender (cf. "Literature Review", this volume, section 6.2).

References

Abo Abdo, Mohammad. 1984. *Atta'areeb wa mashakiloh* (in Arabic). Rabat: Institute for Studies and Research on Arabization.

Al-Abed Al-Haq, Fawwaz, M. 1998a. Language Planning and Term Planning: Criteria for acceptability. In *Proceedings of the International Conference on Professional Communication and Knowledge Transfer, Terminology Work and Knowledge Transfer*. (2). Vienna, Austria. August 24–26, 1998, pp. 2–19.

Al-Abed Al-Haq, Fawwaz, M. 1998b. Towards a Theoretical Framework for the Study of Planning Arabicization. In A. Shunnaq, C. Dollerup and M. Saraireh (Eds.), *Issues in Translation*. Irbid, Jordan: Irbid National University and Jordanian Translators' Association, pp. 53–68.

Al-Abed Al-Haq, Fawwaz, M. 2015. The Attitudes of Governmental and Civic Societies Towards Arabicization: A Case Study of Legislative Authority in Jordan. *Jordan Journal of Islamic Studies*, 11(1), 485–518.

Al-Abed Al-Haq, Fawwaz, M. and Abu-Melhim, Abdel-Rahman, H. 2019. *A Dictionary of Sociolinguistics* (Translated from English into Arabic). Riyadh, Saudi Arabia: King Abdullah Bin Abdulaziz International Center for the Arabic Language.

Al-Abed Al-Haq, Fawwaz, M. and Al-Essa, Sarah. 2016a. *The Role of Term Planning in Nation Building: Business Terms Arabicization, a Case in Point, Language Planning and Language Policy*, (2). Riyadh, Saudi Arabia: King Abdullah Bin Abdulaziz International Center for the Arabic Language, pp. 7–41.

Al-Abed Al-Haq, Fawwaz, M. and Al-Essa, Sarah. 2016b. Arabicization of Business Terms from Terminology Planning Perspective. *International Journal of English Linguistics*, 6(1), 150.

Al-Didawi, Muḥammad. 2007. *The Concepts of Translation: Arabisation Perspective to Transfer Knowledge* (in Arabic). Casablanca, Morocco: Arab Cultural Center.

Al-Oliemat, Ahmad. 1998. *The Attitudes of the Jordanian Members of Parliament towards Arabicization from a Language Planning Perspective.* M.A. Thesis. Irbid, Jordan: Yarmouk University.

Al-Sakran, Laila Sameh. 2004. *Arabicization of Agricultural Terms from a Terminology Planning Perspective.* M.A. Thesis. Irbid, Jordan: Yarmouk University.

Al-Sayadi, Muḥammad al-Mungi. 1980. *Arabisation in the Arab World* (in Arabic). Beirut, Lebanon: Center for Arab University Studies.

Al-Smadi, Muhammad Mansour. 1997. *Language Planning and Arabicization of Military Terms.* M.A. Thesis. Irbid, Jordan: Yarmouk University.

Catford, John Cunnison. 1965. *A Linguistic Theory of Translation.* London, UK: Oxford University Press.

Cooper, R. (1989). *Language Planning and Social Change.* Cambridge, UK: Cambridge University Press.

Coulmas, Florian (ed.) 1997. *The Handbook of Sociolinguistics.* London, UK: Blackwell Publishing Ltd.

Diknash, Sahar Jamil. 1998. *An Evaluative Study of Arabicized Nursing Terms from a Language Planning Perspective.* M.A. Thesis. Irbid, Jordan: Yarmouk University.

El-Fadni, Suliman Issameldin. 2004. *Arabicization in Higher Education: The Case of Medical Colleges in Sudan.* Ph.D. Dissertation. Leicester, UK: University of Leicester.

El-Khafaifi, Hussein. 1985. *The Role of the Cairo Academy in Coining Arabic Scientific Terminology: A Historical and Linguistic Evaluation.* Ph.D. Dissertation. Salt Lake City, UT: The University of Utah.

Emran, Esam. 1993. Etymology: The Science of Language and Technology. (In Arabic). *Journal of Al-Lisan Al-Arabi* 37, 169–174.

Farghal, Mohammed. 2012. *Advanced Issues in Arabic-English Translation Studies.* Kuwait: Academic Publication Council, University of Kuwait.

Halloush, Lana Abdullah. 2000. *Arabicization of Medical Terms in Light of Language and Terminology Planning.* M.A. Thesis. Ramtha, Jordan: The University of Science and Technology.

Hassan, Bahaa-eddin Abulhassan. 2014. *Between English and Arabic: A Practical Course in Translation.* Cambridge, UK: Cambridge Scholars Publishing.

Holmes, Janet. 2013. Doing Discourse Analysis in Sociolinguistics. In J. Holmes and K. Hazen (Eds.), *Research Methods in Sociolinguistics: A Practical Guide.* London, UK: Wiley-Blackwell, pp. 177–193.

Jahr, Ernst Hakon. 1992. Sociolinguistics: Minorities and Sociolinguistics. In W. Bright (Ed.), *International Encyclopedia of Linguistics.* Oxford: Oxford University Press, pp. 169–188.

Jaied, Wamidh Munther. 2010. *Aspectos Semánticos de la Hipérbole en Algunos Textos Árabes Traducidos al Castellano* (in Spanish). Ph.D. Dissertation. Granada, Spain: Universidad de Granada.

Jernudd, Rubin. 1977. *Language Planning Processes* (No. 21). Berlin, Germany: Walter de Gruyter.

Khalifah, Abdel-Kareem. 1978. *The Arabic Language and Arabisation in Modern Times* (in Arabic). Amman, Jordan: Jordan Academy of Arabic.

Kotler, Philip and Gerald, Zaltman. 1971. Social Marketing and Approach to Planned Social Change. *Journal of Marketing* 35, 3–12.

Mahasneh, Basilah Mefleh. 2002. *Evaluation of the Renditions of Internet Terms into Arabic*. M.A. Thesis. Irbid, Jordan: Yarmouk University.
Newmark, Peter. 1988. *A Textbook of Translation*. London, UK: Prentice Hall.
Nida, Eugene. 1964. *Towards a Science of Translating*. Leiden, Netherlands: Brill.
Pool, Jonathan. 1974. Mass Opinion on Language Policy: The Case of Canada. In J. Fishman (Ed.), *Advances in Language Planning*. The Hague, Netherlands: Mouton, pp. 481–492.
Sager, Juan. 1990. *A Practical Course in Terminology Processing*. Amsterdam, Netherlands: John Benjamin Publishing Company.
Shunnaq, Abdullah and Farghal, Mohammed. 1999. *Translation with Reference to English and Arabic: A Practical Guide*. Irbid, Jordan: Dar Al-Hilal for Translation.
Swan, Joan, Deumert, Ana, Lillis, Theresa and Mesthrie, Rajend. 2004. *A Dictionary of Sociolinguistics*. Edinburgh, UK: Edinburgh University Press.

7 New forms of translation
The need for new professional profiles

Lahousseine Id-Youss, Abied Alsulaiman and Frieda Steurs

7.1 Introduction

Translation constitutes an important means of communication. It allows people from different linguistic, cultural, and civilizational backgrounds to interact with each other, a reality which would be impossible had it not been for this practice. Through its diachronic forms, it even makes it possible for people belonging to different historical eras to be understood and appreciated. This communicative aspect in all its manifestations seems to be the element which all forms of translation share, regardless of the technological development of the translation product in question.

Translation has proved to have a great deal of economic and social benefits. Its contribution to the diversification of markets is undeniable. No sooner does a piece of software get localized than new markets and new economic horizons are created for the program developers. At the social level, dubbing, subtitling, and audiovisual description have allowed families and individuals who belong to different speech communities and different social categories to enjoy their favorite films and series. Translation also plays a vital role in ensuring security. Court translation or court interpreting can provide good examples of this, but the prototypical example could perhaps be wiretap interpreting.

Moreover, knowing what is going on in the outside world heavily depends on translation. Thanks to news translation and to the technical relatedness of the different parts of the world through Internet and satellites, people can theoretically follow any event all over the globe. Bielsa and Bassnett (2008) have convincingly demonstrated the fundamental role that news translation with its revolutionized modes plays in this regard. Global news agencies receive news in different languages, and editors must come up with a target text based possibly on multiple source texts and thus posing serious challenges to the traditional view of translation.

Another means by which news stories are spread around the world is through websites, and the localization of these networks of web pages forms an integral component of translation technologies. When Tim Berners-Lee developed the World Wide Web, his hope was to develop a pool of information which could be accessed from any part of the world. It is true that this dream technically became a reality by bringing the Internet and Hypertext technologies together and that any published website can be accessed anywhere so long as one has Internet connection. However, the limitations of the idea to maximally achieve its objective are obvious due to linguistic barriers. How can people benefit from the content of a website – even if they have access to it – if it is written in a language they do not understand? With translation, however, the magnificent idea of a World Wide Web could be realized in terms of both form and content.

Translation methods and formats have evolved drastically over the last decades as a natural consequence of the rapid technological developments. New text genres have emerged posing new challenges and calling on translators to be equipped with new skills and competences, the least of which is the ability to skilfully use computers, which is also referred to as being "tech savvy". The market is in great need for excellent language specialists with technological skills. Some of these new translational forms include wiretap interpreting, software localization, website localization, etc.

In this chapter, we will briefly present some of these new modes of translation, focusing on the extra-linguistic issues associated with them. Linguistic matters are taken for granted in this kind of translation, and the focus is geared toward the technical knowledge which translators are expected to be equipped with. It is indispensable for them to be competent in using computers and efficiently managing files, as some translation projects could be made up of hundreds of files with different filename extensions.

Taking language for granted should not be understood to mean that language is less important in these new translation areas. What is meant is that translators are required to be equipped with additional competences other than linguistic skills, which entails that new professional profiles should be developed where technical knowledge is united with linguistic and cultural knowledge. This could perhaps be the reason for the poor linguistic quality of some localized applications into Arabic, as reported by Id-Youss and Alsulaiman (2019). They demonstrated that technical aspects in software localization sometimes take precedence over linguistic concerns.

This chapter is structurally divided into four sections. The first one addresses some matters relating to wiretap interpreting, and the second sheds some light on the area of website localization. In the third section, some aspects of software localization are introduced. Finally, the fourth one is concerned with two modes of screen translation, viz. subtitling and dubbing.

7.2 Wiretap interpreting

Wiretap interpreting can be seen as one of the most recent forms of translation, and that can perhaps be one of the reasons why it is not yet explored in ample depth from both theoretical and practical perspectives. This can also be partly attributed to the fact that it takes place in secret, confidential circles and that it is not readily available for the public, as is usually the case for most other translation forms, we know. In this section, we will attempt to highlight some aspects of wiretap interpreting, with a focus on the legal implications it brings about and some of the challenges associated with it.

Wiretap interpreting can be defined as the rendering of the content of telephone conversations intercepted by authorities from one language into another. Obviously, the need for translators can be made urgent because these telephone conversations are sometimes held in foreign languages. The term "interpreting" is perhaps preferred over "translation" because the translator deals with oral material, where an oral source message is translated into a written target message. It must be stressed, however, that this form of translation shares some aspects of written translation and some features of interpreting. For a detailed overview, please look at Salaets et al. (2015).

Wiretapping, the practice of intercepting phone calls by the police, can be seen as one of the consequences imposed by globalization, where products, technologies, and information are spread across national borders. According to Diffie and Landau (2010), globalization became possible thanks to the high-quality, reliable, and inexpensive telephone service which has been made possible by optical fibers and computerized central offices.

Some of the delicate matters associated with this form of translation originate from the practice of wiretapping in general, and they concern the tension between the concepts "privacy" and "security" (Salaets et al. 2015). While privacy in most democratic countries is regarded as a universally recognized right of any individual, ensuring security by identifying criminal networks is both a social and a legal necessity. The complexity here lies in how we can ensure security without violating people's private lives through listening to their telephone conversations.

Salaets et al. (2015) demonstrate that the right to privacy is granted to human beings by legislation and declarations on various levels: national (e.g., Belgian legislation), international (e.g., European legislation), and universal (e.g., Universal Declaration of Human Rights). Flaherty (2014) defines "privacy" as the right to autonomy, the right to control information about oneself, and the right to limit access to that information. Moreover, privacy means the right to enjoy solitude, intimacy, and anonymity.

By the same token, laws exist worldwide which provide for the protection of public safety, social order, and national security. Individuals have the right to feel safe and secure. The delicate situation occurs in the event of a conflict between privacy and security. Should we opt for privacy at the expense of security, or the other way around? The answer to the question in non-democratic countries seems to be rather straightforward, as privacy is of little importance. In countries where the rule of law has the upper hand, however, the choice does not seem to be easy.

Different legal systems and jurisdictions handle the tension between these seemingly contradictory notions differently. For instance, in Belgium, wiretapping can be justified under two conditions. First, evidence of strong suspicions that someone is committing a criminal offence must be offered, and the offences that are considered weighty enough for this measure are listed in the Belgian Code of Criminal Procedure (COC; I, article 90ter, §2). Second, wiretapping can only be allowed if providing evidence by another means of investigation is not possible (I, article 90ter, COC) (Salaets et al. 2015).

Now that these legal implications have been demonstrated, we shed some light on the practice of wiretap interpreting from a procedural point of view. The steps in which this form of translation consists may vary from place to place, but the three major ones include language verification, synopsis making, and the translation of the pertinent conversation. The first task that the tap interpreter must perform is to decide whether or not the recorded material falls within the scope of his or her linguistic specialization. Next, a brief synopsis of all the recorded files must be made in the target language in order for the police to determine whether or not there is enough evidence for the alleged crime. If a specific conversation or part thereof contains the sought-for evidence, the tap interpreter renders it in full into the target language (Salaets et al. 2015).

Some of the challenges that the tap interpreter encounters include interpreting para-verbal information and coping with the code language. Para-verbal information/elements refer to issues such as the tone of the speakers, their voice pitch, and the noises which may interfere with the quality of the audio fragment. The tone constitutes an important piece of information that the tap interpreter is supposed to report. A more complex task is perhaps identifying and understanding the code language. One of the ways in which code language can manifest itself is when speakers assign privately agreed upon meanings to lexical items which have nothing to do with those meanings. For instance, in some places, the word "fish" is used to mean "drugs". Obviously, the purpose behind using these non-conventional linguistic strategies by criminals is to mislead the police who may be listening to their conversation. It must be stressed, however, that only experienced tap interpreters can adequately interpret this kind of linguistic usage.

7.3 Website localization

According to Singh (2011: 7) website localization can be defined as the adaptation of websites to conform to the "linguistic, cultural, technical, functional, legal, and other locale-specific requirements of the target market". Even if this definition points to the adaptation of a website, the unit of translation is in fact the web page. Unlike traditional forms of translation, this localization area requires the translator to be equipped with a great deal of extra-linguistic knowledge. In the following paragraphs, we will attempt to shed light on some of these technological extra-linguistic matters such as the language of the web and the structure of the web page.

Web pages consist of two major parts: the header and the body, respectively, where the content of the header section is not generally seen by the human reader (Weideman 2009). Most of the content which is usually seen by users can be found in the body section. The header is reserved for matters such as internal style statements, Java Script instructions, alignment issues, etc.

The language of the web is known as HTML, which stands for Hypertext Markup Language. It defines a set of embedded instructions, called tags, that control how information is to be displayed by web browsers and how browsers are to react to certain events. Tags are words or letters placed inside angle brackets "<>". For instance, the <table> tag is used to create a table. We distinguish two kinds of tags, viz. opening tags and closing tags. Closing tags are structured differently by adding a slash to the tag "</table>".

The HTML language covers three major areas, namely, content, style, and Java Script. The word (content) here refers to the textual and graphical elements presented on a web page. From this perspective, web pages consist of headings, paragraphs, tables, different types of lists – ordered lists, unordered lists, and definition lists – links, images, videos, form fields, different types of buttons – radio buttons, submit buttons, checkboxes, etc. Each of these elements has its own HTML tag that enables it to be displayed properly by a browser (Id-Youss et al. 2014).

The aspect of style settles issues relating to colors, font family, and font size, etc. We distinguish three stylistic categories, viz. inline style, internal style, and external style sheet. While an inline stylistic feature is placed inside a specific HTML element and applies to that specific element, internal styles are placed within the head of the document and apply to the whole web page. A cascading style sheet (CSS), on the other hand, constitutes an independent file with a CSS extension containing all the specified style statements, which can apply to multiple webpages. The connection between each webpage and the external style sheet is established through a link inserted inside the head section (Id-Youss et al. 2014). Java Script, the third element mentioned earlier, is a powerful web programming language in comparison with plain HTML. It "can recognize and respond to user events such as mouse clicks, form input and page navigation" (Khosrow-Pour 1999: 35).

XML (Extensive Markup Language) is yet another important language to invoke in the context of websites. Like HTML, XML is a World Wide Web Consortium Standard, but it allows creators to create their own tags (Pagani 2005). Its purpose is to store any kind of structured information. It is perhaps useful here to point out that some versions of HTML, viz. XHTML (Extensive Hypertext Markup Language) have adopted some rules from XML practice, some of which include tag case sensitiveness, tag closure, and tags' proper nesting (Id-Youss et al. 2014).

Within the source code page, localizers must distinguish between what is localizable and what is not. As a rule of thumb, any text that appears on the screen when the page is launched must be translated. However, it must be noted that some text could be hidden, and it might only appear as a reaction to clicking a button or refreshing the webpage. That sort of text is also supposed to be rendered into the target language. Localizers are not supposed to change HTML tags except for a few exceptions, and their intervention has to be conscious and accurate. As an example, when a website is to be localized from or into Arabic, then the language Right to Left tag <rtl> has to replace or be replaced by the Left to Right tag <ltr> (Id-Youss et al. 2014). Also, the issues of "text expansion" must be mentioned here. Arabic and English, for example, are very compact languages, while German, Hungarian, or Finnish translation of English or Arabic source texts can be 25% or more longer. In software localization, where text fields of particular programs such as games are quantitatively predefined, "text expansion" could be problematic. Localizers are in this case committed to make some compromises by summarizing the lexical or linguistic units appearing on screen. Similar compromises are also done when subtitling films into languages where phenomena such as "text expansion" appear.

To conclude, website localization is a new and interdisciplinary domain. If translation in general has a bearing on linguistics, cultural studies, and language engineering, web localization applications are influenced by even more domains. Some of these domains include international business and marketing, web development, web usability, desktop publishing and graphical design, philosophy, etc. We hope that the short overview here offers a good picture of some of the technicalities involved in localizing websites.

7.4 Software localization

Software localization prototypically falls within the realm of translation technologies. It can safely be described as one of the most technical translation areas. Undertaking such a localization project calls on the localizer to be equipped with a great deal of technical knowledge relating to how programs work and how to use the localization tools available in the market.

According to Kearns (2006), software localization can be defined as the adaptation of computer software packages (user interfaces and resource files as well as their associated documentation) in order for the software to work effectively in another language and in order to suit the requirements of different language markets. Based on this definition, the translation project of a piece of software can be divided into two major parts, viz. the computer program itself and the written documentation, which includes help files, the user manual, etc.

A software is a set of programs developed to carry out operations for a specified task. These programs consist of step-by-step instructions telling the computer how to carry out operations for a specific job (Gupta 2008). One of the aims behind developing a piece of software is to enable "users to perform specific information-processing activities" (Bocij et al. 2008: 125).

Computer programs are sometimes received by localizers as source code and sometimes in binary format (Edwards and Kulczycki 2009). While source code is human-readable computer language (Grossman 2009), and it can be accessed by means of simple editors such as NotePad, binary files are programs or a "data file in machine-readable form" (Nandhakumar 2011: 42), which can only be accessed using specialized localization tools. It must be noted, however, that source codes too can be accessed and translated using specialized tools. These tools are very helpful, as they mark out codes that should not be altered (Id-Youss et al. 2014).

Source code consists of lists of strings, some of which are translatable into the target language, others not. Translatable strings are textual elements that appear in the software user interface when the program is launched for use. Untranslatable strings, on the other hand, are pieces of code used by the computer to execute specific actions, and localizers do not have the right to interfere with the codes, except for some very limited areas, because that can lead to bugs later on in the target version of the software. Furthermore, translatable text is usually placed inside double quotes, but this guideline must be followed carefully because some untranslatable elements could also sometimes be found there (Id-Youss et al. 2014).

From a structural point of view, a piece of software is made up of a number of sections such as menus, drop-down lists, dialog boxes, and string tables. String tables can be seen as the most challenging sections as they contain strings that appear dynamically in combination with other events. Such a dynamic insertion of different elements from different areas in the program with a view to forming a meaningful linguistic unit does not seem easy, especially when the software is to be translated into languages such as Arabic, whose syntax requires agreement between adjectives and the nouns they modify in terms of number, gender, and case, etc.

To cope up with these challenges, specialized localization tools have been developed to adapt graphical user interfaces, that is, dialog boxes, menus, and messages that are displayed on a computer screen (Somers 2003). These localization applications help extract translatable strings and protect untranslatable ones; moreover, they help in resizing dialog boxes and menu items, as they provide the WYSIWYG mode (what you see is what you get). Some of these applications include Passolo Corel Alchemy Catalyst and RC-WinTrans (Somers 2003).

Once the program is fully localized and its associated documentation translated, it proceeds to the last localization phase, viz. the testing stage. The purpose behind software testing is to evaluate the quality of the target version and to ensure that the program does not contain any bugs, be they translation problems or technical ones. Bugs subdivide into functional bugs and cosmetic ones. While functional bugs refer to those errors which interfere with the proper functioning of the software, cosmetic ones are minor problems relating to spelling mistakes, grammar errors, translation issues, text alignment, etc. At the end of this stage, detailed reports are written providing detailed information about the type of every bug and its position in the software. These reports are valuable tools for software debugging (Id-Youss et al. 2014).

7.5 Screen translation

In film making, screen translation constitutes yet another translation form that heavily depends on specialized tools. This concept, which is also termed as film translation or audiovisual translation, encompasses a number of domains, viz. subtitling, dubbing, audiovisual description, etc. The present section will briefly shed some light on the first two types. Subtitling and dubbing differ from each other from both semiotic and linguistic perspectives. Semiotically speaking, while the former is diasemiotic, the latter is isosemiotic. Similarly, while subtitling can be both intralingual and interlingual, dubbing is an interlingual process par excellence.

Subtitling is defined as the "process of transferring the meaning of a piece of speech in a movie or TV series by means of written translation usually placed at the bottom of the screen" (Omar et al. 2009: 181). These written translations are known as subtitles, which are textual versions of the dialogues in films, where the gist of the dialogue is given (Shastri 2011). According to Liu (2014), compared with traditional translation, subtitling raises new challenges such as the constraints of space and time, which are inherent in the subtitling process, the visual conventions as well as the shift of modes from speech to writing.

Another layer of complexity lies in the fact that translation here is not always from one language into another, as is traditionally known, but it can also be within the same language. It is for this reason that Gottlieb (1997) distinguishes two types of subtitling, viz. interlingual and intralingual subtitling. Intralingual translation involves the change of mode only, that is, from speech to writing, and it targets people with hearing impairment – whether partial or total – as well as language learners and karaoke singers. It is interesting to note that this translation mode is common in countries such as the United Kingdom and the United States (Liu 2014). Interlingual translation, on the other hand, targets people belonging to different linguistic communities.

Temporal constraints manifest themselves in the synchronization of subtitles with the audio utterances, which seems to be a real challenge. The key notion here is that of "readability", which refers to the ease in which subtitles could be processed and understood. Thus, subtitles should not be too short nor too long. According to Panek (2010), Tomaszkiewicz (2006: 114) ascertains that subtitles should be displayed from 1.5 seconds to 6 seconds. Otherwise, the subtitle may go unnoticed if the exposure time is shorter than 1.5 seconds. Readability is also related to the level of the target audience and to their reading speed.

Specialized programs for subtitling are vital in resolving this issue and other ones. Examples of these tools include Subtitle Workshop, MovieCaptioner, and Subtitle Composer ETC. They provide subtitlers with precious help in marking where a subtitle should appear and disappear, and these markers are based on SMPTE timecode or film length depending on the nature of the product to be subtitled. SMPTE timecode, a standard defined by the Society of Motion Picture and Television Engineers, is used to label individual frames of the video or film. Frames or frame per second (FPS), which can be made accessible by these software programs, refers to the frequency at which the film's motion-picture gets run through the camera (Andersson and Geyen 2011).

The second area of screen translation which we would like to briefly present in this chapter is dubbing, which can be defined as "an isosemiotic interlinguistic translation from an oral code to another oral code" (Perego and Bruti 2015: 26). The isosemiotic aspect refers to the fact that the source and target texts in dubbing use the same communicative channel, i.e. rendering an oral text into another oral text, and this contrasts with the diasemiotic characteristic of subtitling. In this form of audiovisual translation, the sound portion of the film is first recorded separately and then synchronized with the visual components (Reid and Bojanic 2009). This way, voices of the actors in the original production are fully silenced and are replaced by the newly recorded voices speaking the language of the target audience.

From a technological point of view, dubbing visual materials requires specialized tools, and it is performed in specialized sound studios equipped with all the necessary sound equipment, including isolation booths, in order to achieve high quality sound output. Some methods of dubbing include additional dialogue recording (ADR), which is a system employed in professional audio dubbing studios, enabling "artistes to replace dialogue recorded on location with new, clean dialogue in the controlled conditions of a recording studio" (Gaskell 2003: 186).

7.6 Conclusion

By way of conclusion, we can say that the point which the five translation forms we presented in this chapter have in common is the need for the translator/interpreter to be furnished with both technical and intercultural competence. A divorce between these qualifications would not be adequate. In website localization, for instance, the translators' duty to learn about HTML, CSS, XML Java Script, etc., does not absolve them from rendering the content as professionally as should be. The same thing holds true for the other areas of translation technologies.

Thus, hiring a bilingual professional technician with no translational background to engage in one of these translation forms does not help. Similarly, paying a good translator who was trained to deal with traditional forms of translation to carry out such a task does not solve the problem either. The solution lies in putting forth adequate trainings in which interested translators can broaden their competences in order to meet the new qualification requirements established by these new translation modes. This way, we can ensure that the localized product will undoubtedly live up to the highest standards possible.

These trainings must have a concrete objective of uniting these two types of competences and to strive for striking the balance between them. Moreover, they must be updated on a regular basis so as to catch up with the rapid evolution of technology. Software applications are being developed and updated every now and then, and the new changes and challenges must be reflected there. Here we can refer to advanced postgraduate training programs or master's programs including these translation technology trainings, such as our own postgraduate program. Also, lifelong learning such as the Translation Technology Summer School we organize every first week of September is a good example of an intensive training for professional translators to become acquainted with new technology.

References

Andersson, Barry, and Geyen Janie. 2011. *The DSLR Filmmaker's Handbook: Real-world Production Techniques*. Wiley and Sons.
Bielsa, Esperança, and Susan Bassnett. 2008. *Translation in Global News*. Routledge.
Bocij, Paul, Andrew Greasley, and Simon Hickie. 2008. *Business Information Systems: Technology, Development and Management*. Pearson education.
Diffie, Whitfield, and Susan Landau. 2010. *Privacy on the Line: The Politics of Wiretapping and Encryption*. MIT Press.
Edwards, Stephen H., and Gregory Kulczycki, eds. 2009. *Formal Foundations of Reuse and Domain Engineering: 11th International Conference on Software Reuse, ICSR 2009, Falls Church, VA, USA, September 27–30. Proceedings*, Vol. 5791. Springer Science & Business Media.
Flaherty, David H. 2014. *Protecting Privacy in Surveillance Societies: The Federal Republic of Germany, Sweden, France, Canada, and the United States*. UNC Press Books.
Gaskell, Ed. 2003. *The Complete Guide to Digital Video*. Boston, MA: Muska & Lipman Publishing.
Gottlieb, Henrik. 1997. *Subtitles, Translation & Idioms*. Thesis. Copenhagen: University of Copenhagen.
Grossman, Mark. 2009. *Technology Law: What Every Business (and Business-minded Person) Needs to Know*. Scarecrow Press.
Gupta, Vikas. 2008. *Comdex 14-In-1 Computer Course Kit*, 2008 Edition (With CD). Dreamtech Press.
Id-Youss, Lahousseine, and Alsulaiman Abied. 2019. "Linguistic inferiority in software localization." In *Handbook of Terminology: Volume 2. Terminology in the Arab World 2*. John Benjamins, pp. 218–233.
Id-Youss, Lahousseine, Frieda Steurs, and Alsulaiman Abied (2014). "Translation technologies: Challenging new tasks and competences for translators." *Dragoman* 2, no. 1: 1–14.
Kearns, John. 2006. *New Vistas in Translator and Interpreter Training* (Vol. 17, No. 1). Irish Translators' and Interpreters' Association.
Khosrow-Pour, Mehdi. 1999. *Managing Information Technology Resources in Organizations in the Next Millennium*. Information Science Reference.
Liu, Dayan. 2014. "On the classification of subtitling." *Journal of Language Teaching & Research* 5, no. 5.
Nandhakumar, B. 2011. *Dictionary of Computer Networking*. Excel Books India.
Omar, Hasuria Che, Haslina Haroon, and Aniswal Abd Ghani. 2009. *The Sustainability of the Translation Field*. ITBM.

Pagani, Margherita, ed. 2005. *The Encyclopedia of Multimedia Technology and Networking*. IGI Global.
Panek, Magdalena. 2010. *Subtitling Humor: The Analysis of Selected Translation Techniques in Subtitling Elements Containing Humor*. GRIN Verlag.
Perego, Elisa, and Silvia Bruti, eds. 2015. *Subtitling Today: Shapes and Their Meanings*. Cambridge Scholars Publishing.
Reid, Robert D., and David C. Bojanic. 2009. *Hospitality Marketing Management*. Wiley and Sons.
Salaets, Heidi, Abied Alsulaiman, and Silke Biesbrouck. 2015. "Tap Interpreting: From practice to norm. A Belgian case study." *Turjuman 24*, no. 2: 11–49.
Shastri, Pratima Dave. 2011. *Fundamental Aspects of Translation*. PHI Learning Pvt. Ltd.
Singh, Nitish. 2011. *Localization Strategies for Global e-business*. Cambridge University Press.
Somers, Harold Ed. 2003. *Computers and Translation: A Translator's Guide* (Vol. 35). John Benjamins.
Weideman, Melius. 2009. *Website Visibility: The Theory and Practice of Improving Rankings*. Neal-Schuman Publishers, Inc.

8 The trials and tribulations of the teaching of CAT
The case of Oman

Rafik Jamoussi and Aladdin Al Zahran

8.1 Introduction

Higher education institutions (HEIs) have acknowledged the necessity of integrating technology into the translation curriculum as part of their endeavour to align with industry and workplace requirements, with the consequence that technology has become a standard component of the translation curriculum (Bowker 2015; Jiménez-Crespo 2014: 52; Kenny 1999: 66; Kenny and Doherty 2014: 277) and is unequivocally established in different reference frameworks such as the European Master's in Translation (EMT) or the Process in the Acquisition of Translation Competence and Evaluation research group (PACTE) (Hurtado Albir 2015: 259; Jiménez-Crespo 2014: 45; Massey and Ehrensberger-Dow 2011; Rothwell and Svoboda 2019; Sikora and Walczyński 2015: 122; Toudic and Krause 2017: 9).

Despite this virtually universal acceptance of technology within translation curricula qua principle, much uncertainty has marked the particulars of its integration. The reasons for this are multifarious (cf. Austermühl 2013: 327; Pym 2012: 16). In addition to technical and administrative aspects, pedagogical concerns occupy centre stage among educators. "What to teach and how?" has become a recurrent question (cf. Bowker 2015: 93; Doherty and Kenny 2014: 296; Marshman and Bowker 2012: 72; Rico 2017: 2; Samson 2005: 106). The debate over the "what and how" of technology integration in HEIs' curricula is characterized by a polarization over the education-training dichotomy, where education is meant to serve the long-term purpose of individual growth and development of cognitive capacities and attitudes, allowing the individual to "cope with the most varying (professional) situations" (Bernardini 2004: 19). Training, on the other hand, is rather confined to addressing more targeted questions (ibid.). The major concern in this debate is that the integration of technology into the curriculum could, if not properly undertaken, divert HEIs from their perceived educational role and turn them into professional training centres (Jiménez Serrano 2002: 5). This concern is spelled out by Mossop (in Pym 2000: 232) when he argues for a clear distribution of roles along the lines of this education-training polarity. "The place for training", Mossop maintains "is the practicum and the professional development workshop" (ibid.). It is within these activities that such aspects as software functionalities more naturally fit, he finally adds.

A survey of the literature reveals a variety of answers to the "what to teach and how?" question, contributing, each from a different angle, to what is believed to represent the proper integration of computer-assisted translation (CAT) into a HEI translation curriculum. These answers principally revolve around the focus on transferrable skills, enhancement of critical judgement, adoption of a teaching approach that fosters these skills, and use of CAT tools in translation practice courses. The paragraphs that follow further elaborate on these integration requirements.

8.1.1 Focus on transferrable skills

In addition to being a feature of training sessions, the (exclusive) focus on functionalities that are proper to a specific software package does not serve the long-term purpose of education (Bernardini 2004: 21) as technology tends to evolve rapidly, with the consequence that additional training may be required each time a new iteration of this application is rolled out. Added to this is the fact that graduates who receive focused training on one software package may be severely handicapped if they have to operate in a workplace with a different software environment.

As a response to these reservations, a recurrent plea advocates what can be termed a don't-teach-the-tool-teach-the-principles approach (Shreve in Pym 2000: 271; cf. Kenny 2007: 197; Robichaud and L'Homme 2003: 29). This focus on the underlying principles in operation is meant to counter the aforementioned shortcomings through equipping students with the flexibility to transpose knowledge from one utility to another and therefore to rapidly become comfortable with any application which workplace vagaries may impose.

8.1.2 Critical judgement

Whether directly or indirectly, sessions that provide focused training on a particular application are often meant as a promotion of the CAT tool under scrutiny and reiterate arguments of increased productivity and enhanced consistency and quality which the use of the tool purports to offer. Because of this focus on advantages, these training sessions typically fail to provide the broader picture (Bowker 2015: 97), the detachment that is necessary to form a critical appreciation of the tool.

Yet this critical judgement is necessary (Rodríguez-Castro 2018: 162; Somers 2001),[1] particularly bearing in mind that the technology at stake here is of a kind that has significantly affected the nature of translation (Gouadec in Pym 2000: 226; Kenny and Doherty 2014: 277; Pym 2013: 488). A critical approach heightens users' awareness that technology, though offering considerable advantages, imposes constraints on translation (Jiménez-Crespo 2010: 213–214), and that some of these constraints may have an adverse impact on both translation process and product. For instance, translation memory (TM) output is often affected by what Heyn (1998: 135) calls the "peephole effect", the focus on the micro-textual level resulting from sentence level segmentation. This segment-based functioning of TM systems affects coherence and cohesion and encourages translation that remains close to the ST as well as the recycling of segments that bear the styles of those who originally authored them (Bowker and Fisher 2010: 63).

Likewise, a critical approach to the use of CAT tools should be able to bring students to reflect on the when and why (Bowker 2015: 95), such as deciding whether or not to apply post-editing instead of translating from scratch, figuring out how CAT tools integrate into the translation workflow, gauging whether the nature of a translation job can lend itself to TM, assessing the limitations of these applications, and establishing a comparative evaluation of different tools (Bowker 2015: 96).

8.1.3 Pedagogical approach

The promotion of critical judgement is obviously conditioned on the adoption of an appropriate teaching approach. Over and above the fact that a teacher-centred approach is universally being abandoned (Kiraly 2000), the transmissionist methods that this approach applies are symptomatic, within the teaching of CAT tools, of a focus on software functionalities to the detriment of critical judgement. The adoption of a student-centred approach, including collaborative activities and autonomous learning (Bowker 2015: 97; Kenny 1999: 77; Rico 2017: 3; Samson 2005: 109), therefore becomes crucial for a proper integration of CAT tools into the curriculum.

8.1.4 Integration into practical courses

Finally, there is an emphasis in the literature on integrating CAT tools into practical translation courses and not just confining them to stand-alone courses that focus exclusively on technology. Integration in practical translation courses, where the focus is on translation skills, is a sign that the handling of CAT tools is "transversal" (Enríquez-Raído 2013: 277), woven into the fabric of the whole curriculum, and where this handling becomes a means serving the outcomes of the translation courses rather than being a self-contained "ancillary task" (Marshman and Bowker 2012: 72; cf. Bowker 2015: 96–97; Enríquez-Raído 2013: 277; Rothwell and Svoboda 2019: 38).

Despite the availability of these recommendations on how technology is to be introduced into the translation curriculum, some sources still decry a theoretical gap (Killman 2018: 138) and a persistent reliance on transmissionist methods focusing on instrumental skills (Frérot and Karagouch 2016; Rico 2017: 2).[2]

In Oman, translation is characterized by a relatively short professionalization record and comparatively recently established translation curricula. However, the sector is particularly dynamic and is witnessing a burgeoning interest in CAT solutions, as is attested *inter alia* by the focus of the Third Omani Translators Forum 2018 on this topic: "Translators in the Digital Age". Despite these developments, and other than the work of Shallal (2018), which investigates contextual factors that favour or impede CAT integration, the actual particulars of CAT integration have so far been under-researched. The purpose of this chapter is to contribute to a better appreciation of the integration of technology within translation programs in Oman with a research question that can be formulated as: To what extent does the integration of CAT tools within translation curricula satisfy academic and workplace requirements? This research question can be further broken down into the following sub-questions:

1   How effective is CAT integration in HEIs?
2   Within HEIs, what attitude do academics involved in translator training have towards the use of CAT and its integration within translation curricula?
3   What levels of technology readiness do employers expect of their new recruits?
4   At what stage do employers believe training on CAT should take place?

By answering these questions, the study will capture the particulars of technology integration within translation curricula in Oman and identify the pitfalls that beset this endeavour and will help orient efforts to redress this situation. These findings can contribute to a better understanding of challenges emerging in similar contexts.

8.2 Method

The qualitative research approach was deemed adequate for the investigation intended in this project, and the interview, specifically the e-mail interview, as the method of choice for data collection. Two interviews were developed in parallel, one addressed to academics involved in translation programmes and one to translation professionals and employers.

The questions addressed to academics were of two types; the first focused on factual information depicting different aspects of the integration of CAT tools, while the second elicited the interviewees' opinions about CAT tools and the way they envisaged this technology should be incorporated into the curriculum. The interview questions addressed to employers sought to elicit information about the type of CAT tools they used and their stands on the level of technology readiness they expected from applicants for translation positions as well as the stage at which training on CAT should take place.

For the focus on the means deployed to integrate CAT and their appropriateness, the integration requirements discussed in the previous section were, where necessary, reformulated as objective indicators in the interview questions. These objective indicators provide a fact-based approach where performance is more readily amenable to measurement and evaluation.

For the integration requirement targeting transferrable skills, the first indicator is to be found in course learning outcomes (CLOs) and consequently in course components. Focus on transferrable skills is evidenced through a formulation of CLOs that addresses underlying concepts within CAT and breaks them down into such constituents as alignment, corpus management, concordancing, terminology extraction, etc., all of which represent basic working principles in any CAT tool. Conversely, absence of reference to concepts in CLOs and the almost exclusive reliance on "how to" activities, such as how to create a new project, how to integrate TM and glossary files into the project, etc., and on a course organization that closely follows these steps, are rather symptomatic of an emphasis on the tool. The second indicator of the focus on principles is reliance, at least within practice activities, on more than one software application to demonstrate each of the principles under scrutiny, as exposure to different tools enhances awareness of underlying principles and ultimately serves skill transferability.

As concerns the requirement of critical judgement, the initial indicator is the spelling out of critical analysis as a distinct CLO (Doherty and Kenny 2014: 298–299; Robichaud and L'Homme 2003: 28; Rodríguez-Castro 2018: 162). Here, we are looking for tasks that lead on to reflections on the way a particular tool is helpful in finding solutions or in saving time, limitations of the tools, effects these tools have on the translation process and product, etc. (Bowker 2015: 95–98). Further related indicators for critical judgement are the way this particular CLO is implemented throughout course delivery and whether it is assessed (Doherty and Kenny 2014: 301).

For the teaching approach, indicators are about reliance on projects involving student collaboration (Kenny 1999: 77) and providing the opportunity for first-person engagement with the tools, which alone warrant the development among learners of an informed opinion about the efficiency and limitations of the tool.

Interviews were conducted in the fall of 2019. The first set was conducted with representatives from the five translation programs offered in Oman, all of whom were either directly involved in the delivery of technology-related courses or responsible for the translation curriculum development and implementation. The interviews targeting employers relied on convenience sampling and involved the managers of three leading translation agencies and three heads of translation sections in major institutions.

8.3 Results and discussion

The following paragraphs provide the investigation results and discuss their significance. After an investigation of findings relative to integration facts, the focus will shift to attitudinal aspects identified among both academics and employers.

8.3.1 The situation in HEIs

To the initial question on the adoption of CAT within the translation curriculum, responses indicate that the focus on technology appears with varying degrees of prominence in all five surveyed translation programs. Three of the modules handling CAT appear at the BA level and two at the MA level. However, only two of these modules represent core components (one within a BA, the other within an MA), while the other three are electives. One interviewee reported that a better share was shortly to be given to CAT in a new edition of the translation program his institution was to roll out. Future reviews notwithstanding, the current situation clearly portrays CAT as a niche feature in translation programs. An exploration of the degree to which the four integration requirements are satisfied will further assess the felicity of these integration instances.

As was argued in the section on methodology, two indicators can be used to identify a focus on transferrable skills; CLOs and reliance on more than one software application in activities that purport to provide practical demonstrations. Responses to the question on the objectives of courses involving technology revealed a wide spectrum of practices in our target curricula, from a comprehensive coverage of concepts and processes to the total absence of any reference to them. As for the number of software applications used, four out of the five investigated curricula appeared to make use of a single application. These findings indicate that the objective of fostering transferrable skills is often ill served by course design.

The second on our list of requirements is critical judgement, reliance on which is to be traced in the explicit reference to critical analysis in CLOs. Responses indicate that the element of critical judgement on the use of CAT clearly appears within two of the investigated curricula and is only touched on tangentially, if at all, in the others. When it represents a class focus, critical judgement was reported to be primarily served through class discussions, with the notable additional use of a reflection journal reported in one of the investigated curricula. The already-limited focus on critical judgement as a discrete objective, which these findings indicate, is further minimized by reliance in all but one institution on a single software package. This fact impoverishes class discussion as it removes the element of comparison, whether implicit or explicit, between different competing tools.

The emerging inadequate emphasis on critical judgement is equally corroborated by the rather limited inclusion of this aspect in assessment. Except for one curriculum, where the use of a reflection journal is reported, feedback indicates that critical judgement is assessed only minimally in one curriculum and formatively in another, meaning that in these two cases this aspect does not significantly contribute to the overall mark assessing the students' achievement.

The third requirement addresses the teaching approach, with indicators revolving around student collaboration and the opportunity for first-person engagement with the tools. Feedback indicates that all the curricula under consideration exhibit signs of reliance on student-based approaches. In response to the question on class activities performed around CAT tools, interviewees reported that a typical class includes a demonstration, usually undertaken by the instructor, followed by a set of class practice and take-home activities that are performed through the individual and group variants. Individual and group assignments have equally been found to represent the basis of assessment. One curriculum is reported to involve the use of an additional lab exam and another of oral presentations. These findings indicate that the five investigated programmes satisfy this third integration requirement.

Finally, the integration of CAT tools into practice courses is the aspect where the investigated curricula are found to be glaringly deficient. What emerges from responses is that save for the possible use of CAT tools in the final project module, none of the curricula under scrutiny integrates CAT in practical translation courses, with the implication that CAT remains confined to a stand-alone module. It should be mentioned, though, that all the investigated CAT syllabi feature a focus on translation quality, both in delivery and assessment. Rather than integrating CAT tools into translation courses, CAT courses are infused with some elements of translation practice. However beneficial it may be, this particular focus remains minimal and may even be counterproductive as it consumes some of the already limited time dedicated to CAT in the curriculum, as one respondent argues.

The reasons for this lack of integration are multiple, many of which are intimately related to a conception of CAT integration as a new element to be added to an already existing program. Another explanation for this stand-alone integration is to do with the question of the timing of the introduction of such skills to the translation curriculum. The literature shows discrepant views in this respect, as some argue that students should make use of all the possible translation technologies from an early stage in their training (cf. Jiménez-Crespo 2014: 52), while others give priority to the building of maturity in translation proper and advocate a later integration of CAT (cf. Bowker 2015: 98). The latter position is the one that prevails in the investigated curricula, where focus on CAT is found to appear only at the final stage, that is, year four of the bachelor's degree, or at the MA level in the two HEIs that offer such a degree. Obviously in this case, integration into practical translation courses that are scheduled prior to the CAT course is not possible.

The deficit in the handling of technical and instrumental skills is indisputable in the investigated context and can be considered symptomatic of the recent encounter with CAT, as has already been attested in the literature (Kenny 1999: 66).

8.3.2 HEIs interviewees

Responses relative to personal views on the importance of CAT and the necessity to integrate it in translation curricula reveal that HEI interviewees are often in disagreement with integration aspects in their programs. All interviewees acknowledged the importance technology has come to represent. With responses such as "it is a must", or "working on computer assisted tools is now a core prerequisite [for translators] to be accepted in the translation industry", they reckon that aspects of this technology should be integrated into the translation curriculum. An interviewee even revealed that "some instructors voluntarily guide their students towards using ... [CAT tools] either at BA or MA level", thus testifying to individual initiatives taken to compensate for perceived gaps in their curriculum. The reasons for the obvious schism between respondents' stands and the reality in which some academics operate, especially in institutions where CAT does not figure on the BA program or is only an elective, are believed to be due to administrative complexities that often hamper the timely response of academia to its surrounding context (cf. Shallal 2018: 220–222) as well as the shortage of academics with the adequate background for this type of instruction, "rare birds" in the words of one of the interviewees.

The unanimity identified here vanishes when views on integration details are examined. On the appropriate timing for the integration of CAT tools within the curriculum, the interviewees' arguments are found to diverge along lines delineated in the literature. Thus, some interviewees are in favour of a late introduction, to guarantee that "students are [initially] equipped with translation skills" or that they "are good enough to depend on technology/CAT tools". Others argue that "no stage is too early" for CAT integration, albeit with a careful sequencing of the instruments involved.

On the question of satisfaction with CAT-devoted class time, a similar polarity appears between interviewees who consider the current amount of class time satisfactory and others who do not. One of the interviewees arguing in favour of additional class time described the situation as follows; "currently at the postgraduate level, the course that explicitly addresses technology ... is divided into two parts. ... In an ideal situation this course should be two independent courses". Variation in responses to this question tends to be determined by the interviewees' positions concerning the timing of CAT integration within the syllabus. In other words, the call for increased class time emerges from the belief that CAT should be integrated at an earlier stage and the awareness of the ensuing class time needs.

Polarity among interviewees is further confirmed in relation to the question on the degree of technicality to be targeted in CAT courses. Responses show some awareness that the role of HEIs should be limited to providing a foundation in CAT principles and skills. Further honing of CAT abilities, it is argued in this case, should be sought through professional development programs, whether within or outside HEIs. In the words of one of the interviewees siding with this opinion, "higher education institutions should integrate such CAT tools in their training sessions and classes. Polishing of such technology ... may happen at the workplace". However, this stand is by no means unanimous, as some interviewees were of the view that in-depth training in CAT tools is the responsibility of HEIs. One interviewee mentioned in this respect that "having the skill of using translation software such as TRADOS™[3] is one of the eligibility criteria of translation careers".

The broad picture that emerges from interviews with academics is that despite agreement on the necessity for CAT tools to be integrated within translation curricula, views diverge on the way this integration is to be conceptualized.

8.3.3 Professional interviewees

In an attempt to gain insight into the technology in use in their institutions, employers were asked about the types of software packages they considered essential. The responses they gave show considerable variation, as some interviewees put special emphasis on specific TM tools while others referred to more general office package skills. Interestingly, this unevenness in the use of technology was not reflected in responses to the question on technology readiness, as interviewees unanimously reported that they expected translation job seekers to demonstrate knowledge of CAT tools. Equally important is the variation in the levels of expertise which interviewees referred to. One interviewee expressed this opinion as follows: "I expect them to understand the basics and the importance of using such tools". Still, some interviewees went as far as requesting full mastery, as can be gathered from the statement: "I expect them to use CAT tools used in the translation process".

What emerges from responses to the question on when CAT-related skills should be acquired is that these skills are not considered the responsibility of employers. Here, interviewees indicated that they were of the view that these skills "should be acquired before graduation" and that if they are not acquired through formal academic training, then the onus is on the translator to acquire them through other "out of the box" means, as one interviewee argued. Another interviewee more concretely suggested: "in my opinion, translation graduates [should acquire these skills] with the help of either their own colleagues or [through] private training". This insistence on technology readiness is in line with global trends reported in the literature (Mossop in Pym 2000: 232) and is thought to partake of the employers' standard requirement for new recruits to be all-rounders.

As a cross-section analysis of the local context, the present investigation reveals largely inadequate ways CAT has been integrated in translation curricula, wavering among academics between education- and training-oriented approaches, and gaps, sometimes wide, between employers' professional practices and their expectations about graduate technology readiness. All these symptoms are characteristic of a context that is still grappling with the first stages of the encounter with technology. The context is bound to acquire more sophistication as it evolves through further stages, with market demand expected to play a major role in driving and shaping this evolution and representing an important investigation path to take in further research.

8.4 Conclusion

We started by identifying the main contention, which is that CAT is incorporated in the translation curriculum through a stand-alone module that remains disconnected from the rest of the curriculum and that is designed from the perspective of training towards a specific software. Next, we identified the key requirements for a more comprehensive integration built around the educational role of HEIs. These requirements were further refined into indicators that were subsequently used for the investigation of the focus on CAT in translation curricula in Oman.

Over and above the fact that CAT is a core module in only two out of the total five translation curricula in the country, which in itself shows that the focus on the related set of skills still does not have the share it deserves, the investigation clearly reveals a perception and an integration that do not satisfy academic requirements. This is most obvious in the lack of focus on transferrable skills, use of a single package for demonstration and practice activities, insufficient focus on critical thinking, particularly at the level of assessment, and virtually total absence of the integration of CAT in translation practice courses. In fact, the perception remains closer to training on the use of a specific commercial tool than to education, but without, even in that respect, going the full length down the training path, due to the limited time put into the task.

The observed deficit in the integration of CAT tools and the polarity among academics on how to address the problem have the consequence that the investigated curricula currently satisfy neither the academic education-oriented perspective following clearly delineated integration requirements nor the training-oriented employer requirements. However, the situation is bound for a progressive change following the rolling out of program reviews. The subsequent phases should reflect a better discrimination between CAT as a set of processes and principles and the tools that apply them as well as decisions, both academic and strategic, on which of the education or training paths to take to secure the employability of translation graduates.

Acknowledgements

We express our sincere gratitude to all interviewees who readily accepted to take part in this project and patiently addressed our follow-up questions.

Notes

1 It is to be noted that though Somers is specifically focusing on MT, his statement can easily be generalized to cover CAT tools.
2 According to Rico (2017: 3), this tendency can equally be identified in a number of textbooks produced at the beginning of the period.
3 SDL is now rebranded as RWS.

References

Austermühl, Frank. 2013. "Future (and not-so-Future) Trends in the Teaching of Translation Technology." *Revista Tradumatica* 11: 326–337. https://doi.org/10.5565/rev/tradumatica.46.

Bernardini, Silvia. 2004. "The Theory Behind the Practice. Translator Training or Translator Education." In *Translation in Undergraduate Degree Programmes*, ed. by Kirsten Malmkjær, 17–29. Amsterdam: John Benjamins.

Bowker, Lynne. 2015. "Computer-Aided Translation. Translator Training." In *The Routledge Encyclopedia of Translation Technology*, ed. by Chan Sin-Wai, 88–104. London and New York: Routledge.

Bowker, Lynne and Des Fisher. 2010. "Computer-Aided Translation." In *Handbook of Translation Studies*, ed. by Yves Gambier and Luc van Doorslaer, 60–65. Amsterdam: John Benjamins.

Doherty, Stephen and Dorothy Kenny. 2014. "The Design and Evaluation of a Statistical Machine Translation Syllabus for Translation Students." *The Interpreter and Translator Trainer* 8(2): 295–315. https://doi.org/10.1080/1750399X.2014.937571.

Enríquez-Raído, Vanessa. 2013. "Teaching Translation Technologies 'Everyware': Towards a Self-Discovery and Lifelong Learning Approach." *Tradumàtica* 11: 275–285.

Frérot, Cécile and Lionel Karagouch. 2016. "Outils d'aide à la traduction et formation de traducteurs: Vers une adéquation des contenus pédagogiques avec la réalité technologique des traducteurs [Assisted Translation Tools and Translator Training: Towards a Matching of Pedagogical Content with Translators' Technological Reality]." *ILCEA. Revue de l'Institut des langues et cultures d'Europe, Amérique, Afrique, Asie et Australie* (27). https://doi.org/10.4000/ilcea.3849.

Heyn, Matthias. 1998. "Translation Memories: Insights and Proposals." In *Unity in Diversity?: Current Trends in Translation Studies*, ed. by Lynne Bowker, Michael Cronin, Doherty Kenny and Jennifer Pearson, 123–136. Manchester: Saint Jerome.

Hurtado Albir, Amparo. 2015. "The Acquisition of Translation Competence. Competences, Tasks, and Assessment in Translator Training." *Meta* 60(2): 256–280. https://doi.org/10.7202/1032857ar.

Jiménez Serrano, Óscar. 2002. "Methodological and Professional Challenges Posed by New Technologies in the Teaching of Technical Translation." Simposi sobre l'Ensenyament a distància i semipresencial de la Tradumàtica.

Jiménez-Crespo, Miguel Á. 2010. "The Effect of Translation Memory Tools in Translated Web Texts: Evidence from a Comparative Product-Based Study." *Linguistica Antverpiensia* 8: 213–232.

Jiménez-Crespo, Miguel Á. 2014. "Building from the Ground Up: On the Necessity of Using Translation Competence Models in Planning and Evaluating Translation and Interpreting Programs." *Cuadernos de ALDEEU* 25: 37–67.

Kenny, Dorothy. 1999. "CAT Tools in an Academic Environment: What Are They Good For?" *Target* 11(1): 65–82. https://doi.org/10.1075/target.11.1.04ken.

Kenny, Dorothy. 2007. "Translation Memories and Parallel Corpora: Challenges for the Translation Trainer." In *Across Boundaries: International Perspectives on Translation*, ed. by Dorothy Kenny and Kyongjoo Ryou, 192–208. Newcastle: Cambridge Scholars Publishing.

Kenny, Dorothy and Stephen Doherty. 2014. "Statistical Machine Translation in the Translation Curriculum: Overcoming Obstacles and Empowering Translators." *The Interpreter and Translator Trainer* 8(2): 276–294. https://doi.org/10.1080/1750399X.2014.936112.

Killman, Jeffrey. 2018. "A Context-Based Approach to Introducing Translation Memory in Translator Training." In *Translation, Globalization and Translocation. The Classroom and Beyond*, ed. by Concepción B. Godev, 137–159. Charlotte: Palgrave Macmillan.

Kiraly, Donald C. 2000. *A Social Constructivist Approach to Translator Education: Empowerment from Theory to Practice*. Manchester: St. Jerome.

Marshman, Elizabeth and Lynne Bowker. 2012. "Translation Technologies as Seen through the Eyes of Educators and Students: Harmonizing Views with the Help of a Centralized Teaching and Learning resource." In *Global Trends in Translator and Interpreter Training. Mediation and Culture*, ed. by Séverine Hübscher-Davidson and Michal Borodo, 69–95. London: Continuum.

Massey, Gary and Maureen Ehrensberger-Dow. 2011. "Technical and Instrumental Competence in the Translator's Workplace: Using Process Research to Identify Educational and Ergonomic Needs." *ILCEA. Revue de l'Institut des Langues et Cultures d'Europe et d'Amérique* 14: 1–14. https://doi.org/10.4000/ilcea.1060.

Pym, Anthony. 2000. "Innovation in Translator and Interpreter Training. Report on an on-Line Symposium." *Across Languages and Cultures* 1(2): 209–273. https://doi.org/10.1556/Acr.1.2000.2.5.

Pym, Anthony. 2012. "Democratizing Translation Technologies – The Role of Humanistic Research." Luspio Translation Automation Conference, Rome.

Pym, Anthony. 2013. "Translation Skill-Sets in a Machine-Translation Age." *Meta:* 58(3): 487–503. https://doi.org/10.7202/1025047ar.

Rico, Celia. 2017. "The ePortfolio: Constructing Learning in Translation Technology." *The Interpreter and Translator Trainer* 11(1): 79–95. https://doi.org/10.1080/1750399X.2017.1306995.

Robichaud, Benoît and Marie-Claude L'Homme. 2003. "Teaching the Automation of the Translation Process to Future Translators." In *Teaching Translation Technologies and Tools (3rd Workshop on Teaching Machine Translation)*, ed. by Mikel L. Forcada, H. Somers and A. Way, 27–34. New Orleans: AMTA Association for Machine Translation in the Americas.

Rodríguez-Castro, Mónica. 2018. "Learning Outcomes of Computer-Assisted Translation: Direct Assessment and Self-Assessment." In *Translation, Globalization and Translocation. The Classroom and Beyond*, ed. by Concepción B. Godev, 161–184. Charlotte: Palgrave Macmillan.

Rothwell, Andrew and Tomáš Svoboda. 2019. "Tracking Translator Training in Tools and Technologies: Findings of the EMT Survey 2017." *The Journal of Specialized Translation* 32.

Samson, Richard. 2005. "Computer-Assisted Translation." In *Training for the New Millennium*, ed. by Martha Tennet, 101–126. Amsterdam: John Benjamins.

Shallal, Isamaddin Mahmoud. 2018. "Integration of Computer Assisted Translation (CAT) Tools in the Curricula of Translator Training Programmes in the Omani Context." PhD, School of Languages, Literacies and Translation, University Sains Malaysia.

Sikora, Iwona and Marcin Walczyński. 2015. "Incorporating CAT tools and ICT in the Translation and Interpreting Training at the Undergraduate Level." In *The Translator and the Computer 2*, ed. by Łukasz Grabowski and Tadeusz Piotrowski, 119–133. Wrocławiu: Wydawnictwo Wyższej Szkoły Filologicznej we Wrocławiu.

Somers, Harold. 2001. "Three Perspectives on MT in the Classroom." MT Summit VIII Workshop on Teaching Machine Translation, Santiago de Compostela.

Toudic, Daniel and Alexandra Krause (eds.) 2017. *European Master's in Translation Competence Framework*. Brussels: European Commission.

9 Epilogue
Where do we go from here?

Erik Angelone

9.1 Introduction

The Arab and Middle Eastern perspectives presented in this timely volume highlight the fact that translator and interpreter training is a complex matter influenced by many moving parts beyond the direct stakeholders of instructors and students. Its success hinges first and foremost on awareness of language industry needs in specific markets or regions. These needs are often in a state of flux as a result of such phenomena as technological advancement, ebbs and flows in global markets, and patterns of migration, both physical and virtual. In any event, the scope of stakeholders ideally involved in translation and interpreting (T&I) training transcends students and trainers, and important decision making should include the voices of the companies and organizations in which and for whom students will ultimately work upon graduation.

To a certain extent, the challenges trainers and students face in the Middle East, as outlined in this volume, echo those found in many parts of the world. These include an ongoing lack of recognition of the translation and interpreting professions as bona fide careers that require more in the way of skills and know-how than some nebulous level of bilingualism. A second challenge, and perhaps one that is largely responsible for the lack of recognition just mentioned, is a pervasive disconnect between the industry and academia. On the one hand, this disconnect may be the result of instructors not willing to move outside of their comfort zones in catering to ever-changing industry needs. While instructors are, indeed, often creatures of habit, this would seem to be an overly simplistic explanation. After reading through the content of this volume, one might start to wonder if blame can also be attributed to an over-adherence to Western perspectives and models of translator and interpreter training that tend to still dominate the translation studies literature. These perspectives and models, while often informed by the market needs of the Western world, may fall short in addressing market needs and industry realities in the Middle East. How often, for example, do we see mention of such concepts as religious translation and interpreting for pilgrims, orthographic reforms as part of language planning to facilitate translation, specialized translator training in the domain of wiretapping, and language pairs such as Urdu–Arabic and Pashto–Arabic in the mainstream translation studies literature? These concepts, all highly relevant in the Middle East, highlight the necessity to take a granular approach to translation and interpreting training rather than a broad-brush approach that potentially misses the mark due to a false assumption of universal applicability.

While, on the one hand, T&I training needs to align with local and regional market needs, on the other hand, it is equally important for students to be equipped with knowledge and skills to succeed as language industry professionals on an increasingly global stage. In this day and age, graduates of such programs may find themselves working in practically any part of the world where their language pairs and areas of expertise are in demand. In terms of curriculum design, this necessitates a perpetual balancing act of tending to the local while simultaneously not neglecting the global. This balancing act brings with it a series of inherent challenges faced not only by students and instructors as direct stakeholders but also by more peripheral stakeholders that have – or at least should have – an impact on curriculum design, including higher education administrations, language service provision companies, tool and software designers, and government policy makers, to name a few. The advancement of T&I training and, indeed, the language industry at large, hinges upon open, ongoing dialogue among these stakeholders. This volume will hopefully serve as a call to action in this regard.

Where else might we go from here in optimizing T&I training in the Middle East? This chapter will now put forward some concrete ideas and approaches along these lines for addressing challenges at both the local/regional and global levels.

9.2 Addressing challenges at the local/regional level

9.2.1 The need for empirical, data-driven approaches to curricular optimization

It is in the best interest of any T&I training program to regularly gauge and revise its curriculum in line with changes in market needs and demands. A relatively quick and easy way of doing this is to create corpora consisting of language industry job listings from which high frequency lexical items could be extracted in the form of a word list. High frequency lexical items appearing in a patterned fashion across job listings often shed light on careers, skills, and requirements that are in high demand. Empirical, corpus-based analysis along these lines enables a data-driven approach to curricular change rather than one that is based on held perceptions alone. Ultimately, job listings can feed into a more robust empirical mechanism for gauging curricula. Survey and interview data collected from various language industry stakeholders can also be particularly insightful, especially when alumni of programs are involved. These graduates have a clear understanding of where things worked well and what might benefit from improvement based on the realities they face in the world of work. In any event, a data-driven approach to curricular change and optimization can be helpful in circumnavigating personal likes and dislikes and the ongoing problematic implementation of legacy concepts that may potentially stand in the way of positive, needed change. Al-Batineh and Bilali's 2017 publication on aligning curricula with the language industry can serve as a roadmap of sorts for how to address potential disconnects between academia and the industry.

9.2.2 Thinking beyond English

In the context of T&I training, the Arabic–English language pair will always be prioritized, but this should not come at the expense of preparing students for professional work in other language pairs of documented need, such as those recently put forward by Taibi (2016). A potential challenge in this regard lies in finding competent instructors for some of the less common language pairs, such as Bengali–Arabic or Sinhalese–Arabic, given the fact that there are only so many qualified instructors available (not to mention training programs from which they would come). In the aggregate, translation programs in the Middle East might collaborate in meeting this potential shortage by agreeing on allocations of language pairs so that all are adequately covered, albeit not in any one program alone. This same principle of allocation across programs could also apply to domains that represent areas of need based on empirical analysis of market demands.

Given the status of English as a lingua franca or corporate language, it would also be advisable to focus on its role in the language industry in the Middle East beyond its status as a source or target language in translation or interpreting contexts. If there is a greater tendency for content in certain domains and genres to be created in English from the start rather than translated or interpreted into English, it makes little sense to focus on such content in a translation or interpreting classroom. Again, market analysis will shed valuable light on what role English should play in T&I training. For those domains in which it is not commonly found as a source or target language, but where it plays a pivotal industry role nonetheless, curricular focus may be better placed on English for special purposes instead.

9.2.3 Training for routinized or adaptive expertise

Translators in the Middle East, and, indeed, translators worldwide who are working with the Arabic–English language pair, may increasingly be asked to take on tasks across language industry career strands. We clearly see evidence of this based on the frequent mention of community translation and interpreting as undertaken by the same language industry professionals in public service domains. We are currently seeing a proliferation of language industry career strands (Bond 2018) to an unprecedented extent, brought about in large part by the increasing efficacy of machine translation and artificial intelligence in a broader sense. Translators, for example, are no longer just translating. They are also post-editing, engaging in quality assurance, creating content, and consulting on linguistic and cultural issues, among other things. From a curriculum and training standpoint, this proliferation raises the question of whether it is more prudent to train in pursuit of routinized or adaptive expertise or some combination of both.

Routinized expertise involves consistently superior performance in a relatively narrow, well-defined task domain (Ericsson and Charness 1997). In the language industry, this is what we might expect highly specialized translators to possess. It is accumulated over years of deliberate practice (Shreve 2006) in the narrowly defined domain. Routinized expertise is generally thought to be nontransferable, but, to date, there has been relatively little empirical research on the transferability of routinized expertise across task domains. For example, a legal translator might excel in her or his field, but can this person also leverage expertise to successfully translate in other specialized domains? Adaptive expertise, on the other hand, involves flexible problem-solving heuristics across different task domains and a corresponding tendency to excel in situations involving novelty (Hatano and Inagaki 1986). One might assume a language industry professional with adaptive expertise would more readily be able to take on multiple, changing roles and tasks with general success in each. Perhaps this person would be successful at both translating and interpreting across multiple domains, for example, in the course of a given work week.

This begs the question of what "success" implies, beyond something that is simply in the eye of the beholder. At a very basic level, once again, it is regional market needs and corresponding factors of supply and demand that would provide answers as to whether training for routinized or adaptive expertise is more feasible. Ultimately, the language industry, in the aggregate, calls for both routinized and adaptive expertise. Stakeholders involved in translator and interpreter training in the Middle East, like in all parts of the world, face the important tasks of determining which career paths align with each type of expertise and structuring their curricula accordingly.

9.3 Addressing challenges at the global level

As previously mentioned, translator and interpreter training programs in the Middle East also face a number of challenges from a global perspective. These are not to be regarded as entirely distinct from the local/regional challenges outlined in the preceding section but rather as closely related. Integrating measures to address global-level challenges will ideally make graduates as well as the programs from which they graduate more marketable on a global scale.

9.3.1 Language planning initiatives

As several authors in this volume mention, two paramount, larger-scale language planning initiatives that would stand to benefit T&I programs in the Middle East involve orthographic reform and terminological standardization. Given the importance of transliteration in field-specific translation into Arabic, there is a tremendous need to introduce graphemes in the Arabic language to facilitate communication and mitigate inconsistencies in translation (see Bahloul, this volume). Inconsistencies in terminology across Arabic-speaking countries in field-specific content where standardization would be expected are potentially hampering the dissemination of information and societal advancement in these fields (see Al-abed et al., this volume). What role might T&I training come into play in this regard? At a very basic level, there should be a stronger focus on implementing terminology management skills in and across courses to the extent that sound terminology practices can come to be regarded as a natural component of translation and interpreting project workflows. In essence, translation and interpreting serve as an impetus for introducing terminology to the Arabic language. With this in mind, there should be strong synergies between academia, national translation associations, and bodies involved in the establishment and implementation of terminology standards.

Since translation and interpreting potentially play such as important role in terminological introduction and standardization in the Arabic language, training in each should focus not only on mediation across languages and cultures but also on the role they play in monolingual (Arabic) content creation. Not unlike what we see in many parts of China, where there are hundreds of T&I programs and students from a wide variety of academic disciplines are taking courses in translation and interpreting, the Middle East might benefit from the establishment of learning environments in which T&I students work alongside students from other academic disciplines and vice versa. Training students to leverage big data from reliable sources, for example, from vetted monolingual and bilingual corpora, can lay the groundwork for fostering terminological standardization in academia that could then carry over to the various industries in which graduates work.

9.3.2 Stronger bridges between academia and tool developers

The advent of neural machine translation (MT) is proving to be a game changer in the language industry for many language pairs and domains, having a direct impact on the stages of project workflows and the roles of the stakeholders involved in them. The success of neural MT and computer-assisted translation (CAT) in general, hinges on digitization of content. Optical character recognition (OCR) tool developers need to do more to support the large-scale (semi)-automated digitization of content in Arabic. This will, in turn, enable the teaching and utilization of CAT tools, the training of MT engines, and the compilation of large-scale corpora.

Tool vendors would stand to benefit from tool usability research conducted by academic scholars on Arabic translation, both in training contexts and in the workplace. Fortunately, we are starting to see better support for Arabic from various companies, and students and instructors are eager to integrate them in pedagogical settings. Nevertheless, there is still plenty of work to be done, particularly insofar as segmentation, alignment, and formatting are concerned (see Alanazi 2019).

To facilitate things, tool developers would benefit from extensive direct input on the usability of their products in Arabic from various end users. Outside of the Middle East, academic environments have proven to be a fertile ground for dialogic exchange along these lines. Models and metrics of CAT tool usability have been put forward in the literature (see Krüger 2015; O'Brien et al. 2017). Usability research can take the form of relatively basic surveys and interviews, ethnographic workplace studies, or experimental studies making use of such technology as eye-tracking. Scholars in the Middle East should be encouraged to engage in such research, taking the aforementioned models and metrics as a point of departure, while also bringing to the table facets that are unique to the Arabic language that have been neglected to date.

References

Alanazi, M. (2019). *The Use of Computer-Assisted Translation Tools for Arabic Translation: User Evaluation, Issues, and Improvements*. Doctoral Dissertation, Kent State University. https://etd.ohiolink.edu/pg_10?::NO:10:P10_ETD_SUBID:182552

Al-Batineh, M. and Bilali, L. (2017). Translator training in the Arab world: Are curricula aligned with the language industry? *The Interpreter and Translator Trainer*, 11(2/3), 187–203.

Bond, E. (2018). The stunning variety of job titles in the language industry. *Slator*. https://slator.com/features/the-stunning-variety-of-job-titles-in-the-language-industry/ (last accessed 06 July 2020)

Ericsson, K. A. and Charness, N. (1997). Cognitive and developmental factors in expert performance. In P. Feltovich, K. M. Ford and R. R. Hoffman (Eds.), *Expertise in Context: Human and Machine* (pp. 3–41). Cambridge, MA: MIT Press.

Hatano, G. and Inagaki, K. (1986). Two courses of expertise. In H. Stevenson, H. Azuma and K. Hakuta (Eds.), *Child Development and Education in Japan* (pp. 262–72). New York: Freeman.

Krüger, R. (2015). Contextualising computer-assisted translation tools and modelling their usability. *trans-kom*, 9, 114–148.

O'Brien, S., Ehrensberger-Dow, M., Connolly, M., and Hasler, M. (2017). Irritating CAT tool features that matter to translators. *HERMES – Journal of Language and Communication in Business*, 56, 145–162.

Shreve, G. (2006). The deliberate practice: Translation and expertise. *Journal of Translation Studies*, 9(1), 27–42.

Taibi, M. (2016). Curriculum innovation in the Arab world: Community interpreting and translation as an example. In M. Taibi (Ed.), *New Insights into Arabic Translation and Interpreting* (pp. 22–46). Bristol: Multilingual Matters.

Index

Page numbers in *italics* and **bold** indicate Figures and Tables, respectively.

acceptability errors 93
acceptability-oriented translations 92
acceptability principle 10
accuracy errors 104
acquisition planning of Arabicization 116–117, 123
acronym disambiguation 75–77
acronyms: challenging **77**; disambiguation of 75–77; of /p/, /g/, and /v/ graphemes **79**; pairs transliterations **76**; transliterations of 74–75, **75**
adequacy errors 93
adequacy-oriented translations 92–93
Ain Shams University 26–27, 28
Alexandria University 28
American Translators Association (ATA) Framework for Standardized Error Marking 95
analytical translation quality assessment methods 92–95
appositive elements 50
Arabic as a Foreign Language (AFL) 72
Arabic dialects: in Arabic-speaking societies 68–69; in classrooms 70–71; disconnect between spoken and written languages 68–69; intelligibility between 68; linguistic environment *87*; Modern Standard Arabic vs 69–72; native languages 68–69; *see also* English to Arabic transliteration
Arabic Internet Corpus 24
Arabicization: agricultural terms 118; attitudes toward terms 118; business terms 118; English internet terms 118; Jordanian parliament attitudes toward 117; medical terms 117–118; military terms 117; nursing terms 117; planning stages of 116–117; stages of 123; terminology planning and 122; as translation strategy 122–123; *see also* Arabicization study
Arabicization study: adoption, assessment for 130, **131**; adoption, mean value for 132; assessment criteria correlations 132, **133**, **134**, **135**; data analysis methods 120; data collection 119–120; evaluation, assessment for 126–127, **127**; evaluation, mean value for 130; knowledge, assessment for 125–126, **126**; knowledge, mean value for 130; methods and procedures 119–120; participants 119; procedures 120; proficiency, assessment for 129–130, **129**; proficiency, mean value for 132; purpose of 118–119; recommendations 138–139; research questions 124; results 135–137; significance of 121–123; of sociolinguistic terms, attitudes toward 134–135, **136**, 137–138; terminology assessment 125–130; terminology assessment criteria 130–132; translated term acceptability criteria 124–125; usage, assessment for 127–128, **128**; usage, mean value for 131–132; word formation guidelines 124
Arabicized translation, definition of 116
arabiCorpus 24
Arabic script: diacritics **80**; script base **80**; worldwide use of *88*
Arabic-speaking societies: Arabic dialects in 68–69; educational system 72–73; English language teaching (ELT) field in 71–72; list of 82n1; map of *86*
Arab League 82n1

Arab universities: corpus-related courses 26–31, **32**; corpus-related courses summary *40*; course descriptions *33*; translation movement 1–2; *see also individual universities by name*
assessments: criterion-based methods 96–97; error typologies and (*See* error taxonomies/typologies); idiomatic expressions and 50; norm-referenced methods 96; performance 41, 49–50; of translators' competence 9–10; *see also* Arabicization study, error analysis of machine translations, source text study, translation quality
audiovisual translations 149–150
"automatic reflexes" 46

back-translation 15, 16
Berners-Lee, Tim 142–143
bilingual competence vs language teaching 50–51
bottom-up reading processes 42, 54n2
British Academy 58

Calibration of Dichotomous Items (CDI) method 96
calibration translation quality assessment methods 95–97
Cambridge University Press 58
CAMeL Lab 25
Canadian Language Quality Measurement System (Sical) 93
cascading style sheet (CSS) 146
checking 17
Check Your English Vocabulary for Law (Wyatt) 15
classrooms 8, 21–24, 27–28, 35, 41, 167; *see also* education, training, translation curriculum
code language 145
communicative aspects of translation 142
communicative innovation 115
competence 3–4, 9–10
computer-assisted translation (CAT) tools: as core module 162; devoting class time for 160; disagreement with integration of 159–160; employers' standard requirements 161; integrating into education curriculum 155–156, 159, 160, 162; integration timing 160; interviewees' opinions of 156; professional translators view 161; success of 169–170; teaching of 169–170; tool developers 170; tool vendors 170; university courses on 27; usability metrics 170; *see also* machine translations
computer corpora *see* corpora
computer programs 148, 149–150
concordances 18, 23, 25
contemporary approaches to translators 5
contextual text analysis 44–46
corpora: Arabic resources 24–25; challenges of 23; in the classroom 21–23; course titles relating to **33**; definition of 17; online repository 35; specialised 35; of spoken Arabic dialects 24–25; student-centeredness focus using 23; tools 25; translation problems solved by 23; transliteration issues 71; use of 22; *see also* parallel corpora, translation technologies
corpora resources 3
corpus Arabicization 116, 117, 123
corpus linguistics courses: in Gulf universities 28–31; in North Africa/Middle East universities 26–28; in the West 21
Corpus of Contemporary Arabic 24
corpus terminology planning 121
corpus-use skills 34
cosmetic bugs, software 148
criterion-based assessment method 96–97
cultural equivalence in target language 115

data-driven learning (DDL) 17–18
decision making, terminology planning as 114–115
declarative knowledge 8, 51
descriptive equivalence in target language 115
diacritics 80, **80**, **81**
Dialectal Arabic (DA) 68–69
discriminating power, definition of 96
dot diacritics *see* diacritics
dubbing 149, 150

economic benefits of translation 142
education 153; *see also* classrooms, translation curriculum
education-training polarity 153–154
Effat University 30
English language teaching (ELT) field 71–72
English to Arabic transliteration: acronym disambiguation 75–77; challenges of 62; common words, sample of **60**; of consonant /g/ 62–66; consonant

graphemes and phonemes 60–61, **61**; of consonant /p/ 66; of consonant /v/ 67–68; diacritics 80, **80**, **81**; reversibility criterion 59–60; of voiceless bilabial stop /p/ **66**; vowel sounds 62, **62**; *see also* transliterations
ENTRAD 17
error analysis of machine translations: common error categories **104**; human translation vs post-edited machine translation 98–99, **99**; machine translations vs post-edited machine translations 100–101, **100**; in rule-based machine translations 100–103; in SMT and RBMT **101**; TM-based (translation memories) translations 103–106; word sense disambiguation 103
error taxonomies/typologies 4; acceptability errors 92, **108**; accuracy errors 104; adequacy errors 93, **108**; agreement errors 101; assessments and 89; categories 105; confusion of senses 101–102; error analyses 89–90; error types in different 90; grammatical errors 103; language-related errors 107; MeLLANGE error typology 94, 107; misordering errors 101–102, 103; misselection errors 101; mistranslation errors 103; models 89; model selection 90; overview of **108**; SAE J 2450 93–94, 107; sample of **106**; SCATE taxonomy 90, 94–95, 102, 107; style and register errors 150–156; translation aids generating 105; untranslated words 103; word order errors 103; wrong choice 101–102
European Language Resources Association (ELRA) 24, 25
European Master's in Translation (EMT) 153
experience-based training 19

"false friends" phenomenon 46
film translations 149–150
functional bugs, software 148–149
functional equivalence in target language 115

GALE Arabic Newswire Parallel Text Project 25
globalization 21, 74, 144
Google Translate (SMT) 102, **102**
graphemes: acronyms and **79**; Arabic 69; Arabic orthographic system accommodating 79–81; in Arabic writing systems 71–72; consonant 60–61; for English consonants 78–79, **78**; f-like 67
Gulf universities, corpus-related courses 28–31
Gumar corpus of Gulf Arabic 24

Hamad bin Khalifa University 29
higher education institutions (HEIs) 153; *see also* translation curriculum
high-quality translations 91
holistic translation quality assessment 92
HTML (Hypertext Markup Language) 146

idioms 46–47, 50
Imam Muhammad Bin Saud University 29–30
information mining 8
information-quality translations 91
instructional time 8
instructor-centered training 15–16, 18
instructors: CAT tools and 160; corpora, use of 17; as facilitators 18; industry-academia disconnect and 165; qualifications of 7, 167; as stakeholders 165–166
interlingual translations 149
Internet 24, 30, 118, 142–143
intralingual translations 149
isosemiotic interlinguistic translations 150

Jacquemond, Richard 1–2
Java Script 146
Johns, Tim 17
Jordan Academy of Arabic 117–118, 120, 138

King Fahd School of Translation 27

language pairs 167
language planning: as branch of sociolinguistics 123; communicative innovation in 115; definition of 123; equivalence in target language 115–116; initiatives 169; models for 113–114; as organized activity 122, 123; terminology management skills 169; *see also* Arabicization, terminology planning
language teaching, bilingual competence vs 50–51
layout, in legal translations 11
learner-oriented training 18; *see also* student-centered training

Lebanese American University 27
legal terms, sensitivity of 15
legal translations: assessment of 9; audience focus in 15; difficulty of 10; layout 11; positive and negative connotations 13–15, *13*; of Quran 12–13; as restricted 10–11; structural/stylistic differences in 11; syntax problems in 11; vocabulary usage 12–13
lexical choices 11–12, 15, 16, 103
linear-combination models 71
Linguistic Data Consortium (LDC) 24, 25
linguistic diversity 74
LISA standards 103–104
literary translations 35–36, 43
Localization Industry Standards Association 103–104

machine translations: Arab university courses and 26–31; error analysis and (*See* error analysis of machine translations); grammatical errors in 99; human translation vs 98–99; neural machine translation (MT) 103, 169; researchers in 71; training of 26; *see also* corpora
MeLLANGE error typology 94, 107
Modern Standard Arabic (MSA): Arabic dialects vs 69–72; as language of instruction 68–69; limited use of 70–71; in monolingual educational systems 70; as second language 70
Moses-based MT systems 100–101, 103
Multidimensional Quality Metrics (MQM) framework 90, 94, 107
Multilingual Student Translation (MUST) project 35

neural machine translation (MT) 103, 169
news translation 142–143
norm-referenced translation assessment methods 96
North Africa/Middle East universities, corpus-related courses 26–28

optical character recognition (OCR) tool 169
orthographic reforms 3, 59, 69, 79–82, 165, 169

PACTE Group 44, 53
Pan-Arab identity and nationalism 117, 118, 134
parallel corpora: Arabic 25; data-driven learning and 17–18; definition of 17; real-world translations through 18–19; for teachers and researchers 35; *see also* corpora
para-verbal information 145
particles 11–12
pedagogy 21
peephole effect 155
performance assessment 41; *see also* assessments, source text study
phonemes: Arabic 81; English consonants 60–61, **61**, 62; English vowels 62; orthographic reforms for 58; systematizing transcriptions of 81
polysemy 76
Prince Sultan University 30
privacy 144–145
Process in the Acquisition of Translation Competence and Evaluation research group (PACTE) 153
process-oriented training 16
product-oriented training 16
professional translators: adaptive expertise 168; definition of 41–42; faulty renditions by 45, 46; hiring of 150–151; lifelong learning 151; performance assessment 49–50; routinized expertise 168; sense-oriented translation approach 49–50; text segments comparisons **48**; wiretap interpreting and 144
proficiency: Arabicization study 120, 129–130, **129**, 132, 136–137; definition of 7; dilution of 74; professional translators' level of 50; student translators' level of 8; terminology planning and 114–115
promoting and marketing terminology 4
publication-quality translations 91
Pym, Anthony 7

Quran, legal translations and 12–13

RBMT corpus 103
readability principle 10, 149
reading comprehension 42, 43, 50, 51
revisions 17

SAE (Society of Automotive Engineers) International 93
SAE (Society of Automotive Engineers) quality metric 93–94, 107
Sager, Juan 121
SCATE taxonomy 90, 102, 107
screen translations 149–150
security 142, 144–145

self-evaluation 16
Shami Dialect Corpus 24–25
Sharjah University 31
Sketch Engine 24
Skopos theory 92
Smart Computer-Aided Translation Environment (SCATE) error taxonomy 94–95
SMPTE timecode 150
social benefits of translation 142
social constructivist training 15
social media 3–4, 69, 115
Society of Motion Picture and Television Engineers 150
sociolinguistics 115, 123, 134–135; *see also* Arabicization study
software, definition of 147–148
software debugging 148–149
software localization 147–149
source codes 148
source language text 9, 42, 50, 92–93, 115–116
source text study: classifying problem solutions 44; contextual text analysis 44–46; data analysis 44–47; data collection 42; faulty renditions 44–45, 46; performing translating task 43–44; professional translators 43, 45, 46; reading comprehension 42, 43, 50, 51; results 47–49; source text 55; source text significant segments 42; subjects 42–43; text segments comparisons **48**; trainee translators 42, 44–45, 46; translation problems instrument 56–57
specialised corpora 35
stakeholders 115, 122, 138, 165–168, 169
status Arabicization 116, 123
status terminology planning 121–122
string tables 148
student-centered training 18, 23, 158–159
subtitling 149–150
Sultan Qaboos University 28–29
synonyms 12
syntax problems in legal translations 11
System of Transliteration from Arabic into English (Cambridge University Press) 58
Systran (RBMT) 102, **102**

tap interpreter 145
target language (TL): acceptability in 109; equivalent translations to 115–116; error taxonomies/typologies 90–95; language industry and 167; learner's ability 17; legal translations 145; monolingual corpora 105; source codes 148; training and 51–53; translators' competence and 9; university courses on 27; website localization 147
task-based translation teaching 8–9
team/group work 8
technologies *see* corpora, translation technologies
TED Parallel Corpus 25
terminology: allocation 122; definition of 123; dimensions of 125; as field of study 121
terminology planning: as communicative innovation 114; as decision making 114–115; definition of 113, 121; equivalence types in 115–116; influential people in 114; management skills 169; as marketing 114; model for 139; as organized activity 122; types of 121–122; *see also* Arabicization, language planning
Third Omani Translators Forum 156
top-down reading processes 42, 54n1
TRAD-Arabic-English Mailing Lists Parallel Corpus 25
traditional instructor-centered training 15–16
trainee translators: definition of 42; faulty renditions by 44–45, 46, 49; form-oriented translation approach 49; learning environments 169; textual competence in L2 reading comprehension 50; training modules for 51–53
training: academic institutions 1; approaches to 8–9; Arabic-English language pair 167; corpus skills and 34; education-training polarity 153–154; error taxonomies for 4; formal training 1; global level challenges 168–170; improvement recommendations 34–35; industry-academia disconnect 165; language teaching 50–51; modules for 51–53; multicomponent competencies development 7; post-translation phase 53; pre-translation phase 52; for routinized/adaptive expertise 167–168; stakeholder involvement in 165; transfer phase 53; in undergraduate programs 3; *see also* education, translation curriculum
transcriptions: orthographic 71–72; of speeches 100; systematizing 81; of voiced velar stop /g/ 63–64

translation curriculum: CAT tools (*See* computer-assisted translation tools); course learning outcomes 157; critical judgement 154–155, 157, 158; data-driven approaches to 166–167; integrating computer-assisted translation tools into 155–156, 159; job listings and 166–167; language pairs and 167; local/regional level challenges 166–168; objective indicators 157; pedagogical approach 155; student collaboration 157, 158–159; technology integration in 156; transferrable skills focus 154, 157, 158; underlying operation principles 154; *see also* classrooms, trainee translators
translation forms: news translation 142–143; wiretap interpreting 143–145
translation market *see* technologies
translation memories (TM) 29, 89, 98, 103–106, 155, 161
translation quality: acceptability/fluency 89, 107; adequacy/accuracy in 89, 107; automatic assessments 97; definition of 91–92, 107; error analysis and 98–100; human evaluation assessments 92–97; translation method's impact on 97–106
translation strategies **73**
translation technologies: advances in 18–19; bugs 148–149; cascading style sheet (CSS) 146; HTML (Hypertext Markup Language) 146; Internet 24, 30, 118, 142–143; Java Script 146; optical character recognition (OCR) tool 169; software localization 147–149; software testing 148–149; source code 148; string tables 148; tools in 21–22; XML (Extensive Markup Language) 146–147; *see also* computer-assisted translation (CAT) tools, corpora
translators *see* professional translators, trainee translators

transliteration diversity 74
transliteration projects 58–59
transliterations: acronym disambiguation 75–77; acronym pairs **76**; of acronyms 74–75, **75**; of bilabial stop /p/ **75**; of challenging acronyms **77**; definition of 59; of English consonant /g/ **63**; standardization and 74; of voiced labiodental fricative /v/ 67–68, **67**; of voiced velar stop /g/ 63–66, **64**, *65*; of voiceless bilabial stop /p/ 66; *see also* English to Arabic transliteration
transmissionist teacher-centered training 8
Tunisian Arabic Corpus 24

UAE University 31
Undergraduate Learner Translator Corpus (ULTC) 35
United Nations Council of Orthography and Transcription of Geographical Names 58
United Nations Parallel Corpus 25
United States: adopting unified transliteration system 58; Board on Geographic Names (BGN) 58
University of Jordan, School of Foreign Language 27
University of Tunis 27–28

web pages 146
website localization 4, 24, 142–143, 145–147
What-if Principle 16
wiretap interpreting 143–145
word formation guidelines 124
World Wide Web 142–143

XML (Extensive Markup Language) 146–147

Yarmouk University 27